SIYYID MUṢṬAFÁ RÚMÍ

Hand of the Cause of God, Apostle of Bahá'u'lláh

SIYYID MUṢṬAFÁ RÚMÍ

Hand of the Cause of God, Apostle of Bahá'u'lláh

Memoirs compiled and edited by
IRAN FURÚTAN MUHÁJIR

BAHÁ'Í
PUBLISHING
WILMETTE, ILLINOIS

Bahá'í Publishing
401 Greenleaf Avenue, Wilmette, Illinois 60091

 Published 2020
Printed in the United States of America on acid-free paper

10 9 8 7 6 5 4 3 2

ISBN 978-1-61851-157-7

Book design by Patrick Falso
Cover design by Carlos Esparza

CONTENTS

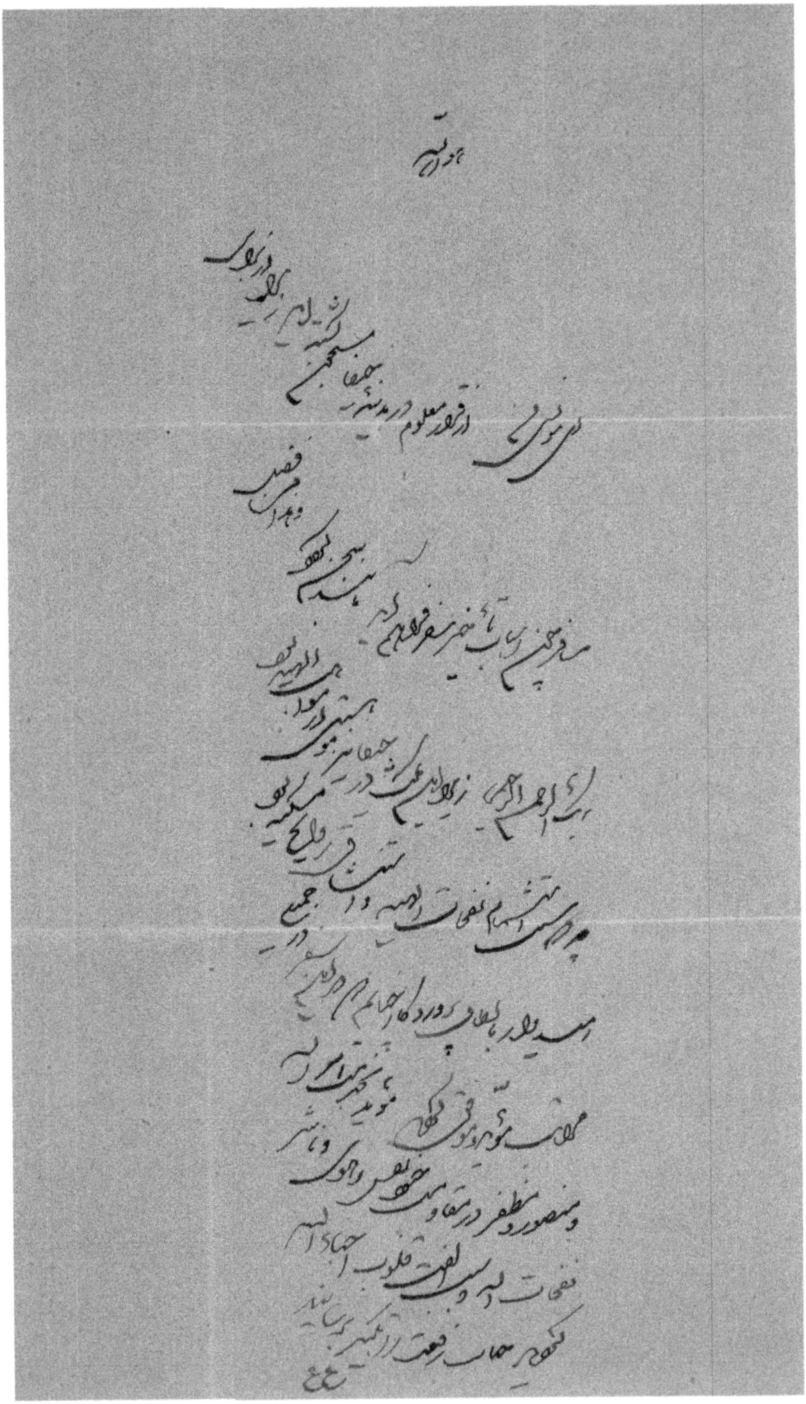

Tablet in the handwriting of ʻAbdu'l-Bahá, addressed to Siyyid Muṣṭafá Rúmí.

O thou my companion!

It seems that thou hast become a prisoner in the city of Haifa, for whenever the means of travel are delayed, the place becomes like unto a prison for the traveler. This, verily, is a bounty from thy Merciful and Compassionate Lord, inasmuch as this pause in Haifa hath become a means of receiving divine blessings, and an opportunity to inhale the heavenly breezes and the musky fragrances. My prayer during thy sojourn is that the Almighty in His loving kindness will confirm and assist thee, and graciously aid thee to serve this Cause. May thou be triumphant and victorious in resisting the hosts of self and passion, in promoting the divine sweet savours, and uniting the hearts of the beloved of the Lord.

—'Abdu'l-Bahá

Dear and most prized co-worker:

What you will place on record regarding the history of the Faith in India and Burma will acquire tremendous significance and influence in the days to come. It will serve to instruct, inspire, and cheer countless souls among the rising generation, and will add fresh laurels to those you have so deservedly won in the service of God's immortal Faith. No words can adequately convey the gratitude I feel in my heart for your continued and inestimable services. Your true and affectionate brother,

Shoghi

ACKNOWLEDGMENTS

I am grateful to the Universal House of Justice for the provisional translations of the Tablets of 'Abdu'l-Bahá appearing in this book.

I offer my thanks to the National Spiritual Assembly of the Bahá'ís of India for giving me access to Siyyid Muṣṭafá Rúmí's archival documents.

To Mr. Kenneth Bowers, Secretary of the National Spiritual Assembly of the Bahá'ís of the United States of America, for his encouragement and for facilitating the work on the manuscript.

To my dear friend Ramin Abrishamian, who, with his precise engineering mind went over the memoirs with me and put them in the correct sequence. He not only toiled over the manuscript with me, but with his dear wife Diana provided kind hospitality for weeks during my stay at their home.

To my editor Bahhaj Taherzadeh for his conscientious attention to the final editing of the manuscript.

FOREWORD BY IRAN FURÚTAN MUHÁJIR

Each stage of the promulgation of the Faith and development of the Bahá'í community in the vast subcontinent of India—a region that included the present-day countries of India, Myanmar (Burma), Pakistan, and Bangladesh before their division into independent states—was undertaken at the direction of the Central Figures of the Faith.

During the Ministry of the Báb, there were at least three Indians who recognized His station as a Manifestation of God and embraced His Faith. Nabíl-i-A'ẓam, in *The Dawn-Breakers,* offers a brief account concerning Shaykh Sa'íd-i-Hindi, the eighth Letter of the Living:

> Among the disciples whom the Báb had instructed, in the early days of His Mission, to disperse and teach His Cause, was a certain Shaykh Sa'íd-i-Hindí, one of the Letters of the Living, who had been directed by his Master to journey throughout India and proclaim to its people the precepts of His Revelation. Shaykh Sa'íd, in the course of his travels, visited the town of Multan, where he met . . . Siyyid Básir, who, though blind, was able to perceive immediately, with his inner eye, the significance of the message Shaykh Sa'íd had brought him.[1]

Contact with Shaykh Sa'íd was cut off after his travel to Multan, and no more is known of his history.

Nabil recounts details of the life of Siyyid-i-Basir, who was taught the Faith of the Báb by Shaykh Sa'íd-i-Hindi:

> The vast learning he had acquired, far from hindering him from appreciating the value of the Cause to which he was summoned, enabled him to grasp its meaning and understand the greatness of its power. Casting behind him the trappings of leadership, and severing himself from his friends and kinsmen, he arose with a fixed resolve to render his share of service to the Cause he had embraced. His first act was to undertake a pilgrimage to Shíráz, in the hope of meeting his Beloved. Arriving in that city, he was informed, to his surprise and grief, that the Báb had been banished to the mountains of Ádhirbayján, where He was leading a life of unrelieved solitude. He straightway proceeded to Ṭihrán, and from thence departed for Núr, where he met Bahá'u'lláh. This meeting relieved his heart from the burden of sorrow caused by his failure to meet his Master. To those he subsequently met, of whatever class or creed, he imparted the joys and blessings he had so abundantly received from the hands of Bahá'u'lláh, and was able to endow them with a measure of the power with which his intercourse with Him had invested his innermost being.[2]

Nabíl also provides an account of Qahru'lláh, ". . . a dervish who had come from India and who, as soon as he met the Báb, acknowledged the truth of His Mission. All who met that dervish, whom the Báb had named Qahru'lláh, during his sojourn at Iski-Shahr, felt the warmth of his enthusiasm and were deeply impressed by the tenacity of his conviction. An increasing number of people became enamoured of the charm of his personality and willingly acknowledged the compelling power of his Faith. . . . He was often heard to relate the following: 'In the days when I occupied the exalted position of a navváb in India, the Báb appeared to me in a vision. He gazed at me and won my heart completely. I arose, and had started to follow Him, when He looked at me intently and said: "Divest yourself of your gorgeous attire, depart from your native land, and hasten on foot to meet Me in Ádhirbayján.

In Chihríq you will attain your heart's desire." I followed His directions and have now reached my goal.'"

The Báb instructed Qahru'lláh to "return to India and there consecrate his life to the service of His Cause. 'Alone and on foot,' He commanded him, 'he should return whence he came. With the same ardour and detachment with which he performed his pilgrimage to this country, he must now repair to his native land and unceasingly labour to advance the interests of the Cause.' No sooner had Qahru'lláh received the message from his Master than he arose to carry out His wishes. . . . Alone, clad in the meanest attire, staff in hand, he walked all the way back to his country. No one knows what ultimately befell him."[3]

In the 1800s "a few members of the Afnán family had established a trading company and later a printing press bearing the trade mark 'Násirí' in Bombay, India. This was the first printing press in the Bahá'í world to produce several volumes of Bahá'í writings. As a result of this enterprise Bombay became a place where Bahá'ís would congregate and to which Persian Bahá'í pilgrims traveled on their way to and from 'Akká. When the Afnáns realized that there was receptivity towards the Faith among the Indian population, they sent a petition to Bahá'u'lláh for a Bahá'í teacher with knowledge and experience to go to India, and offered financial assistance towards this meritorious enterprise."[4]

Bahá'u'lláh chose Sulaymán Khán-i-Tunukábání, also known as Jamál Effendi, for this purpose. 'Abdu'l-Bahá explains:

> *Sulaymán Khán was the emigrant and settler who was given the title of Jamáli'd-Dín. He was born in Tunukábán, into an old family of that region. He was cradled in wealth, bred to ease, reared in the comfortable ways of luxury. From his early childhood he had high ambitions and noble aims, and he was honor and aspiration personified. At first he planned to outdistance all his fellows and achieve some lofty rank. For this reason he left his birthplace and went to the capital, Ṭihrán, where he hoped to become a leader, surpassing the rest of his generation.*

> *In Ṭihrán, however, the fragrance of God was borne his way, and he listened to the summons of the Well-Beloved. He was saved from the perturbations of high rank; from all the din and clatter, the glory, the pomps and palaces, of this heap of dust, the world. He threw off his chains, and by God's grace, discovered peace. To him, the seat of honor was now no different from the place where people removed their slippers at the door, and high office was a thing soon gone and forgotten. He was cleansed from the stain of living, his heart was eased, for he had burst the shackles that held him to this present life.*
>
> *Putting on the garments of a pilgrim, he set out to find his loving Friend, and came to the Most Great Prison. Here for a time he rested, under the protection of the Ancient Beauty; here he gained the honor of entering the presence of Bahá'u'lláh, and listened to momentous teachings from His holy lips. When he had breathed the scented air, when his eyes were illumined and his ears attuned to the words of the Lord, he was permitted to make a journey to India, and bidden to teach the true seekers after truth.*
>
> *Resting his heart on God, in love with the sweet savors of God, on fire with the love of God, he left for India.*[5]

Soon after his arrival in India, Jamál Effendi traveled to Madras (present-day Chennai). It was there that he encountered the young Siyyid Muṣṭafá Rúmí, who quickly became enamored of this holy man and the teachings he had brought, and started to travel with him as his translator. Siyyid Muṣṭafá soon embraced the Cause, and, in the years that Jamál Effendi was traveling throughout the Indian Subcontinent to teach the Faith at the behest of Bahá'u'lláh, he accompanied and served him.

After the Ascension of Bahá'u'lláh, although heartbroken and despondent, Siyyid Muṣṭafá remained steadfast and immediately expressed his obedience to 'Abdu'l-Bahá. The Master's love for Siyyid Muṣṭafá is evident in the tens of Tablets He revealed for him in which He addressed him in the most glowing and loving terms:

O thou who art firm and steadfast in the Covenant!
O thou faithful friend of 'Abdu'l-Bahá!
O thou who hast been chosen for the great bounties of the Lord!
O thou harbinger of the Covenant!
O thou promulgator of the Faith of God!
O thou My companion!

Siyyid Muṣṭafá was a great administrator as well as a great scholar and teacher of the Faith. As soon as there were enough Bahá'ís in a town, he organized them into groups and thus laid the foundation for the Spiritual Assemblies that would be formed in the future. He was among the first Bahá'í teachers to implement systematic teaching projects by repeatedly sending teachers to specific areas to promulgate the Faith and strengthen the new believers.

The Ascension of 'Abdu'1-Bahá in 1921 did not shake Siyyid Muṣṭafá's steadfastness in the Covenant. He became a staunch defender of the Will and Testament of 'Abdu'1-Bahá against the allegations of Covenant-breakers, and transferred the devotion and love he felt for 'Abdu'l-Bahá to Shoghi Effendi, the Guardian of the Faith. He emphasized that as long as he lived, there would not be any opposition to the Guardianship in Burma.

He revered and loved the Guardian and in spite of his advanced age tried to follow his advice and instructions to the best of his ability. As can be gleaned from the Guardian's messages to him, this love was reciprocated:

No words can adequately convey the gratitude I feel in my heart for your continued and inestimable services. I will ever be reminded of your glorious and exemplary services to the Abhá Revelation.

You have, in the evening of your life, added fresh laurels to the crown of immortal glory which your many services have won for you and which the future generations will gratefully and joyfully remember.

> *You belong to the heroic age of our Beloved Faith—an age to which you have richly contributed.*
>
> *Future generations will glorify and extol your service rendered with such devotion, zeal and love. I feel extremely grateful to you, and am proud of your record of service.*
>
> *My heart overflows with gratitude for all that you have achieved in His path.*
>
> *You have set an inspiring and unforgettable example to the rising generation. The concourse on high is proud of and extols your splendid achievements. Be happy and confident.*

The beloved Guardian encouraged Siyyid Muṣṭafá Rúmí to write his memoirs, stating: *"What you will place on record regarding the history of the Faith in India and Burma will acquire tremendous significance and influence in the days to come."*

Siyyid Muṣṭafá obeyed and wrote his recollections, spanning more than seven decades, not only of his own life but of the early history of the Bahá'í Faith in the region. These memoirs, written with utmost humility and simplicity, indicate how under the tutelage of Jamál Effendi, Siyyid Muṣṭafá became a great teacher of the Bahá'í Faith and dedicated his life to the service of God. His knowledge of multiple languages of India and Burma, combined with his gentle and loving manner, attracted many souls to the Faith. Bahá'u'lláh praised him in several Tablets, in one of which He addressed him with these loving words, *"Be thou thankful for that thou hast been remembered by this Wronged One, and that there hath been revealed for thee that which shall abide for as long as earth and heaven shall endure."*

Siyyid Muṣṭafá Rúmí continued to serve the Faith in love and humility until his life ended in martyrdom. Shoghi Effendi, bestowed upon him the title of "Hand of the Cause of Bahá'u'lláh," and described him as an "Apostle of Bahá'u'lláh," a "Pioneer," and "Martyr."

May his shining soul be a guide for all of us, and aid us to serve our beloved Faith.

Iran Furútan Muhájir
November 2019

Siyyid Muṣṭafá Rúmí.

INTRODUCTION
BY SIYYID MUṢṬAFÁ RÚMÍ

On 21 January 1931, I received a loving letter dated 15 December 1930 from our revered Bahá'í friends Mrs. Mariam Haney and Mr. Stanwood Cobb, the editors of the Bahá'í magazine *Star of the West,* expressing their heartfelt desire that "I might care to write an article for their magazine on the subject of 'the coming of the Bahá'í Cause into Burma'" as my name had been given to them as a person capable of writing such an article. They "hoped with all their hearts that" as a faithful and old obedient servant of the beloved Guardian, His Holiness Shoghi Effendi Rabbani, I would "render this service at once."

After two unsuccessful attempts to perform such a duty, this was a golden opportunity for me to render this service to the supreme Cause.

While I was in the holy presence of my beloved Master 'Abdu'l-Bahá in 1914, a well-known learned Bahá'í teacher who had recently returned from a tour of France, Germany, and England to the holy threshold of the supreme Lord asked me to write in Persian while on pilgrimage about my life and about the history of the Bahá'í movement in India and Burma. In obedience to his loving request I wrote about fifty pages, which was highly appreciated by my fellow-pilgrims when it was read to them. Unfortunately the said teacher suddenly became ill and was sent to Beirut by our Lord for treatment. Also this humble servant and other pilgrims from Bombay were commanded by 'Abdu'l-Bahá to return to India and Burma. The Master predicted that the disastrous world-devastating Great War was at hand. He instructed me to remain in Burma, and not to travel.

Thus, after returning to Burma, I resigned to His Will and occupied all my time in translating some holy scriptures, such as the book of Íqán into Burmese, and writing other booklets for the enlightenment of the Bahá'ís of Burma. I also tried to complete the history of the Faith in India and Burma in Persian. . . .

Now I am extremely happy that I was able to accomplish this arduous task notwithstanding my advanced age. . . .

I confess frankly that it was my bounty to be bestowed with many accolades such as "teacher of the Cause, proclaimer of the Covenant, promulgator of the Divine Cause" and so on by my Lord 'Abdu'l-Bahá and the beloved Guardian through their supreme merciful grace and clemency. However, I know my limitations. I am a humble servant, unschooled, without any qualifications, and seek no name or fame.

The diadem of my qualification is only, if it is acceptable in His holy presence, to be a most humble servant of all servants of the holy threshold of the Báb, Bahá'u'lláh, 'Abdu'l-Bahá, and the beloved Guardian of their divine Cause, Shoghi Effendi Rabbani. I earnestly desire to sacrifice my worthless life in the glorious path of their love.

Most humbly and devotedly in His supreme service,

Siyyid Mustafa Roumie
Mandalay, Burma
15 September 1932[1]

- 1 -

CHILDHOOD AND YOUTH

My ancestors came from the Shí'ih community of Iṣfahán (Persia), from the Sháhshaḥán quarter. They left their native country to permanently reside in Karbilá, where they lived in a house opposite the residence of Ḥájí Siyyid 'Alí-Naqí, the Mujtahid. My father, Siyyid Muḥammad, was an Arabic scholar, who, because of some family disputes, left his home in Karbilá during the reign of Sulṭán Maḥmúd II (1785–1839) for Syria and later Constantinople, Turkey. He was the son of Siyyid 'Alí, who was the son of Siyyid 'Abdu'l-Raḥím. At the age of thirty he was appointed as Qáḍí (Cadi), an Islamic judge for the Shafi'i and Sunní Sects in Constantinople. During the Janissary Uprising,[1] he left Constantinople for Baghdád and Karbilá and later returned to India as it was not safe for him to remain in the Turkish-ruled areas. For many years he toured India with the surname of Roumie, derived from the historical Islamic name for Constantinople, Roumatu'l-Kubra (Great Roman City).

He studied Sufism in India and in a short time became highly esteemed and honored as a spiritual leader. He soon had thousands of disciples in Baroda (Gujrat), Hyderabad (Deccan), and the Madras and Malabar coasts, among them princes and subjects of the ruling principalities.

Years later he returned to Karbilá and married my mother, Ṭayyibih, from the noble Babush-Shaikhi Arab tribe of Iraq. I was born in Karbilá on 12 Rabí'u'l-Avval 1268 A.H. [January 5, 1852].* I was seven days

---

* There is some discrepancy regarding the date of Siyyid Muṣṭafá Rúmí's birth. This appears to be based on the belief that he was approximately ninety-

old when my mother passed away and my father entrusted me to the care of my maternal uncle and left for India. He returned when I was twelve years old. My uncle asked for a handsome compensation before my father could take me to live with him. My father was traveling with his new wife, Munavvar Jahán; their infant son, Siyyid Maḥmúd; and his mother-in-law, who was of the family of Dúst Muḥammad Khán, the king of Kabul, Afghanistan.

My father purchased a house near the "Baghdád Gate" and opened two fabric stores, mostly of Bengali, Syrian, and Chinese silk cloth, one in Baghdád and another in "Bazaar Dangchinyan" in Karbilá. He left the management of the store in Baghdád to a partner and managed the one in Karbilá with the help of an Indian servant.

Unfortunately, he lost a great portion of his wealth during the dreadful famine of Iraq. Also, when Náṣiri'd-Dín Sháh of Persia visited Karbilá, his dignitary companions swindled my father and he was unable to reclaim the money owed him even by going to court. In spite of all his problems he distributed a large sum as alms among the starving people.

Another matter pressuring him in Karbilá at this time was the question of the ownership of his house. He had purchased the house for a considerable sum and had made sure that the title was lawfully clear and that the deed of sale was drawn by an expert lawyer and duly registered in the Turkish Government Registration Office in Baghdád. However, after a few months, some dishonest people went to the well-known mujtahid, Shaykh Zaynu'l-'Ábidín, by the referral of Grand Mujtahid Mírzá Faḍlu'lláh, both of Mázindarání origin. They filed false claims as heirs of the deceased owner of the property and obtained a decree from the grand mujtahid that the sale was null and void, and the executors had no legal right to execute the deed of sale. My father was summoned to personally

---

nine years of age at the time of his martyrdom [see 'Abbás-'Alí Butt, "An Account of the Services of Siyyid Muṣṭafá Rúmí," *Bahá'í World,* vol. X, p. 519], which is reported to have taken place on 13 March 1945. This would place his birth circa 1846; however, it is possible, as was common at the time, that his date of birth was uncertain and his precise age was unknown to his contemporaries.

appear before the grand mujtahid with all the deeds to the property. He was not acquainted with the law courts and legal proceedings, as he had never been to civil or criminal courts although he had served as a religious justice. He was sure that if he appeared before the mujtahid he would be disgraced and defeated, and he had no trustworthy person to appoint as an agent for himself. He kept quiet until the opposite party filed their suit in the Turkish Civil Court of Baghdád as legal heirs and absolute owners of the property. As a testimony to their claim, the plaintiffs filed the final decision of their religious leader—ordering to set aside the sale.

The case was postponed from time to time and was prolonged for more than a year for want of evidence. Several judges changed until at last the case was decided in favor of my father by a new judge who had arrived from Constantinople. The suit was dismissed with cost. Immediately after the judgment, the plaintiffs ran away to Persia as the instigators of the case refused to help them, fearing they might be prosecuted for the trial cost, which amounted to more than the price of the property.

This incident disheartened my father, who bitterly lamented the regretful condition of the people of Karbilá who polluted that sacred spot through their irreligious misdeeds without understanding and repentance. He felt he could not peacefully pass the remaining days of his life in Karbilá and sold all his moveable and immoveable belongings at sacrificial prices and migrated to India on a permanent basis.

During our stay in Karbilá my father sent me to the school of Shaykh Báqir of Iṣfahán, who was a very cruel teacher. One time he slapped me so harshly that I fainted and drops of blood from my nose fell on my book. The next day my father went to the school, rebuked the shaykh, and took me out of that school. He employed a teacher, Shaykh 'Alí-Arab, to teach me for a couple of hours a day at home. I could not speak Persian, but I could read and write in Arabic. Sometimes, when my father was free, he would command me to read a book for him. My lessons were quite unsystematic, irregular, and unsatisfactory. However, at home I learned a little Persian and to a certain extent Urdu as my stepmother and her mother spoke these two languages.

I accompanied my father to Bombay, where he was cordially welcomed by his disciples and lived there for four or five years. In Bombay I was taught Persian by Áqá Ḥájí Muḥammad Ḥusayn Tavakkulí of Shíráz. Although I was very keen to learn the other languages prevailing in Bombay, such as Gujrati, Marathi, Kachchi, Urdu, and English, my father did not agree. However, I gradually picked up Gujrati from Parsee friends and Urdu from some Indian acquaintances. I learned to speak Kachchi from some of my father's disciples—who belonged to Katch-Bhooj, a small island near Bombay—and Marathi from our neighbor. Unfortunately I had no one to teach me English.

Ḥakím Muḥammad Háshim, the maternal uncle of my stepmother, who was the elder of their family, decided to transfer the residence of the family to Salem, a town in the Madras province that was known to have cholera epidemics in some months. They left first, and my father and I left Bombay for Calicut, another seashore town of Madras, which was the nearest town to Salem. While traveling by ship, I had a dream that my stepmother, Munavvar Jahán, had died. I was terribly upset and when I woke up I wept while telling my father about the dream. He felt that it was just the dream of a young boy and was not disturbed by it.

We arrived at the harbor of Calicut (Kozhikode) on the Malabar Coast, where my father was warmly received by his disciples. We continued our journey for Salem by the recently constructed railway. Upon our arrival in the evening we gave the carriage driver the address of Ḥakím Muḥammad Háshim's house in the Noor-Mangalam quarter. The driver was surprised and informed my father about the death of the newly arrived niece of the Ḥakím. My father started wailing and weeping for his irreparable loss. His loud moans continued for days and no one could console him. I was greatly loved by my deceased step-mother, even more than her own son, Siyyid Maḥmúd, thus I also felt and lamented her loss. The next morning we all went to the cemetery to perform prayers for the soul of the departed. My father in his agony did not want to return to the house but was finally persuaded to do so. His pathetic condition continued every time he visited his wife's grave. She was supposed to be his last companion among the twenty-three or twenty-four wives he had married during his long life. He had lost thirty-five sons and many daughters. People were afraid that in this lamentable and agitated circumstance he might become insane. He did not stay long in Salem and suddenly disappeared, leaving all his affairs in my charge. My step-grandmother also could no longer stay in the house where her daughter had died. She advised me to move with her to Madras, where I could find many of her friends as well as sincere disciples of my father.

My father had not written a single line to inform us about his whereabouts. Thus I asked permission from my step-grandmother to make a quick tour to search for him before leaving for Madras. I went from town to town, and after a month or so suddenly came across him in the town of Madurai. He was the guest of the Raja of Shiva Shanghla State, Prince Dorasingha Tavar. He embraced me in public and I thanked God that he was healthy. He introduced me to the Raja and I stayed with him for a few days and then took leave to return to my step-grandmother. In addition to the presents that I received from the Raja, my father gave me a few hundred Indian rupees and brought me to the railway station. I kissed his hand and said goodbye to him. He prayed for my long life and happiness and repeatedly told me to go to Madras with his mother-in-law and son Siyyid Maḥmúd, and to take all his belongings with me.

After my arrival at Salem it took me several days to pack and leave for Madras. We rented a house on a public road in Tirmal Khedi near the big mosque of Walajah, the late ruling Raja of Madras. I registered Siyyid Maḥmúd in an English school and became associated with the many friends and disciples of my father.

I did not have a frivolous upbringing and was fortunate to have been brought up in a circle of elderly learned sages according to the ancient customs, and was prohibited from associating with playmates. Therefore, during my life to my present age I have not been to any sporting events, playgrounds, race courses, theatres, or any other recreational venues. I liked to associate with those who were interested in spiritual discourses. My father used to speak about the advent of the Imám Mihdí according to the long ode of the celebrated saint of Islam, Sháh Nematu'lláh Valí, which said "He will appear in the year of "shin, re and seen," which is numerically equal to the Persian alphabetical number of 1260, Hijrí, or 1844 A.D. However, he did not investigate the truth from the Bábís, who believed that the expected Imám Mihdí had appeared in the appointed time. My father was well acquainted with Ḥájí Siyyid Javád-i-Karbalá'í[2] but thought that the traditions of Imám Ja'far-i-Ṣádiq[3] might have been misinterpreted by some clerics of the past. Thus, despite all his knowledge of the holy scripture and traditions, he remained deprived of all the bounties and blessings of the golden age.

I always observed my father after his daily prayers asking God for the speedy advent of the Imám Mihdi, and saying in Arabic: *Al-Ajal Al-Ajal Al-Ajal* and *As-saeh As-saeh As-saeh,* "O Imám appear hastily, hastily, hastily, immediately in this hour and moment." I imitated him, and after my daily prayers always repeated the same words. Sometimes, while meditating alone in the neighborhood mosque at midnight, I would tell myself that if the Imám had already appeared His light would shine forth on me due to my chastity, piety, and sincerity in seeking Him.

One day a disciple of my father, Ḥájí Isháq, a member of the Kutchi (Cutchi) Memons, a Sunní Islamic community of Bombay, came to see me and in a kindly tone told me that "it is not wise to pass this life idly, particularly in such a distressful time when famine is overwhelming the whole region of Madras province. I came to you to entreat you for your help in my business of rice trade." He said that he had trust in me to go to all towns and cities where his employees were selling rice, and to collect and bring the proceeds of the sales to his office in Madras. He offered me a share in the profits and said that he would provide a moderate sum for my living and would pay all my travel expenses. After consulting with my step-grandmother I accepted his offer.

I joined the service immediately, and, with a servant from the office to accompany me, journeyed from town to town and city to city where the company's rice business was situated. It was an arduous task for an inexperienced young man, but I discharged my duties honestly and once every month returned to the central office to bring the cash that I had collected. My service was highly appreciated by my employer

After one year it was estimated that the business was losing money. My employer lovingly expressed his regret that he could not give me any dividends but offered an honorarium of five hundred rupees. I refused to take it and said that I was not entitled to receive any bonus or dividend in case of such a loss, and left the office. Ḥájí Is<u>h</u>áq personally visited my house and insisted that I accept his offer as a token of his loving appreciation and a mark of his respect. After that visit he very often came to me and cordially invited me to once more join his business, but I declined his offer and decided to start my own business on a small scale in the trade of Kashmiri wool shawls.

It was during my time in the rice business that I had an extraordinary experience. One day I was in the city of Tiruchirappalli in a rice stall, taking the proceeds of sales from the agent, when I saw a Persian dervish walking in the street and chanting a Persian poem. He was an elderly man of above sixty years. He approached me, stood before the shop and asked me if I would spend some time with him to talk. I invited him to come in and to talk to me. He said "Thou art a very fortunate man of the Holy Shrine of Imám Ḥusayn in Karbilá, why tarry so long in vain? No more expectation and longing for the advent of our Qá'im. He appeared in 1260 of Hijrí. In Mecca as well as in Persia, thousands of people believe in Him and have sacrificed their wealth, family, and life in His path. Thy forehead is shining with His splendor and has attracted my soul and drawn me near you; go thou and search for it, sacrifice thy life for Him."

I asked him what the poem was that he was chanting, and he commenced to chant loudly in a melodious voice, saying "A youth of tender age, speaking our own language (Persian) has appeared and has come with a shining brilliant face, following in His path are thousands of Angels and Ḥúríes (Virgins of Paradise). He is God, He is Muḥammad Muṣṭafá, He is the essence of all prophets." I was extremely moved. The dervish did not stay long, and disappeared. But as the people are against such manifestations I dared not utter a single word about this incident. I kept quiet until in Calcutta the dynamic force burst from my innermost heart and soul, and I accepted the Cause of God.

- 2 -

THE ARRIVAL OF JAMÁL EFFENDI IN INDIA

It was during my years in Madras that my spiritual father and revered benefactor, Sulaymán Khán-i-Tunukábání, also known as Jamál Effendi or Jamálu'd-Dín Sháh, arrived in India. He was a venerable figure of an advanced age and a great scholar of Arabic, Turkish, and Persian. His selfless striking character and personality with courteous manners most eloquently testified to his noble birth and high rank. As a firm believer since the early days of the Báb's declaration, he was well aware of the prophecies regarding the Manifestation of Bahá'u'lláh and readily embraced Him. He left his home in Persia, renounced all his worldly possessions, cheerfully gave up his official rank and position, and traveled to the presence of Bahá'u'lláh and offered most humbly and meekly to sacrifice himself at the Holy threshold of his Lord so that he might attain His supreme pleasure.

Bahá'u'lláh revealed a Tablet conferring upon him the title of "Lámí'á" (the brilliant one), the opening words of which are: *"O thou the brilliant one! We have conferred upon thee the title of the brilliant one so that thou mayest shine forth in the universe in the name of thy Lord the possessor of the Day of Distinction."*

At this time Ḥájí Siyyid Mírzá and Ḥájí Siyyid Muḥammad Afnán; both sons of Ḥájí Mírzá Siyyid Ḥasan; Afnán-i-Kabír; and Ḥájí Siyyid Maḥmúd, a grandson of Ḥájí Siyyid Muḥammad; had a very successful business in Bombay as general merchants and commission agents, trading under the company name of Messrs. Ḥájí Siyyid Mírzá and Mírzá Maḥmúd Co.

The Afnáns, realizing the potential for teaching the Faith in India, beseeched Bahá'u'lláh for a Bahá'í teacher to be sent there, and offered to defray the expenses.

Jamál Effendi was chosen by Bahá'u'lláh and was commanded to proceed to India in the company of his kinsman Mírzá Ḥusayn, and at all times to consult with the Afnáns in his activities. These two noble and heroic souls at once set out from the Holy Land with unflinching determination to serve the divine Cause and took the first boat available from Port Sa'íd to India, and landed in Bombay around the year 1872–73.

Since ancient times, all those who promulgated Islam in India were Persian sages and mostly dervishes in appearance. As the Indian Empire was formerly ruled by the Moghul Dynasty, when Jamál Effendi came to India, although India was under British rule, the majority of the people were well-acquainted with the Persian language and its literature. Jamál Effendi spoke very high Persian and traveled all over India in a princely manner with two or three companions, and by his gentle behavior of exemplary independence and virtue, and by his venerable appearance and eloquent discourses, attracted the people to him.

On arrival in Bombay, with the guidance of the Afnáns, Jamál Effendi used the garb of a dervish. At that time there were many unsavory people from Persia in Bombay who traded in selling horses and thus open teaching of the Cause was not advisable.

Jamál Effendi's first residence in India was the Ḥusayníyyih, a building in Bombay dedicated by its founder, Babri Ali, a zealous Shí'ih philanthropist from Lucknow, India, for the celebration of the mourning ceremony for the Imám Ḥusayn.

During his stay in Bombay, Jamál Effendi, in spite of the language barrier, managed to deliver the great message to many distinguished Persian residents, such as the late Áqá Khán (the then head of the Khoja Ismá'íliyyih community, and grandfather of the present well-known leader of that community) and the Persian High Priest of the Shí'ih

Ithná-'Asharíyyih Mosque, Siyyid Muhammad. The latter accepted the message and proved to be one of the most confirmed and devout believers.

Within a short period, Jamál Effendi became a known figure in the public, and the nature of his activities became widely publicized. The Afnáns advised him that in the interest of the Cause, and for his own protection, he should leave Bombay and visit the interior provinces of India. He left Bombay and traveled through many important towns, proclaiming the glad tidings everywhere.

It was very easy for him to speak with the rulers of the states and high officials of the government. During his two years in India he visited many important parts such as Jaipur, Gwalior, Baroda, Hyderabad Deccan, Rampur, Rohilkhand, Benares, etc., and was given warm and excellent receptions by the rulers of the states wherever he visited. In each place he delivered the great message of love and peace and explained the requirements of this new age to everyone.

In Rampur, Rohilkhand, Uttar Pradesh,[1] which was ruled by a native chief, Navváb Kalb-i-'Alí Khán, an orthodox Sunní Muslim, Jamál Effendi was the guest of the chief's uncle Colonel Navváb Asghar 'Alí Khán. During his stay there, the chief arranged a meeting of the Muslim clergy of his state at his palace for a discussion with Jamál Effendi about the Bahá'í doctrine of the "nonexistence of evil."

Jamál Effendi told the audience that Bahá'ís do not believe in the existence of positive evil in creation. According to Bahá'í belief all is good. The Creator of all things is but one God. He is good, and therefore His creation is good. Evil does not exist in His creation.

At the end of his discourse the high priest of the state, who was noted for his learning, pointed to the fire on the hookah that the chief was smoking and questioned Jamál Effendi: "Is this not a positive evil? It may burn the palace and reduce to ashes all present here in no time."

Jamál Effendi answered the question with great eloquence. He asked the audience to imagine what would be the consequence if fire did not exist on earth for a moment. In its absence the very existence of human life would be impossible, as it is a principle element in the creation system. Humanity ought to be thankful to the Creator for such a useful creation for preservation of life. How can one justly call it a positive evil! It is the same with all the natural qualities of man. If they be used and displayed in an unlawful way they become offenders and blameworthy. The gist of the divine laws in all religions is to use each and everything in its proper place as ordained by its Author. Then each thing is termed as good and lawful. Only when used in a wrong manner is it called unlawful, evil, or sin. The chief object of the Prophets of God is to teach this doctrine to mankind according to the conditions and necessity of the time. Thus "commandments" and "prohibitions" are ordained.

He also illustrated the same principle with a penknife that was shown to him by the chief. Referring to it he said, "How useful an article is this. But its misuse—for example, if it is used for the purpose of stabbing—is an evil. The creation of metal is not evil in itself. It is one of the necessities of our life. But when men turn it into a deadly weapon it becomes evil."

The chief and the whole assemblage of learned men applauded his scholarly exposition and many became interested in the teachings of the new age.

Jamál Effendi became known and the clerics of the city rose to oppose him. Thus he decided to return to Bombay. In his previous stay in Bombay, the wife of Áqá 'Alí Sháh, the new head of the Khuja after the passing of Áqá Khán, had asked Jamál Effendi to pray for her to have a child. Now she had a son and believed Jamál Effendi had great powers. On his arrival in Bombay, she greeted him with great reverence and sent him Persian sweets. Many of the Áqákhání followers also visited him.

To prevent another incident, the Afnáns suggested that Jamál Effendi should leave Bombay once more and travel to Pune, Hyderabad, and Madras. He agreed with this advice and left for Deccan, Hyderabad.

He was greeted with respect and was given accommodation in a house belonging to the chief. A group of officials accepted the Cause—among them Mawlawí S̲h̲áh Reza, Áqá Muḥammad-'Alí Ḥakkák, and Áqá Siyyid 'Alí, who was a confidant of the chief Navváb Mukhtaru'l Mulk, and Mir Siyyid 'Alí K̲h̲án, who was a S̲h̲í'ih. Shamsul K̲h̲án, a captain of the army, who was a Hindu, became a Bahá'í and without fear announced his conversion.

Many high officials and women of the haram heard about the Cause. As the old Navváb had passed away and his successor was a minor, according to the custom they brought him to Jamál Effendi and received a prayer for his long life. It was placed in an amulet that was hung around the child's neck. He wore it to the end of his life. All the new believers received a Tablet from Bahá'u'lláh.[2]

At this time, a historic gathering was held in Delhi, the ancient capital of the Moghul Empire in India, on the occasion of the assumption of the title of the "Empress of India" by her Majesty Queen Victoria (January 1, 1877). Almost all the rulers of the various native states along with their entourage, high officials of the British government, and many other notable persons, Indian as well as non-Indian, were present at this gathering. Jamál Effendi did not hesitate in taking advantage of this unique opportunity. He came in contact with almost all the celebrities of India and quietly informed them about the great mystery of the age. He met Swami Devanand Saraswati, the founder of the Arya Semaj, and found in him a true and sympathetic friend of the Cause.

After this event he proceeded to Deccan, Hyderabad—the Nizam's dominion. The Nizam was very young at that time, and Jamál Effendi was introduced to the Prime Minister, Sir Salar Jung Mukhtaru'l Mulk, who was a staunch S̲h̲í'ih. Through the magnetic personality and eloquence of Jamál Effendi this statesman soon became deeply interested in the Bahá'í Cause and eventually a Tablet from the Supreme Pen was revealed in his honor. (According to the laws of the Kingdom, high officials could not openly accept any religion except their ancestral faith declared on oath, even though they were ruling monarchs.)[3]

Prince Mahboub 'Alí Khán, the young Nizam.

The regent, Sir Salar Jung.

Jamál Effendi's next move was toward Madras in southern India. While in Hyderabad and Madras, he conceived the idea of visiting Burma and unfurling the banner of *Yá Bahá'u'l-Abhá* on the shores of the Irrawaddy River. He had received information that King Mindon of Burma was a monarch of exceptionally generous disposition and absolutely unprejudiced mind, and, though himself a Buddhist, was tolerant of all forms of worship.

In those days the steamships running between India and Burma were very few, so he had to wait for some time before he could catch a boat to take him to Rangoon. While he was waiting, he received a message from the ruler of Rampur State, asking for his immediate presence. The brother of the chief, Navváb Muḥammad-'Alí Khán, had displayed a tendency toward atheism and it was the conviction of the chief that Jamál Effendi was the only person qualified to demonstrate to his brother the absurdity of his belief and bring him around to the true faith of Islam.

Jamál Effendi readily accepted the invitation. Before proceeding to Rampur, he sent Mírzá Ḥusayn with all his belongings and a servant to Rangoon by cargo boat.

It was in Madras that I (Siyyid Muṣṭafá), the writer of this account, met Jamál Effendi for the first time. I was then a young man and was preparing to return to my native country, Karbilá, and Bag͟hdád, after having settled my dues in consequence of a heavy loss sustained in the rice business. I saw a venerable figure, advanced in age, with a brilliant countenance surrounded by heavy luggage and many companions. I approached him at once. He questioned me about my name, my parentage, my native place, and my business. I disliked such questions at first but I kept quiet when he said that he had already seen my father in the city of Bangalore and gave me my father's message that he would come to Madras very soon.

Jamál Effendi's eloquent address, his silvery voice, and his flowery language frequently attracted large gatherings around him. I was one of his ardent admirers and soon became so devotedly attached to him that I approached my father, Siyyid Muḥammad, for permission to accompany Jamál Effendi to Rampur. My father, who was a very learned Muslim divine and was held in great esteem and reverence by the Muslim public, did not approve of my proposal; although he did not know that the theme of Jamál Effendi's talks was the Bahá'í Revelation. He not only refused permission but prohibited me from entering Jamál Effendi's house. However, I was determined to accompany Jamál Effendi to Rampur and succeeded in doing so.

At that time he had with him two other Bahá'ís, Ráfi'u'd-Dín K͟hán of Hassanpur and Ḥájí Ramad͟hán of Rampur, as his constant companions. After leaving Madras, our journey was broken for a couple of days at Gulbarga,[4] where friends and officials from Hyderabad came to meet him. After a short trip to Bombay, we set out for Rampur. On our way to the Cawnpore Railway Station, Jamál Effendi met the brother of the ruler of Rampur State for whose sake he had undertaken this long journey. The Rampur ruler, to form a closer acquaintance between Jamál Effendi and his brother, had sent him to Cawnpore to meet Jamál Effendi and travel with him to Rampur State.

Jamál Effendi on this occasion stayed about a month and a half in Rampur, in the mansion of the ruler's brother, and availed himself of this opportunity to hold several public and private discourses on the ideals and ethical teachings of the Bahá'í religion. Within a few days the ruler's brother and those who were prompting him to oppose Jamál Effendi were silenced, their atheistic doctrines were thrown into the shade, and all their reasoning proved to have no real foundation. In this way Jamál Effendi incurred the displeasure of one Nazír Aḥmad Ḥasan of Aligarh, a most zealous proponent of atheism, who wielded considerable influence over the ruler's brother. By some treacherous means, he had cheated the ruler's brother out of more than thirty thousand rupees that had resulted in much heated argument and correspondence between them. The ruler's brother was indignant at the conduct of this old atheist friend and had him imprisoned. From his prison he wrote to Jamál Effendi, asking him to intercede for his release. Jamál Effendi did so and he was duly released, but had to leave the state. He swore vengeance against Jamál Effendi, although from him he had received nothing but kindness. He declared he would make Jamál Effendi and his wrong doctrines public in newspapers. Jamál Effendi penned an answer to him saying that he would be grateful if he did so, as the Cause would be proclaimed and become famous. To thank the Nazír he also sent him two Kashmiri shawls.

On arrival in Moradabad, the two companions of Jamál Effendi asked permission to remain in their native town, and Jamál Effendi and I continued our travels. Accompanied by a servant, we left Rampur for Lucknow via Kashipur and Moradabad.[5] In Lucknow the chief of police and the head of Arya Semaj, who had met Jamál Effendi in Delhi, visited him. He also met the Rajas of Asethi and Balarampur States, who accorded him a very cordial reception. Meanwhile the Raja of Kashipur arrived and took him to meet the Governor of United Provinces (Uttar Pradesh, India). The Rajas gave us a letter of introduction to the Maharaja of Benares, the sacred city of the Hindus.

We proceeded to Benares. The Maharaja, a Brahmin and a very staunch Hindu, was also the religious head of the Hindu community. He sent his special guards to accompany us to his home and we were his guests for fifteen days in his palace, situated at the bank of the Ganges River. His Muslim servants and cooks took care of our needs.

During this short period we became acquainted with many leading citizens of Benares, Hindus as well as Muslims of all schools of thought. One was Áqá Muḥammad Taqí Benarasí of Khurásán, at whose house we met Ḥájí Aḥmad Bindaní, an influential and wealthy citizen of Rangoon, and several leading Persian Muslims of Calcutta.

At the very first gathering, the conversation gradually turned to the question of the time of the appearance of the Imám Mihdí, the Qá'im, and the Raj'at-i-Ḥusayní according to Shí'ih belief. A learned Shí'ih theologian who was present declared that no time had been specifically mentioned either in the Qur'án or in the sacred traditions of the revered Imáms. Jamál Effendi cited several passages from the Qur'án and the traditions of Imám Ja'far-i-Ṣádiq[6] that pointed to the year 1260 A.H. (corresponding to 1844 A.D.) as the time when one should look for the coming of the expected Mihdí Who would be born like other human beings. Jamal Effendi refuted the theory of the sudden and phenomenal appearance of a youth of one thousand years of age from the strange and unknown region of "Jabulqa" and "Jabulsa."[7]

Jamál Effendi explained that the Qá'im on his appearance would introduce a new Cause, a new Dispensation, a new revealed book, and a new divine law for the guidance of mankind. He also quoted numerous passages from the sacred traditions to the effect that the Qá'im would be subjected to all kinds of persecution, humiliation, and opposition, and eventually he and his followers would be martyred by men of his own ilk and class. It was an exceedingly interesting discussion that went on for a couple of days. At the conclusion, the learned divines protested that although there was some force in Jamál Effendi's argument, they were not justified in accepting it since there was no appearance of the Antichrist or Sufyání. Jamál Effendi then, in his usual friendly manner, said:

"Let us jointly pray for divine guidance and endeavor to grasp the true significance and correct meaning of the words of the Holy Book, which according to the saying of Imám Ja'far-i-Ṣádiq could be comprehended only by chosen ones and faithful servants whose hearts are pure."

From Benares we proceeded to Calcutta, visiting Patna on the way. We arrived at Patna at dusk and went directly to an inn, where we spent the night. Early the next morning, we were informed that the police had surrounded the inn the previous night and had been checking the arrival and departure of the guests. Shortly thereafter some high European officials came directly to Jamál Effendi and informed him that the chief commissioner wanted to see him, and that he should accompany them. We went with them to Danapur, the seat of government at that time. On arriving at Danapur, we were ordered to wait in a room under police surveillance and remained there for four hours without knowing the cause of this sudden arrest. I felt that Nazír Aḥmad Ḥassan, the atheist, who had been against Jamál Effendi in Rampur, must have had something to do with this little surprise. My surmise proved to be correct. A clerk came to Jamál Effendi with one of the letters he had written to Nazír Aḥmad Ḥassan, and began to question him about it. Realizing that the reason of the arrest was some misunderstanding about this letter in the mind of the officials, I asked for permission to produce the letter of Nazír Aḥmad Ḥassan to which that one was a reply. Upon receiving permission I promptly produced the letter in question, a reference to which at once cleared all doubts. We were immediately set free and all our effects were returned to us. Thus the attempt of an atheist to do mischief to the Cause was frustrated.

As this incident took place during the month of Muharram (Islamic New Year) the majority of the high-ranking citizens—such as Navváb Muḥammad, Navváb Wiláyát-'Alí Khán, and other illustrious persons—gathered around Jamál Effendi and invited him to their homes, where he had the opportunity to deliver the Bahá'í message freely in their large meetings.

After two weeks we left for Calcutta, and went to live in a house that had been prepared for us by Navváb Safdar-'Alí Khán, the paternal uncle of the Rampur Ruler. Here, too, within a very short time the magnetic personality of Jamál Effendi and his affable manner attracted many leading citizens of Calcutta and its neighborhood. He soon became a well-known figure in the community, particularly among men of religious and philosophic mind. Jamál Effendi always eagerly sought the opportunity to deliver the great message of universal love and peace, the message of the wonderful Revelation of God's mystery, and the message of the advent of the new age.

An opportunity came about when he met Ḥájí Mírzá 'Abdu'l-Karím Shírází, a renowned Persian merchant of Calcutta, at whose residence leading Muhammadans met every day to discuss current topics. This was the time of the Russo-Turkish war of 1877, and the main subjects discussed were the events of the war as they appeared in the newspaper reports. In the course of these discussions, Jamál Effendi, as often as possible, directed the attention of the audience to various prophecies in the holy Qur'án and the tradition of the Prophet regarding the signs of the appearance of the Promised Redeemer. His eloquence and his unique method of presenting the subject made a great impression on all present.

A Muslim man who was preparing to go on the Ḥájj sent five hundred rupees as a gift for Jamál Effendi. He refused it with thanks and sent him a message that he did not accept gifts. The Ḥájí thought that the amount had not been sufficient and sent a thousand rupees. I took the money to Jamál Effendi who became angry and told me to take it back with a message from him that said, "You have spent a large amount for this trip and are now leaving for pilgrimage to Mecca. It is better if you spend this money for this blessed journey. We will always pray for you."

I told Jamál Effendi that we really could use that money as we did not have any left for our expenses. He answered, "Do you want to shame us in front of God and the people? This is not how the people of Bahá work." He then opened his small coffer, took out a small gold coin that was about nineteen mit͟hqáls [two troy ounces] and told me to go to the market and sell it to cover our living expenses. This made me stronger in my belief.

About this time Jináb-i-Ḥájí Mírzá Muḥammad-'Alí Afnán and his assistant Áqá Mírzá 'Abdu'l-Ḥámid arrived from Hong Kong. They were on their way to Persia via Bombay. Jináb-i-Afnán was the maternal uncle of His Holiness the Báb. Both these gentlemen had business in China and came to see Ḥájí Mírzá 'Abdu'l-Karím in this connection and were his guests. They were known to Jamál Effendi, and the unusual joy expressed by these friends on their sudden and unexpected meeting and the extraordinary warmth and affection manifested as they inquired about each other's welfare, astonished all who were present at the gathering. The people then began to realize that Jamál Effendi was a member of the new sect.[8]

On the following day people again came to see Jamál Effendi, and after a long conversation about the war and much discussion of various passages of the Holy Tablet of Bahá'u'lláh—the Lawḥ-i-Ra'ís, Tablet to the Ottoman First Minister, 'Alí Pás͟há—relating to prophecies concerning Turkey, Jamál Effendi asked me to chant the Tablet for his two honored guests. It was the first time that I had heard these supreme utterances, and as I was chanting the Tablet, I became conscious of a sudden flash of heavenly light and was quite overwhelmed with an inexpressible divine illumination. I could not at the time fully realize the cause of this strange emotion that overwhelmed me. After the chanting of the holy Tablet was over, the revered guests and Jamál Effendi discussed between themselves the fulfillment of Bahá'u'lláh's prophecies, His teachings for the uplifting of mankind, His noble ideals raising the standard of morality, and the majesty of His mission; all of which I listened to attentively as if spellbound.

At the termination of the discussion, I confessed the truth of Bahá'u'lláh's claim and decided to dedicate my life to the service of the divine Cause. The three veterans at once embraced me affectionately.

Jamál Effendi, then in his supplication to the Sacred Threshold, submitted my name, and a holy Tablet was revealed on my behalf in Arabic:

He is the Glorious, the Most Glorious! O Mustafá!

There hath come before Us a letter from Jamál . . . him who hath soared in the atmosphere of the love of thy Lord, the All-Possessing, the Most High. Thy name was mentioned in this letter; wherefore do We now make mention of thee through the power of truth, that thou mayest read and be of them that are thankful.

Say: O God of the world. Thou Who art manifest in the Most Great Name! I ask Thee by them who are the Essences of being, whom neither the hosts of the world have hindered from turning towards Thy face, nor the kings of the earth deterred from gazing upon Thy horizon, to write down for me with Thy Most Exalted Pen that which beseemeth Thy generosity, O Thou, Who art the Possessor of all Names and the Creator of the heavens!

O Lord! I bear witness unto that which Thou didst Thyself witness before the creation of the heavens and the earth, and I confess to that which Thy tongue did itself confess ere the kingdoms of Thy Revelation and of Thy creation were made manifest: that Thou art God; no God is there but Thee. Thou hast from eternity been powerful to do what Thou hast willed, and unto everlasting Thou shall remain as Thou hast been from time immemorial.

O Lord! I have hearkened unto Thy call and turned my face towards Thy face. I ask Thee to draw me ever nearer unto Thy horizon; ordain then for me, O my God, that which shall profit me in every world of Thy worlds. Thou, verily, art the Almighty, the All-Highest, the Exalted, the Great. We now make mention of him who hath been named Mustafá, that he may yield thanks unto God, the Lord of the Throne above and of the earth below, and that he may be of the steadfast. O Mustafá! Heed thou the call that hath been raised from the direction of this Prison: "Verily, there is none other God but Him, the Almighty, the

All-Knowing." Blessed art thou for having turned towards Him, and for having attained to that whereby thy name shall live for as long as the Names of Thy Lord, the Ever-Forgiving, the Most Bountiful, shall endure. Say: "O My God, and My Master! I ask Thee by Thine own Self to cause me to remain steadfast in Thy Cause. Thou, verily, art the Almighty, the Most Exalted, the Omniscient, the All-Informed.[9]

After staying for a few months in Calcutta, Jamál Effendi moved to Garden Reach near Calcutta at the invitation of Mir Ramazán-'Alí, Munshí-us-Sulṭán Bahadur, the private secretary to Wájid 'Alí Sháh the former Raja of Oudh. The main object of going to Garden Reach was to deliver the holy message to the former Raja. Jamál Effendi was told that he was an orthodox Shí'ih Muhammadan and was ardently expecting the advent of the twelfth Imám with a passionate devotion that almost amounted to madness. He always kept dozens of horses saddled day and night, ready at the gate of his palace so that he would not lose even a moment in going to the Imám if he heard of his appearance, to assist him in his fight against infidels. Jamál Effendi found him absolutely hopeless; he had no inclination for any religious or serious discussion of any kind. He was blindly following what he was told by his ancestors. Surrounded by luxury of every description, he spent all his time in pursuit of nothing but pleasure. Jamál Effendi, in spite of his efforts to enlighten the Raja, eventually had to leave disappointed. However, the Raja's secretary, the Munshí-us-Sulṭán, became a firm Bahá'í and with God's assistance, a Bahá'í Center was established in Garden Reach before his passing.

The following is a translation of the Tablet that Munshí-us-Sulṭán Bahadur received from Bahá'u'lláh:

He is predominant over all things.

Thy supplication which verily speaketh of thy facing towards God and of thy severance from all things save Him, was submitted in the presence of this wronged one. We pray to God that He may bestow upon thee confirmation in His Cause and may draw thee to the nearness of that greatest ocean, every wave of which proclaim: Verily there is no God but He the Wise, the All-Knowing.

Blessed art thou as thou hast rent asunder the veils and turned towards the horizon which nothing is seen therefrom but the effulgence of the face of thy Lord the dignified the generous. Say O ye group of the heedless ones! Verily the portals of knowledge are thrown wide open and the dawning place of the Cause of the merciful became manifest in the universe, testifying that which God hath testified before the creation of heaven and earth; were ye among the hearers.

Blessed is he who has thrown away all that he possessed and took hold of that which is given onto him by the Powerful, the Mighty. Thus the fragrance of the significances is wafted upon the universe so that all that is concealed in it may become apparent therefrom. Verily He is the All-Knowing Educator.

Harken Thou therefore to My voice and perform that which this Wronged One commandeth thee from this remote region. Catch hold of the rope of favor of thy Lord and cling unto the hem of His generosity, severing from those who are diverted from the straight path. Say praise be to God the Lord of the universe.[10]

Jamál Effendi finally received the necessary documents from the consulate in Bombay and the foreign department of the government of India to enable him to proceed to Burma.

Before moving to Garden Reach from Calcutta, Jamál Effendi had dismissed the servants who had joined him in India; therefore only I remained in his company. Later, Ḥakím 'Abdu'l-Rahim Khán, a Bahá'í friend from Rampur State, sent his eldest son Imtiyáz Ḥusayn Khán, now known in Burma as Dr. 'Abdu'l-Ḥakím, to serve and to be educated by Jamál Effendi. He arrived just a few days before our preparation to leave for Burma.

- 3 -

FIRST VISIT TO BURMA

Our stay in Calcutta became prolonged. Jináb-i-Ḥájí Siyyid Javád had informed the Afnáns that the younger brother of a Bahá'í in Egypt, Ḥájí Siyyid Mihdí Shírází, lived in Rangoon and knew about the Faith. The Afnáns wrote Jamál Effendi to contact Siyyid Mihdí and inquire about Mírzá Ḥusayn who was sent from Madras to Rangoon with all of the luggage.

We wrote a letter to him, and after some time the answer came with the tragic news that Mírzá Ḥusayn had passed away and had been buried in the Shí'ih cemetery (his gravesite is next to the grave of a young boy named Naṣru'lláh Shírází). All our belongings had been taken by the authorities for safekeeping. As a Turkish subject, Jamál Effendi wrote a letter to the Consul General in Bombay for a letter of introduction to the authorities in Rangoon. After a long time the letter of introduction arrived.

We left Calcutta in May 1878 and as steamers at that time were very slow we reached Rangoon (present-day Yangon) after a trip of seven days. Although we had no acquaintances in this city, the news of our journeys had been widely spread and the difficulties in regard to our belongings and the police department had been noised abroad. Thus all the inhabitants of Rangoon were aware of our arrival. At the wharf many people had come to meet us, among them Ḥájí Siyyid Mihdí Shírází of Egypt. We had written to him about our coming and had requested him to procure a suitable place for our residence. This he had attended to and was at the wharf to meet us.

Upon our arrival in this picturesque country we saw everything new—new faces with new style of dress and new language, new manners, new food, new religions, and new forms of worship that were not known in India. The few Persians there were rich merchants and had their own Persian Vice Consul. Some Chinese and Indians were occupied in different lines of business. The Rangoon town seemed very small and with a poor population. Ḥájí Mihdí had rented a large building on a monthly rental for us in the business quarter on Merchants Street, but we had to move from that place to the adjacent street, called Moghul Street, as it was the month of May and the beginning of monsoon and the old building was badly leaking.

Every day people of all nationalities, creeds, and casts came to see us. Jamál Effendi was gifted with faculties to speak to each and every soul in accordance with the wisdom that is commanded in the divine scriptures by Bahá'u'lláh, and his eloquent speech was satisfying and to the taste of every individual truth-seeker.

Jamál Effendi, was determined to discharge his material affairs as soon as possible and proceed to Mandalay to see the Burmese King Mindon Min and deliver the great message of Bahá'u'lláh to him. This was the main purpose for our coming to Burma. As soon as possible we met the Chief Commissioner of British Burma, Sir C. U. Atchison K.C.S., with some introductory letters from the eminent personages and government high officials of Calcutta, such as Mr. Siyyid Amír 'Alí M.A., a parliament member and legislator of Muhammadan Law in England; Mr. 'Abdu'l-Laṭíf, a presidency deputy magistrate of Calcutta; Mr. Amír-'Alí Khán, the prime minister of the ex-king; Wájid 'Alí Sháh of Oudh India; and Hussein Effendi, the Turkish Consul general in Bombay to the foreign secretaries Sir Alfred C. Lyell and his assistant secretary Sir Mortimer Durand.

The chief commissioner cordially received us and heard our statement of the affairs with kind attention. He promised to help us by all means possible and gave us a letter of introduction to the chief secretary, Mr.

J. E. Bridges. The next day we went to the secretary's office and were received warmly by him. He was very kind to us, and after due inquiry into our affairs, sent us to see the deputy commissioner with an introductory letter, and through him to go inspect our luggage that was still in the custody of police. The deputy commissioner, Major Evanston, a military officer, after a short conversation directed a police officer to go with us to the town locker where all our luggage was stored. Jamál Effendi was upset to find the boxes mostly empty. His valuable writings and the merchandise comprising of precious stones, Kashmir woolen shawls, stitched costumes, pebbles, and a gold frame [all gifts intended for King Mindon] that were sent from Madras with Mírzá Ḥusayn were all missing. We inquired from the police inspector in charge whether they made a registered inventory of articles at the time of taking them and whether, as was customary, it was handled in the presence of some respectable persons and the headman of the concerned quarter. No satisfactory reply was given.

The next day we went to the chief secretary and put the matter before him. He advised us to see the chief commissioner again and inform him about the situation. We went to the chief commissioner on the appointed day and explained the facts to him. He promised to investigate the matter officially and to let us know soon. Meanwhile the police constable and subordinate officers tried their level best to maliciously set out a plot against us in order to drag us to the police court, or if possible to murder Jamál Effendi and I, but we continued with care.

The chief commissioner finally directed us to take legal steps concerning our grievances and loss. After due consideration, we engaged Mr. Vartanness, an Arminian lawyer, to follow the case. We had to file a suit before the Recorder, which was the highest Tribunal Court in British Burma.

The case was prolonged and we were compelled to wait for the final decision. Jamál Effendi was a Turkish subject according to the passport given to him by that government in Constantinople. The decree finally said that, "whereas the plaintiff Jamál Effendi had written in his signature 'Faqir Jamáluddin' and his passport proves that he is a Dervish, so it is not proper to grant a decree for such an enormous amount of over 70,000 against the British Government. As a Dervish, it is the same to him whether he obtains such a large amount or not, and no harm was done to his dignity and nobility. The appeal should be submitted and lodged lawfully from this Court in the Privy Council at England instead of the Indian High Courts."

Jamál Effendi had applied for a certified copy of the whole proceedings with the judgment. It was a voluminous book. He felt quite disheartened, and, realizing that the matter was merely a waste of time and money, we dropped the idea of proceeding further. Thus ended the matter of our litigation. Though the police authority repeatedly asked him to come and take away the residual things belonging to him, Jamál Effendi did not bother to collect them. The affairs in court had prolonged and delayed us for more than a year.

The King of Burma, Mindon Min, died on October 1, 1878, about five months after our arrival in Rangoon and we were deprived of the privilege of his royal presence. This was an irreparable and tremendous loss for us and our main sacred purpose. We had to change our course and lofty thoughts for the time being and continue as ever before in promulgation of the divine Cause among the general public.

As a result of this mission of Jamál Effendi in Rangoon many wonderful souls accepted the Faith, and in a very short time the Cause was widely promulgated. Then a peculiar incident occurred due to the zeal of our Rangoon friend, Ḥájí Siyyid Mihdí Shírází. Being a novice in the Cause and untrained in the best way of giving the Bahá'í message, he took it upon himself in a moment of great zeal, to go to the Shí'ih mosque during the Friday worship and make a stand, loudly calling upon the congregation and inviting them to visit the Bahá'í teacher, Jamál Effendi. "Don't pause or tarry for a moment," he said, "come immediately. The appointed time foretold in the Holy Books has arrived. The prophecies have been fulfilled. The Promised One has appeared. The glad tidings of His Manifestation are widely known in Persia and all over the world. Thousands of people in Persia have accepted this Cause, and have sacrificed lives, family, and wealth in its path. Come immediately and hear Jamál Effendi in his wonderful way expound this Movement. You will see with your own eyes the new heaven and the new earth, the new sun and the new moon, the new religion and the new Cause."

This ill-timed discourse created a great commotion and turmoil among the fanatical Shí'ih congregation in the mosque. Outcries, curses, and abuse were raised from every side. A terrible excitement reigned. Ḥájí escaped and slipped out of the mosque, otherwise he would have received injuries from the mob and perhaps been killed. The Muhammadans called a meeting to deal with this "infidel." A mullá named Áqá Siyyid Javád, a visitor to Rangoon, who was brought to officiate at the Feast of Muharram, rose to the pulpit and denounced, abused, and cursed Ḥájí Mihdí, mentioning him by name. He tried to rouse a mob and urged them to unite in force and violence and to expel the Bahá'ís from Burma. He said that the Ḥájí should be expelled from the Shí'ih mosque and be excommunicated and killed before the whole province was won over by the heretics.

This provocative sermon impressed only a few among the audience and the majority did not pay much attention to it. We were unaware of this event because Ḥájí Mihdi was ashamed to give us information concerning the situation.

What he did was to bring a charge of defamation of character against the mullá who had delivered the violent sermon about him. After full investigation of the suit, brought before the District Magistrate Court, it was decided against the fanatical mullá. He was obliged to execute a bond for keeping the peace for six months. Feeling disgraced, he left Burma for Calcutta by the next boat.

Ḥájí Mihdí brought half a dozen of his relatives and friends to us to hear the Bahá'í message from Jamál Effendi. His father-in-law—a well-known merchant—had died and his wife had inherited the property and rule of the family. She did not sympathize with the Ḥájí in his new Faith, and he left his kindred and became separated from the family.

The Ḥájí's zeal in the mosque did not cause any violent hindrance to the work as we had feared, but it took some time for the poisonous effect of the incriminating sermon of the mullá to die down. However, some positive results did occur from the Ḥájí's public announcement in the mosque of Jamál's mission, as people who heard it were curious to investigate the truth of the matter.

One afternoon a young Persian man of about thirty came to see us. By his appearance he seemed to be of a high class family, but he was rude and coarse in his manner to us and we soon noticed that he was drunk. He was under the impression that we were people of low class. As soon as he entered into the presence of Jamál Effendi and recognized his culture and station in life, he realized his mistake, became silent, and remained only a little while. He asked permission to come and see Jamál Effendi the next day.

He came punctually, now a perfect gentleman, both in manner and clothes. We welcomed him warmly and as Jamál Effendi talked to him with love and wisdom, gradually the young man's face shone as the result of the effect of the divine message with which he seemed to be delighted. He remained seated for a long time in silence, a soul enchanted. Then Jamál Effendi told him to come again the next day, for he should take time now to digest what he had heard, which was enough of a lesson for the present.

Jamál Effendi learned upon inquiry that the young man was a descendant of the "Kad Khoda"[1] family of Sh͟íráz, Persia, and his name was Áqá Muḥammad Kaẓím Sh͟írází. He had come to Rangoon to visit his uncle and cousins, who had settled here many years ago and were cloth merchants.

This youth came every day to see us and soon was a confirmed Bahá'í. Later he told us how he had come to see us as a foe, and purposely had made himself intoxicated in order to inflict some fatal injury upon us.

But what a miracle, he said, that he had returned the next day and the next and the next, impelled by his attraction to the Cause. This youth received several wonderful Tablets from Bahá'u'lláh. In Rangoon we had many believers from the Sunní and some from the Shí'ih communities.

In the Sunní community were Mawlawí 'Abdu'l-Subḥán Qurashí, his five sons, his wife and his wife's sister and mother, as well as other relatives belonging to his family. This composed the largest Bahá'í family in Rangoon. They subsequently received Tablets from Bahá'u'lláh and 'Abdu'l-Bahá.

Among the Shí'ih community there were many who received Tablets from Bahá'u'lláh and 'Abdu'l-Bahá, and a group of them journeyed to Haifa in 1899; they were the pilgrims who went with the sacred marble sarcophagus, made in Mandalay, for the remains of His Holiness the Báb.

Early in 1879, after the establishment of the Cause in Rangoon, we left for Mandalay with several Persian companions. These were: Imtiyáz Ḥusayn Khán, now known as Dr. 'Abdu'l-Ḥakím; Dr. Khabíru'd-Dín and his young son, Shamsu'd-Dín; and, Fakir Muḥammad, a servant that had accompanied our departed friend, Mírzá Ḥusayn.

As there was no railroad connection at that time, we had to go by a slow river steamer that ran once a week from Rangoon to Mandalay, capital of the then independent kingdom of Burma.

The trip to Mandalay was long and tedious, as the boat did not run at night, and it took us more than ten days to reach our destination. We arrived at Mandalay about an hour before sunset and had great difficulty in finding lodgings. At the advice of the chief of customs (Mullá Ibrahim from Surat near Bombay), who was a Muhammadan, we took shelter for the night at a mosque (Joon Pulli) where we slept as well as we could in an open shed adjoining the mosque.

Fortunately the next morning a Calcutta friend, Ḥájí 'Abdu'l-Karím (in Burmese Ko Sho Bo), upon hearing of our arrival came to see us with his son, Ḥájí 'Abdu'l-Aziz (Ko Po Ob). Both were dealers in precious stones and were well-known and respected by the Muslim communities of Burma and India. We asked them to find a house for us, which they did—a residence in the Muslim quarter not far from the mosque called Obo, on 83rd Street. The rent was fifteen rupees, which was high due to a rush of visitors to Mandalay because of the opening of gambling houses by the permit of the Burmese government. Our landlord was Ko Shwe Bon, who loved the dervish.

There were many obstacles in our work in Mandalay. We did not know the Burmese language and had no arrangements for a place to stay or for contact with the natives and had to manage by ourselves until we were fortunate in finding a Persian from Calcutta who knew us and who gave us our first opening in the city. Also, under the rule of the new despotic Burmese king, teaching the Cause was extremely dangerous. Promulgation of a new religion was, by Buddhist law, to be punished either by banishment or execution by torture.

But, did we not have a Tablet in hand from Bahá'u'lláh giving us the divine command to proceed to Mandalay and establish the Kingdom of Abhá there? This was our spiritual duty. What difference did it make to the lives of obedient servants if they were killed in the path of duty? We considered nothing to be our own; all belonged to our Lord.

News of our arrival spread through the Muslim community of Mandalay, and men of all classes came to see us, asking many religious questions. One gentleman who had already accepted the Cause in Rangoon, Áqá Muḥammad Kaẓím Shírází, and his wife who was from Persia, rejoiced to see us, and became regular and enthusiastic visitors thereafter. Our Calcutta friend Ḥájí 'Abdu'l-Karím also came regularly to ask some questions from Jamál Effendi on problems connected with Muslim law.

As far as possible, we tried to mingle with all races, creeds, and nationalities in our travels, but the people brought to us were mostly Muhammadans. Thus we felt it necessary to observe all Muhammadan rites. For instance, the observance of the Fast of Ramaḍán, and the Feast that followed it (Eid-al-Fitr) and all the obligatory prayers. Although we were associating in this way with Muhammadan Burmese, we were not able to converse with them in the Burmese language and our Calcutta friend Ḥájí Karím interpreted for us.

Our days went on in this manner until one evening stones were suddenly thrown at us from the darkness opposite our house. At the time we were seated in front of the house in conversation with friends. Fortunately no one was hurt. The landlord came out, shouted loudly, and the stoning ceased. The next morning Ḥájí Karím told us that the people of the quarter disliked our presence there and it would be better for us to move somewhere else. We thought it best to comply with their wish and moved into a house with a compound at some distance from this one. Our friends continued to meet with us, occasionally bringing new seekers of truth. Jamál Effendi welcomed and entertained them in the kindliest way, conversing with them on spiritual subjects, and they left strong admirers of him and of the message which he had presented.

This quiet and unobtrusive method of teaching led to some important results. One of our new friends, 'Abdu'l-Waḥíd, who, like many other Muhammadan merchants in Burma, had taken the Burmese name, Ko Thin, carried the news of Jamál Effendi and his spiritual message to his uncle 'Abdu'l-Sattár (U Koo) a well-known silk merchant, a man of great intelligence and influence in his circle. 'Abdu'l-Waḥíd related to his uncle all that he had heard and seen during his visits with Jamál Effendi. The old gentleman, 'Abdu'l-Sattár, an ardent seeker of truth, told his nephew to invite us both to dinner in his home, an invitation which we accepted with great pleasure.

They came to fetch us with a bullock cart, the main vehicle in Burma at the time. We found our host eagerly awaiting us. We were the only guests, and after dinner and the usual exchange of greetings 'Abdu'l-Sattár had many queries for Jamál Effendi relating to Ṣúfí mysticism. Jamál Effendi with great promptness and brilliancy answered all his questions and solved all his spiritual problems to his satisfaction. We talked until the early morning hours and it was about two o'clock when we made our apologies and took our leave. Later we heard that our aged host, due to the sheer delight and pleasure he had in conversing with Jamál Effendi, was unable to sleep that night.

The next day, to our great surprise, his nephew came with a bullock cart and a chariot to take us with all our belongings to a house that 'Abdu'l-Sattár had assigned to us. Upon arrival there we found the old gentleman busily at work, engaged in constructing a meeting place on a vacant piece of land adjoining to the home assigned to us. Soon this meeting house became a center that attracted a sincerely devoted audience. This was the real beginning of the divine Cause of Bahá'u'lláh in Mandalay. It is evident that the chief credit for the opportunity to spread the Cause in Burma must be given to 'Abdu'l-Sattár and his nephew. They were the first to become believers in Mandalay, each of them noble souls, who were the recipients of several Tablets from the Blessed Beauty.

Gradually the number of believers increased until it reached to two hundred or more. These were busy and happy days. Indeed we worked day and night, and I was kept busy translating Tablets and verses from the Qur'án and the traditions regarding the time, place, and person of the divine Manifestation prophesied in these holy books into the Urdu language. This work finally extended itself into a book of some three hundred pages, The Standard of Truth or Reality, which I wrote for 'Abdu'l-Sattár.

How grateful we were to God that in a city where there was such danger in spreading the message of Bahá'u'lláh, we had been protected by the friendship and influence of our new Bahá'í brother, 'Abdu'l-Sattár. This was our salvation, for although the Persian <u>Sh</u>í'ih community publicly denounced Jamál Effendi as a Bahá'í and incited the people to do us injury, yet so great was the influence of 'Abdu'l-Sattár that no one dared to oppose or obstruct the Movement.

Meanwhile our Persian friend, Áqá Muḥammad Kaẓím <u>Sh</u>írází, was working independently within the circle of the Persian <u>Sh</u>í'ih community where he was able to guide many souls to the truth, among them Áqá

Muḥammad Ṣádiq, a partner of his in his Mandalay shop, and others who had become natives of Mandalay.

In the course of time the prejudice of the Persian Shí'ih community decreased. Two well-known merchants, Mírzá Muḥammad-'Alí Iṣfahání and Áqá Muḥammad Ibrahim Shírází, each invited us to dinner in their homes where we found gathered all the notable Persians of Mandalay. Jamál Effendi took advantage of this wonderful opportunity to deliver a most convincing address on the expected Qá'im and the Messiah. The audience received this address in the most respectful silence, except for a few polite questions.

The cleric of the Chinese Muhammadan Mosque, a learned sage, came to see us bringing with him a written question, a spiritual puzzle, which he wanted made clear. Jamál Effendi accomplished this to his great satisfaction, pointing out how the Báb and Bahá'u'lláh had fulfilled all these prophecies. The Chinese gentleman retired completely satisfied with his answers.

We stayed in Mandalay for eighteen months. When the time came to leave, 'Abdu'l-Waḥíd was appointed as our representative and through him we were able to continue communication with the Mandalay friends. In order to prepare him for this responsibility we had been teaching him the divine principles of Bahá'u'lláh every day.

Having finished our duties in Mandalay for the present time, we felt that much of importance had been accomplished and that the supreme Cause of Bahá'u'lláh was well founded there. We returned to Rangoon by the same river steamer in which we had arrived. Our safe arrival at Rangoon delighted the hearts of the friends and uplifted their spirits. Many holy Tablets revealed by Bahá'u'lláh for the friends in India and Burma, as well as for ourselves, were awaiting us.

First, we stayed in a house in Lewis Street and then moved to the last block of 39th Street. As we planned to stay for a while in Rangoon, we thought it best to undertake some kind of business in order to earn our own living and pay our own way. We finally decided to open a pony market and a line of hackney carriages and a shop for the sale of animal fodder. Jamál Effendi wrote to Áqá Muḥammad Kaẓím Shírází in Mandalay and it was arranged to send some ponies suitable for the Rangoon market. In time the business became profitable.

The Cause of God was gradually progressing, but although there was a good number of believers, they were exclusively of our own nationality. We felt the Cause should be promulgated among the natives of the land. Otherwise the Bahá'í Faith in that country would not be strong enough to build upon. Although a considerable number of the foreign population might accept the Faith, they would likely return to their respective lands, and gradually the Faith would die away.

We had two Bahá'í households in Rangoon, that of Jináb-i-Áqá Ḥájí Siyyid Mihdí Shírází, from amongst the Shí'ih, with his son Áqá Siyyid Ismá'íl Shírází and Mawlawí 'Abdu'l-Subḥán Qurashí. However, they were not natives of Burma, as they were from Persia and India respectively and had become naturalized citizens of Burma. We did our best to attract the native Burmese to the Faith, but our efforts were not effective.

After the lapse of one year we took a second trip to Mandalay to see the friends upon their invitation and continual requests. During this trip, a member of the Shí'ih Persian community of Mandalay instigated one Mírzá Mehdí, a professional cook, who had been with us in Hyderabad, to falsely start a civil suit against us for 176,509 rupees at the Burmese Court, stating that he had sold goods to us in Hyderabad for which he had not been paid.

At the time the Courts in Mandalay were completely lawless and unjust and were well-known for their bribe taking. Many bona fide claims had been dismissed as false, and many false claims had been decided as right. Many defendants and some of the plaintiffs had been sent to jail and violently tortured before the preliminary court hearing.

The friends, particularly 'Abdu'l-Sattár, an influential Bahá'í, managed to secure from the Court all the details of this claim and a copy of the complaint. We also had an interview with Prime Minister Kewun

Mingyi, through the kind intervention of Mullá Ismá'íl, a Bahá'í friend who was the chief commissioner of the Burma Customs. After listening to our story he promised to give us justice. The next day when the case was called in his court, the case against us was dismissed on the grounds that "whether true or false, the transaction had not taken place in the jurisdiction of the Burmese Court; therefore, the proper procedure is for the plaintiff to present his claim in a proper court where the transactions had taken place. We dismiss the suit against the defendant, Jamál Effendi, who is known to us as a leader of a religion and not a worldly man. The principal cause of action in this suit seems to be nothing but religious antagonism and hatred toward the personage of the defendant in this extra-judicial case."

The Mandalay friends were anxious about these events and had no peace of mind even after the decision in our favor. They knew about the lawlessness of their courts. Anybody might bring an action, civil or criminal, against any person without much trouble and expense. Therefore, after a few months we decided to return to Rangoon.

We arrived in Rangoon distressed and heartbroken that we had not achieved much in Mandalay. But we could not sit in idleness and lament. We had to earn our living. A few months after our arrival in Rangoon, I was sent with some ponies and some ruby stones to Calcutta and returned with great profits. I was sent on another trip with the same kind of livestock and gems to Penang in the Malay Peninsula. This was a new part of the world for me, but I managed to find lodgings on my arrival in the house of a well-known leader of mysticism, Tuan Omar Khalid, a man of Malay descent. He was about sixty years old with half a dozen grown-up sons and daughters, most of whom could speak Arabic. This island was quite small and within a week I became a conspicuous figure everywhere. Although I did not find any interested souls, I did not neglect my duty to deliver the message of Bahá'u'lláh. Finally after the favorable sale of all my ponies and gems, I returned to Rangoon. After a couple of months I was sent to Calcutta with ponies and precious stones and returned to Rangoon by the end of the year 1884.

In the year 1886 Jamál Effendi and I decided to go on a long trip through India and, if possible, around the Malay Peninsula and the Java islands. The friends in Rangoon agreed with our decision. We left our business of livestock and hackney carriages in the charge of Dr. Kabíru'd-Dín and Imtiyáz Ḥusayn Khán of Rampur (India), and took the first boat to Calcutta.

Most of the friends in Calcutta had either moved or had passed away, so we did not stay long and left for Dacca,[2] an important city in Bengal. We visited Goa, the largest city in Bengal and the seat of the Navváb. Although all these areas are now under the rule of the British government, the previous rulers are still revered. Here we met several times with Navváb 'Abdu'l-Ghani.

We always kept in touch with the Afnáns in Bombay, as they were our liaison for all communications with the Holy Land. We received a cablegram from them in Dacca stating that our presence in Bombay was immediately needed.

Upon our return to Bombay, Jináb-i-Ḥájí Siyyid Mírzá Afnán took Jamál Effendi to a private room. He came out to the visiting room after a few minutes and told me about the arrival of Mírzá Muḥammad-'Alí, the son of Bahá'u'lláh, in Bombay.

I was instructed that I should bow reverently before him and fall prostrate at his feet when he came out to see us. Mírzá Muḥammad-'Alí appeared in the hall and I was presented to him by Jamál Effendi, but I did not prostrate at his feet. My attitude created great annoyance for Jamál Effendi, the Afnáns, and the audience.

After salutations and the usual greetings, Mírzá Muḥammad-'Alí went out for a walk with Nazír Abu'l-Káẓim. But we remained seated with the Afnáns, occupied in conversation about the progress of the Cause. We were told that Mírzá Muḥammad-'Alí was sent to India by Bahá'u'lláh for the purpose of printing the original holy writings such as the Kitáb-i-Aqdas, the Lawḥ-i-Haykal, Iqtidárát, Kitáb-i-Mubín, Íqán, and the Tablets of Ṭarázát, Ishráqát, and Tajallíyát.

After a long conversation, when we were about to leave, Ḥájí Siyyid Mírzá Afnán asked me why I did not prostrate at the feet of Muḥammad-'Alí. I answered that according to the text of the Kitáb-i-Aqdas it is prohibited to prostrate before any individual (whosoever it may be), except the Almighty God, whose Great Manifestation on earth is the Blessed Beauty, Bahá'u'lláh. We are only commanded to treat the branches of the Sacred Tree reverently and respectfully. The Afnán was truly annoyed and told Jamál Effendi that he should not bring me with him to their office anymore.

We remained in Bombay for about three weeks and left for Madras, where we had about four hundred Bahá'ís. The number of believers considerably increased after our arrival there. I was busy every night giving public lectures in various quarters of the town. I was also happy and grateful to once again see my father, Siyyid Muḥammad Roumie, who was now one hundred and fourteen years old.

Many eminent persons accepted the Faith, among them Navváb Fírúz Ḥusayn Khán; Navváb Maḥmud Míyán, the chief contractor for Madras harbor; Siyyid Kaẓím 'Alí; Osman Khán; Major Bahadur, the Aid-de-Camp of the Governor of Madras; Siyyid Dawood, the high priest of the Navváb Walajah's mosque, among the Sunní sect of Islam; and, the great scholar of Arabic from the Bohra community of the Ismá'íliyya sect, Mullá Muḥammad-'Alí Rampuri, and his nephew, Morad 'Alí, a merchant.

After staying for a couple of months in Madras we left for Singapore.

Jamál Effendi

- 4 -

TRAVELS IN CELEBES AND MACASSAR

Jamál Effendi and I, accompanied by two servants, left Madras on board the ship *SS Minatchi* and arrived in Singapore eleven days later. We were cordially received by the representatives of the Turkish Vice Consul, Abú Bakr bin Omar-al-Joneia, and were his guests during our stay in Singapore. He was a well-known merchant from the province of Hadhramaut (Arabia).

From there we sailed for Batavia (Jakarta), the chief seaport of Java and the seat of the governor general of the Dutch government. On arrival at the port we were taken to Customs, where the police in charge told us different nationalities traveling in Java were to be under the supervision of a police of their own nationality.

Jamál Effendi had his Turkish passport with him and it was easy for him to get a permit from the Dutch authorities to visit Java. I had great difficulty in getting a visa but finally secured one from the British passport office for myself and the two Indian servants. However, we were allowed to travel in seaport towns and only for six months. We rented a place, and, after putting our belongings in order, went to see the Turkish Consul General, 'Alí Gh<u>h</u>álib Bey. As Jamál Effendi was well versed in Turkish, he was warmly received and was promised that all necessary actions would be taken to make his travels easy. However, during all our travels in Java we were closely watched by detectives and spied upon everywhere, as the Dutch government was afraid of religious propaganda in Java. We were also hampered by lack of knowledge of the Javanese language. Jamál Effendi spoke Turkish, Persian, and Hindi. I knew several languages, and in a few weeks picked up the Malay language and could translate for him.

From Batavia we went to Surabaya where we stayed for a couple of months. Our landlord, Siyyid 'Akkíl-bin-Há<u>sh</u>im-al-Ḥaba<u>sh</u>í, was the descendant of Hadhramaut Arabs but did not know Arabic. He was very kind to us and became a true seeker. He embraced the Cause with his family and children. People used to come and go, and we had religious conversations with all of them. Many were interested, but it was difficult for them to forsake their own beliefs.

Siyyid Há<u>sh</u>im advised us to go to the island of Bali Lombok, where Siyyid 'Abdu'lláh was the chief collector of customs. He was known to be the descendant of a Siyyid in Ba<u>gh</u>dád, whose ancestor was the celebrated Sunní <u>Sh</u>ay<u>kh</u> 'Abdu'l-Qádir Gílání. However, he did not have a genealogy document and therefore the Hadhramaut Arabs did not accept him as a Siyyid.

Siyyid Há<u>sh</u>im asked us to take 'Abdu'lláh's son, a twenty-year-old youth, who had been angrily discarded by his father, with us. We agreed to his proposal, considering it to be a good opportunity for our preliminary introduction to the chief collector. After two months in Surabaya, we left for Bali.

The chief collector of customs, Siyyid 'Abdu'lláh, received us at the harbor in his royal boat. Soon after our arrival, we made private inquiries about the chief's genealogy, and I immediately prepared a decent chart of his genecology from the information that I had gathered. Siyyid 'Abdu'lláh arranged for a sumptuous grand feast with Arabian dishes and invited all citizens of the Muslim community—consisting of Arabs, Javanese, Malay, and Buginese—and asked me to read out and present the chart of his genealogy to him in the presence of that crowd. He thankfully received the document, which was highly esteemed by him for the confirmation of his descent from the Prophet. At the same time he cheerfully embraced his son.

The inhabitants of Bali originally were Hindu and Buddhist, but they did not adhere to these faiths. The ruler of this province did not practice any religion, but called himself a Buddhist. His queen, who was a Muslim by birth, was anxious to meet Jamál Effendi. She sent some high officials with two ponies to escort us to the palace. Accompanied by our friend the chief commissioner of customs, who served as interpreter for us, we reached the palace and were cordially welcomed. For hours the king and queen questioned us about spiritual subjects. It was a most interesting conversation. Finally, after partaking of coffee and some sweets, we received permission to retire.

This province was rich and fertile in rice plantations. Spinning and weaving gave the population good income as the cloths were exported by Chinese merchants.

After a couple of days, we sailed for the Celebes Islands, the chief seaport of which is Macassar, now the seat of the Dutch Governor. We landed there safely and the police instructed the porters to take us with our luggage to the Arab quarter where we were to be under the supervision of its chief who had been born and brought up there. We were greeted cordially by him and he assigned a large brick building with an iron gate for us. We occupied only two rooms on the top floor, one for Jamál Effendi, and one for our luggage and I. As experienced travelers, we decided to carefully inspect the whole building. We locked the doors of all vacant rooms and took particular care to lock the huge gate that opened to the public road. It took long to lock the gate with utmost difficulty. The building, owned by a rich Chinese merchant, seemed to have been abandoned for many years. News of our arrival and of the location of our lodgings had spread in the town and we soon witnessed the wisdom of this precaution.

In the morning, to our amazement, we saw a throng of people outside the building. With great astonishment they asked us how our lives had been spared that night. Had no ghosts, demons, or evil spirits disturbed us? How was it that we were not harmed? Had we overcome the Monstrous Devil? Previously those who had spent the night in this building were found dead in the morning, from no known cause. So terrible had been the reputation of this residence that the heirs of the Chinese owner of the building did not dare to live in it. We told them that we had driven out the evil spirits, ghosts, demons, and devils from the house and made it habitable.

Knowing the Chinese have many superstitions and a great fear of demons, we concluded that some deaths in this house had led them to believe that it was haunted. To our amazement we learned that their fears were not groundless. The chief of this Arab quarter, who was in charge of the house, had usually given it as a shelter to inexperienced and unknown fellow countrymen who arrived in the city. They would retire for the night, assured of the protection of the Arab chief without taking any precautions. Once they were sound asleep, some of the chief's men would creep in, dressed as demons, and choke them to death. The next morning they would be buried by the chief, and their belongings would be taken away for supposed safe custody.

In our case the evil designs of the chief were thwarted. His men came to the gate, and tried hard to force it open. I was awakened by the noise and shouted loudly in Arabic, "Who is there?" and looking out saw men running away from the gate. In spite of this knowledge we dared not disclose to the chief our awareness of his villainy, for we needed his help in all of our movements. Thus, instead of confronting him we deemed it best to present him with a gem worth twenty dollars and thanked him for his kind protection.

'Alí Gh̲álib Bey, the Turkish Consul, had asked us to visit a blind Turkish soldier, Muḥammad Effendi, in an interior town while we were in Celebes Island. On the second day of our arrival we went to see the Dutch governor, Mr. Brooghmann, to ask for approval of our visas to visit him. He asked us the cause of our traveling to the interior of the Island, which was ruled by the Bugis native chiefs, and where the protection and responsibility of the Dutch government was not available. The people of the interior were said to be rude and wild, and apart from rice and coconut oil, no proper food was available. We replied that our main reason was to visit the old and blind former Turkish soldier and would not prolong our stay there. He said that our visa was only good for another four months and we should return to Macassar before its termination. We said we would respectfully abide by the Dutch government's rules and the governor's order. Our passports were duly examined and endorsed with visas for further travel.

The people of Macassar treated us cordially and thought of us as experts in healing the sick and eradicating evil spirits, and they were not willing to let us leave. We were able to deliver the message of Bahá'u'lláh to everyone that came in contact with us.

Finally with utmost difficulty we were allowed to depart. The captain engaged a small sailing vessel for us and we proceeded toward Paré-Paré, which was ruled by the independent Bugis native chief, Fatta Aron Matua Aron Raffan, meaning the great monarch and king of all kings. At about 3:00 in the afternoon we arrived at the port of Paré-Paré. I went ashore and went directly to the customs to ask permission for landing. The officer in charge gave me a pony to ride and followed me to the Royal Palace, which was built of Bamboo, to obtain permission from the king. The king was about sixty years old, and was watching our approach through a telescope in the window of his palace. As soon as I entered into the royal presence, the king got up from his seat and embraced me and said that he had eagerly waited to meet his honored guests and enquired about the whereabouts of Jamál Effendi. I replied that he was in the ship awaiting the royal permission to disembark.

Two envoys sent by the Dutch Governor of Macassar were also present. They carried a private letter to the king that indicated our arrival, and asked him to refuse any help that we might want. The reason given was that we were magicians and would use our art to subdue the chiefs and their subjects for our mystical religious attainments. The king became furious and in an angry tone told the two envoys, "These venerable visitors are my guests and under my protection. The Dutch governor should not interfere in our religious affairs. This is the answer to his offending letter and an official message that should be conveyed by you to him." The envoys were thunderstruck and immediately left.

The customs officer was commanded to apologize to Jamál Effendi on the king's behalf for not being able to arrange for a public reception, and told that he should accommodate the guests comfortably in his own house in a separate compound. It was done accordingly and Jamál Effendi was honorably received by the customs authority.

The next day we were invited to the palace for an audience with the king. We were warmly received and the king embraced us both and asked us to sit close to him. After the usual salutations and due homage and exchange of loving expressions, he made inquiries about our lengthy voyage and the reason for our unexpected arrival at such an unfrequented spot. We explained our reason of travel to his satisfaction. The king asked us to call again the next morning. The next day we rode the ponies sent by the king and went to the palace which was about two miles from our residence. We were introduced to the king's daughter, Princess Fatta Sima Tana, the wife of the king of Sedendring Province and the queen of Fatta Talloo Latta.

The king was suffering from psoriasis. His whole body was covered with scabs like fish scales and his skin itched all the time. He was confident that Jamál Effendi could cure his painful disease and asked him to do so. Jamál Effendi replied that we were not qualified physicians for bodily sufferings, but that we would earnestly pray for divine guidance and would try to find out some remedy through heavenly confirmations.

After returning home we consulted and went out to the adjacent woods to find some medicinal herbs as we had nothing with us. We found many Cassia Fistula trees with abundant fruits, and collected some of them. We also found wild mint plants and picked their leaves. We continually said the Greatest Name while we were engaged in this extraordinary activity. We brought the gathered leaves home and prepared a purgative from the Cassia Fistula fruits. We also had a few cakes of carbolic soap with us. We prepared three bottles of purgative with added vinegar and sugar and the next day took all of these and the soap with us to the royal palace. Every alternate day we gave four doses of the purgative to the king for cleansing the bowels, and gave him nourishments during the interval days. Every day he had a hot bath, using the carbolic soap, and applied the balm we had made. It took more than a month to soften his skin. Finally through divine confirmation and the glorious power of the Greatest Name, we succeeded to lessen the psoriasis to a certain degree.[1]

His belief in us cured the old king, and we asked him to supply us with a boat that we might go to visit the old blind Turkish soldier, Muḥammad Effendi. The boat was supplied and we went to see him. He lived on a small island, thirty miles away, with his wives and concubines and more than a dozen grown-up children. Their income was from dry fish that was exported by the Chinese traders to other towns. We were welcomed by him. This was the first occasion that he had seen a Turkish speaking person. We informed the Turkish Consul at Batavia (Java) about our meeting.

With the royal edict and the king's escort we journeyed inland to the town of Sedendring, which was on the border of an extensive lake with a river as its tributary. Here the officers in charge arranged three long canoes with twenty oarsmen in each to expedite our voyage to the province of Padali Lama, which was ruled by Fatta Radali, Orang Fammana. The lake and the river were full of large crocodiles that dived in the water upon hearing the loud singing of the oarsmen. We arrived after sunset near the palace of the king, and a lamp was hoisted as signal of our arrival. The king's officials came running to the boat and went back to report our arrival. The king ordered accommodation for us as guests in a very nice house on the shore. As the duty of the escorting officers and the boatmen terminated at this point, they asked permission to present the introductory edict to the king, which had been issued by their monarch, and then to return with the news of our safe arrival.

The next morning we went to the palace. King Fatta Chikourdi of Radali and the Queen Diammaral welcomed us warmly and asked us to have an audience with them every day. We felt that people there were not interested in religious matters and decided to move further to Boonai. But unless the king provided us with canoes and all voyage requirements we could not move; moreover it might have annoyed the king if we departed early. We waited for the opportunity with earnest prayers.

To our surprise, suddenly there came news that a smallpox epidemic had broken out in the principal towns of Padali Fammana and in the houses close to the palace. The loss of many children alarmed the king and he implored us for assistance. I had no knowledge about smallpox but Jamál Effendi instructed me to get some ordinary needles and tie them tightly together and pick some live scabs from the affected children, put them in a small phial, and add to it a little milk. With these needles I then scratched the arms of the children.[2] In this way we daily vaccinated up to five hundred children. One percent could not be cured but the lives of the remaining ones were saved. In those days we were able to deliver the message to everyone but we could not find out the result before leaving for Boonai.

We were supported by the king and supplied with all necessary voyage equipment, consisting of three long canoes with full escort. We said goodbye to him and all others and started our journey. Very few crocodiles were seen in this trip. We reached our destination before sunset. We had not noticed that there was an Arab man among our companions and found out only after our arrival.

In Boonai we were warmly received by the king and his officials, and the government rest-house opposite the palace was appointed for our residence. After dinner we were called to the audience chamber and were greeted enthusiastically by the king and queen. The king was younger than the queen as he was the only match available from her distant royal blood of the ancient dynasty of Goach, a town located near Macassar. The province was inherited by her as the sole heir of her royal ancestors. The king was a learned and intelligent man. At the first meeting we became very friendly and he posed all sorts of questions, material and spiritual, and recited a mystical prayer in Arabic called "jeljelutieh." The Arab Yemeni man who was with us corrected the king's Arabic and this made the king very angry, and he ordered the man out of the palace. The king was happy with Jamál Effendi's heart-stirring and sweet talks and until 2:00 a.m. engaged us in answering his questions.

After this first meeting, we were summoned by the king to the audience chamber every day to answer his religious questions. After a few days he asked us to write an essay in Arabic describing principles for the administration of his state, and another to teach colloquial Arabic. I wrote it in Persian and Jamál Effendi translated it into Arabic. We tried our best to incorporate the Bahá'í principles in our essays.

Although we treated the Arab man with kindness, he kept a grudge against me. One day while I was busy writing he made loud banging noises by hitting the bamboo floor of the house. I politely asked him to be quiet, but he struck my head with a heavy piece of wood. I was bleeding but did not notice it. The queen was watching from the palace window that faced our rooms and immediately informed the king. The king rushed into my room with his servants and arrested the Arab man and commanded his execution. We begged the king for hours to grant clemency and finally he agreed to banish the man to Macassar with a criminal record. The king kindly allowed us to give a gift of cash and some clothing to the Arab man before he was sent away.

We completed the essays and named them Fáṭimih Qá'imatu'd-Dín, which was the title of the queen. They were appreciative and promised to spread the Cause in all provinces of the Celebes Island. Thus we raised the standard of Yá Bahá'u'l-Abhá and made preparations to return. With sad hearts the king and queen arranged all that was necessary for our voyage.

We arrived at Padali Fammana before sunset and occupied our former residence. We received many cordial presents from the parents of the children that we had vaccinated during our short stay in this place. We were getting ready to leave Padali when we were informed about the death of the aged king of Paré-Paré, Fatta Orang Matua. His funeral ceremony was to take place on the following day. Fatta Chikourdi of Padali and all of his officials were to attend. We were invited by Princess Fatta Sima Tana, the daughter of the deceased king, to join the ceremony as the king had wished that one of us attend this sorrowful event.

Before sunset of the same day I went to the funeral house. I was astonished to see that the people of this island, although Muslim, had placed their king in a coffin and kept it for forty days. During those forty days his subjects had surrounded the coffin day and night, chanting mourning songs.

I spent the night in the home of an Arab and the next morning attended the ceremony. It was a majestic occasion. All native chiefs who had come for the funeral went onboard the Dutch government man-of-war to meet the governor, who had come from Macassar to attend the funeral ceremony and express his condolences. As was the custom, each of the native chiefs received a gun-salute suitable to their respective ranks

The secretary to the governor told me to go also, for the governor was eager to meet me. In front of all the chiefs he joked that perhaps I might be arrested and carried off to Macassar for breach of the rules as my visa had expired. The native chiefs unanimously declared that they would also volunteer to be detained with me. They said that they were responsible for the offense, if any.

I was supplied with a boat to go to the ship after the native chiefs had completed their respective interviews. However, all of them surrounded the ship when I went onboard to see the governor. The governor cordially welcomed me and asked whether I had married a princess, had purchased a piece of land, or whether we had established an alliance of the Turkish government with the native chiefs. He of course knew all about our daily movements, reported to him by his officials. I denied all the allegations and told him that we had no intention to bother anyone, and were staying with native people who did not have their daily needs, such as butter, tea, and sugar, which were not available in their areas even with payment of a high price. This statement satisfied the governor immensely. He left his seat and shook hands with me and told me to convey his good wishes to Jamál Effendi and ask him to return to Macassar as soon as possible.

When I said goodbye and left the ship, all the native chiefs who had anxiously waited for me applauded loudly with cheers and followed me to shore. That evening, in a large gathering, the Arabs and the natives with their rulers, congratulated me and chanted some songs in Arabic. In response I expressed my loving sentiments and thanked all of them and explained the reason of our visit. Thus I delivered the message of Bahá'u'lláh according to the capacity of the audience. As Jamál Effendi was alone at Padali Fammana, I asked the mourning queen and other native chiefs for permission to return, which was granted after three days. I returned with a servant who led the way, and on arrival informed Jamál Effendi about all that had passed there, which he highly approved and appreciated.

As soon as Fatta Chikourdi, the king of Padali, returned from the funeral ceremony to his royal seat, we asked permission to leave. He reluctantly granted permission and kindly arranged all that was necessary. After saying goodbye to him at his palace, we left for Paré-Paré via Sedendring. Unfortunately, on our arrival at Sedendring, our native servant, who had served us throughout our journey, passed away, and the people of Sedendring took him away for burial. We arrived at Paré-Paré before sunset. The next day we went to see the queen, Fatta Sima Tana, and expressed our deep feeling for her lamentable bereavement. We asked her permission to return to Macassar as early as possible after performing the fortieth day ceremony for the late king. We prayed for her long life. By her command the officers in charge arranged all necessary things for our voyage and we left by a small sailing ship for Macassar.

The next day the captain of the Arabs, 'Alí Matar, took us all to the governor who welcomed Jamál Effendi warmly. We left for Surabaya by the first boat, and after a couple of days reached there. Our friend Siyyid Háshim warmly welcomed us, and after a week we left by boat for Batavia. The Turkish Consul General, 'Alí Ghálib Bey, had left for home some months before our arrival and a French Consul General was in charge of the Turkish Consulate in addition to his own official duties.

We delivered the great message to many souls, even to the government officials. A great sage, Siyyid Osman bin Háshim, and Siyyid 'Abdu'l-Rahmán-bin-Akkíl, who were our neighbors, and several others, accepted the message of Bahá'u'lláh. We had several prayer meetings before leaving them. We left on a mail boat and soon arrived in Singapore.

The French Consul General of Batavia had given us a letter of introduction to the French Consul General in Siam as well as one to the King of Siam (Thailand) who was his friend. Therefore, Jamál Effendi wished to go to Siam. He sent me to buy some precious stones as a present for the King of Siam. I left for Rangoon, and Jamál Effendi remained in Singapore. I successfully accomplished all tasks within a fortnight and returned to Singapore.

After my return we left for Siam. The French Consul General treated us kindly and sent his office servant to open the government rest-house on the banks of the river Nai Wang, near the palace. It was accordingly done and we stayed there. Unfortunately, we had arrived at an awkward time as the king had lost his mother a few days before our arrival and as he was in mourning he could not receive visitors. After staying a month or so, we left without seeing the king. During our stay there we delivered the message to a Persian Shí'ih shopkeeper who had married a Siamese girl and had lived there for a long time. We also taught the Cause to one Siyyid 'Alí Yamani and another prominent Siamese.

We returned to Singapore and immediately left for Rangoon. Before our departure, a Bahá'í from the Bohra community, called Muḥammad-'Alí, who was a managing agent of Hakimji Rajbhoy and Company, called to see us off. The captain of the ship was a Bahá'í from Calcutta, Faizi Sarhang, who had accepted the Cause during our first trip to Rangoon in 1878.

- 5 -

RETURN TO RANGOON FROM SOUTH ASIA

On our arrival at Rangoon we found everything in turmoil. The Burmese Empire was taken over by the British government, and the Burmese king and queen had been overthrown and imprisoned, all within twenty-four hours, without any fighting or discussion. They were later exiled to India and were imprisoned in Ratnagiri near Bombay. Dr. Khabíru'd-Dín had sold all our carriages and livestock and joined his former service in the Rangoon General Hospital. Imtiyáz Ḥusayn Khán seemed to be vagrant everywhere and nowhere. Mawlawí 'Abdu'l-Subḥán Qurashí, the brilliant faithful Bahá'í, had ascended to the Abhá Kingdom. The piece of land that we had applied for from the government, situated in a central spot for a Bahá'í center, was given to the Christians and they were busily engaged in building a church on it.

We were quite disheartened that so many changes had taken place in a short time during our absence and were at a loss as to what to do next. We had no place to stay; therefore, we engaged a house for a month on the second block of 42nd Street. Meanwhile we informed everyone in Bombay, the Afnáns, and also the Holy Land about our arrival in Rangoon. We received replies from all centers and detailed Tablets were revealed in the name of Jamál Effendi and myself.

The one addressed to me by the Blessed Beauty is as follows:

He is the All-Knowing, the All-Informed!
O Mustafá!

Be thou thankful for that thou hast been remembered by this Wronged One, and that there hath been revealed for thee that which shall abide for as long as earth and heaven shall endure. Consider and call to mind the day on which Muhammad the Messenger of God appeared with the signs of God, the Help in Peril, the Self-Subsisting: some among the people denied Him, others turned away from Him, yet others mocked Him, and still others rose up against him in such grievous fashion as to sentence Him to death without any clear proof from God, the Lord of all being. Verily, He said: "Fear God, O peoples of the earth! Bear ye witness unto His unity and oneness, and follow not your idle fancies and vain imaginings. Join not partners with God, O people, and worship not that which your own hands have fashioned! Better is this for you, if ye be of them that understand." The more strenuously He admonished them, the greater waxed their enmity and hatred. Thus doth the Pen of the Most High recount unto thee from this Glorious Abode. Be thou steadfast in the Cause, and proclaim this Name through which the traces of Jibt and Tághút have been obliterated. Names of false deities worshipped in Arabia before the advent of Muhammad. The Glory of God be upon thee and upon all those who have quaffed the choice sealed wine from the hands of the bounty of My Name, the Self-Subsisting.[1]

We then decided to visit Mandalay and as there was no railway connection between Rangoon and Mandalay, we had to take the trip by flotilla boat. We stayed in Mandalay for only a few days to see the friends. The Rangoon friends convinced Jamál Effendi to agree to send me back to Mandalay to establish a business with his friend Abú-Ẓáfir Quras͟hí. I opened a business office in central Mandalay near "Zaijo," the big market. The business was successfully carried on for about four months and was running briskly with considerable profits beyond our expectation. Suddenly Jamál Effendi wrote me to immediately return to Rangoon for some urgent matter. I left the business in the charge of Mr. Abú-Ẓáfir Quras͟hí's brother-in-law and left for Rangoon.

In a Tablet addressed to Jamál Effendi, he was given permission by Bahá'u'lláh to return to the Holy Land.

FIRST MARRIAGE

Upon my arrival, Jamál Effendi told me that the reason for my recall was that he was leaving for the Holy Land, and that before his intended departure he had arranged for my marriage. He had settled all necessary affairs with the responsible guardians of the bride in full confidence that this proposal would meet with my cheerful agreement. He said: "The majority of the friends in Burma agreed that you should remain in Burma as their guide during my absence." Jamál Effendi thought this decision was wise and advantageous for the Cause of God. There was no time left for further consideration as the marriage ceremony was to take place the next day and the invitations had already been printed and the guests invited.

This heartrending, unhappy news caused me unspeakable grief, as there was no time to consider my total deprivation in attaining the holy presence of Bahá'u'lláh—the real object of the creation of humanity. I was dumbstruck and was unable to comprehend this deplorable situation. I constantly wept about my ill fate. On the one hand, this was a fatal blow, and from the other, Jamál Effendi, with the eager desire of the majority of the Bahá'ís of Burma, had decided to leave me here for service to the Cause in Burma. Therefore, he had decided to arrange my marriage to the daughter of the late Mawlawí 'Abdu'l-Subḥán Quras͟hí, the first person who, with his family, had accepted the Bahá'í Cause during our first trip to Burma. I could not refuse this decision as Jamál Effendi would be disgraced in public and among the Bahá'ís. Also this whole family, and perhaps other families of the Burma Baha'is, would cease to follow the Cause and consequently hinder its progress. I thought deeply about the circumstances. There was no alternative except to submit to the Will of the Almighty God and obediently follow Jamál Effendi's decision.

The marriage ceremony took place in September 1886 A.D. The management of the marriage feast was supervised by the bride's elder brother, who had defrayed all expenses of about 2,500 rupees. Due to my marriage, Jamál Effendi and I were separated forever. Jamál Effendi later repented his decision in vain. It was difficult for him to do anything without my assistance. Before his departure for the Holy Land he declared that as I was a thoroughly qualified person and could easily earn my living comfortably, he was not going to give me any money to use as capital to start a business. Thus I was left completely empty-handed.

Jamál Effendi was exceedingly depressed, but nothing could be done as I was also drowning in a deep ocean of sorrow, not knowing what my future life would be.

Jamál Effendi left for the Holy Land by a steamer going directly to Port Sa'íd. He regularly wrote to me from every port until he arrived in the Holy Land. He submitted my supplication at the holy presence of His Holiness Bahá'u'lláh and the following Tablet in Arabic was revealed:

O Mustafá!

Upon thee be the peace of God, the Possessor of the earth and the Creator of the heavens. Our servant in attendance hath brought thy letter into the presence of this Wronged One, and read it out before Our face. We, verily, have heard it, and made reply thereto in these perspicuous verses . . . verses that shall draw thee nigh unto God, the Lord of the worlds.

This is a day on which, at every moment, the Crier crieth out: "The Kingdom is God's, the Lord of the Day of Reckoning." This is a day on which every steadfast soul hath attained, every ear hath heard, and every eye hath witnessed that which hath shone forth in refulgent splendor above the horizon of the will of God, the Lord of the mighty throne. He, verily, hath desired naught but to sanctify His servants and to purify them from lust and wickedness, from evil and transgression. He, verily, is the most merciful of them that show mercy.

Shouldst thou hear the call raised from the Most Sublime Horizon, and quaff the choice wine of utterance from the bounteous cup of Him Who is the Lord of the Kingdom of Names, then say: O God, My God! I bear witness that Thou didst not create Thy servants save to recognize the Dayspring of Thy signs and the Dawning-place of Thy testimonies; that Thou didst not create their ears save to hearken unto the shrill voice of Thy Pen; that Thou didst not create their eyes save to behold the effulgences of the horizon of Thy Revelation; that Thou didst not create their hands save to take hold of Thy Book with a power deriving from Thy presence and a sovereignty vouchsafed by Thee; that Thou didst not create their hearts save to turn towards the Kaaba of Thy knowledge, Thy glory, and Thy command; and that Thou didst not create their feet save to attain unto Thy Straight Path.

I ask Thee, by the faces that have been stained crimson by the blood spilled in Thy path; by the breasts that have been pierced by the shafts of Thine enemies for the exaltation of Thy Word; and by the souls that have neither been overawed by the ascendancy of the oppressors nor affrighted by the fearsome weapons of destruction arrayed against them by the infidels, but who, in Thy Name, have set themselves towards the Manifestation of Thy Self, and who, in their eagerness to meet Thee, have circled around His pleasure, to assist me under all conditions to lay fast hold on the cord of Thy Cause, and to arise to serve Thee and to extol Thy Name amongst Thy servants.

O Lord! I am Thy servant and the son of Thy servant and Thy handmaiden. I find my self bewildered by the matchless tokens of Thy Revelation, by the wondrous evidences of Thy dawning forth, and by Thy signs and traces that have encompassed both Thy heaven and Thine earth. I beseech Thee to adorn my head with the crown of detachment, and to bedeck my temple with the robe of humility and lowliness before the revelation of Thy laws and Thy commandments.[2]

- 6 -

RETURN OF JAMÁL EFFENDI TO BURMA

Jamál Effendi did not stay long in the Holy Land. Bahá'u'lláh commanded him to return to India. He traveled via Aden, where he stayed over a month to see the Sultan of Lahej.[1] He had several long discussions with the sultan and delivered the holy message to him. In a large gathering of 'ulamá it was decided to send a deputation to Mecca and consult about the advent of their promised Imám Mihdí and Rúḥu'lláh (Christ), as they were unable to decide the matter by themselves.

Jamál Effendi and his companion from the Holy Land, Jináb-i-Ḥájí Faraju'lláh, left Aden for Bombay. There he delivered the message of the advent of the promised Hushidár and the divine manifestation of Shah Bahram, the Prince of Peace, to the Parsee community of Persians according to their holy book Zend-Avesta. Many of them accepted the holy Cause. Jamál Effendi then left to visit several towns and villages to deliver the message of Bahá'u'lláh to all native chiefs and eminent persons of India. His traveling expenses were defrayed by Prince Navváb Safdar-'Alí Khán, the president of Rampur State. He visited Calcutta, Delhi, Lucknow, Kanpur, Moradabad, Rampur, Bareilly, Jaipur, Jodhpur, Gwalior, Fatehgarh, Bhopal, Indore, Ujjain, Malwa, Lahore, Gujrat (Punjab), Kailashpur, Amritsar, Peshawar, Hyderabad (Deccan), Madras, Bangalore, Shimla, Hyderabad (Sind), Khairpur, Jammu, and Kashmir and Poona. He also visited Bombay several times during his tour. Jamál Effendi did not rest for a moment in spite of his advanced age and did not care for his comfort or ease.

Jamál Effendi singlehandedly attended to all his communications. Sometimes he wrote me to assist him with his letters to the friends in Urdu and Hindi. During this period several holy Tablets were revealed by Bahá'u'lláh for the Indian native chiefs of the states that Jamál Effendi visited. Also, an exhortation was addressed to the head of the Bohra Ismá'íliyyih sect of Islam, Siyyidáná-Najmu'd-Dín of Bombay.

Mullá Muḥammad-'Alí Rampuri of Madras, a great scholar in Arabic from the Bohra sect, who declared himself a believer after reading that Tablet, went to Bombay and in a large gathering of the great sages of that community handed the Tablet to their chief and discussed it with strong and convincing demonstrations, quoting from their own traditional books. The audience listened with complete silence. The mullá wrote to Jamál Effendi about his success and promised to promulgate the Cause among his community. After Mullá Muḥammad-'Alí passed away, most of the former Bahá'í followers of Bohra Ismá'íliyyih, due to appeals and financial promises by their leaders, left the Cause and rejoined their former community.

It is exceedingly hard for the members or followers of that community to embrace the Bahá'í Cause. There are many obstacles in their way that prevent them from declaring their faith publicly. Firstly, there is the question of their livelihood. Secondly, there is the problem of matrimony as their wives do not consent to assume any new religion, and finally, their bonds of relationships are so strongly linked that they are helpless and cannot deviate from their beliefs. Although we had many beautiful souls who believed in the truth of this Dispensation, all were forced to hide their belief. Owing to severe cold in Kashmir and the high elevation of the mountainous regions, Jamál Effendi could not travel in winter. He waited for spring, and in April 1889 went on a journey from Kashmir to Ladakh. He was the guest of the Chief Secretary of the British Resident, Mir Man<u>sh</u>í Aḥmadu'd-Dín, and from there he went to Leh and Gilgit up to Pamir, "the Roof of the World." On the way he came in contact with the nomad tribes and gave the message of Bahá'u'lláh to all of them according to their capacity of understanding as they were all illiterate. On this trip, because of a severe snow storm, Jamál Effendi suffered frostbite in his toes. He was in much pain and decided to change the course of his journey and go to Kandahar, the well-known city of Afghanistan. This city was populated with all nationalities such as Persians, Bokhara Turks, Arabs, Chinese, Hindus, and Tibetan Mongols. The majority were Afghani, consisting of various tribes. He was the guest of the governor of Kandahar.

After the frostbite was partially cured, he wanted to return to India via Kabul. He wrote to the ruler of Kabul, Amír 'Abdu'l-Rahmán Khán, describing his suffering and requesting permission to go through Kabul to return to India. However his application was denied. In his reply the king blamed Jamál Effendi for taking a wrong track to that city that caused him to sustain such painful suffering, and stated that "though the king, was a keen admirer of Jamál Effendi's beautiful Persian handwriting, and his flowery metaphorical style used in that letter, yet the king honorably advises him to return to India through the same route he came, lest he may cause his hand to be mutilated in addition to his foot; the applicant is disallowed to pass through the capital."

Jamál Effendi took the route through Kashmir. He wrote me and other friends that on this trip, in a particular mountain pass, he had to climb up on foot for about four hours, and his luggage with books and sundry articles had to be carried by a carrier and some bullocks. However all the luggage being carried by bullocks fell off into the sweeping Murghab River below and was lost. In addition, a Persian in Bombay who had pretended to call himself a Bahá'í, swindled him out of 800 Rupees that was entrusted to him by Jamál Effendi for safekeeping.

This was the only occasion that Jamál Effendi wrote to the friends in India and Burma to help him. The friends responded lovingly to his urgent call, and he was able to start his travels once more.

THE ASCENSION OF BAHÁ'U'LLÁH

Jamál Effendi was still in India when the heartrending news of the Ascension of Bahá'u'lláh was communicated from the Holy Land. The Afnáns in Bombay published the "Kitáb-'Ahd" and announced that Ghuṣnu'lláhu'l-A'ẓam, the Greatest Branch, His Holiness 'Abbás Effendi, Sarkár-i-Áqá, the Exalted Master 'Abdu'l-Bahá, was appointed and universally accepted by all the Bahá'ís of the world as "the Center of the Divine Covenant" and the Expounder of the Divine Books. All the friends of Burma and India were protected by my humble efforts from the poisonous influence of the violators of the Divine Covenant.

Jamál Effendi was called back to the Holy Land, by the beloved Master, 'Abdu'l-Bahá. Before returning to the Holy Land, he visited Burma one more time. The first and foremost eminent believers in Mandalay, 'Abdu'l-Waḥíd (alias Khalifa Ko Thin) and his uncle 'Abdu'l-Sattár (alias U Koo), had ascended to the Abhá Kingdom, and there was no one to represent the Cause and to conduct the memorial meetings. Ḥájí Faraju'lláh, who had accompanied Jamál Effendi by the command of Bahá'u'lláh, passed away in India. A young man, Munír, who had served him in his travels, accompanied him to the Holy Land, and became known as Isfandíyár. He is now serving as the coachman of 'Abdu'l-Bahá. Another young man from Burma who was taken to the Holy Land by Jamál Effendi was Khusraw, who to his last breath was a loyal servant in the holy household.

Jamál Effendi returned to the holy presence of the benevolent Master 'Abdu'l-Bahá with absolute loyalty. He ascended to the Abhá Kingdom on November 9, 1898, and was buried in the Bahá'í cemetery of 'Akká. His tombstone is engraved with a verse in Arabic by the command of 'Abdu'l-Bahá:

> *Verily Jamáluddin the itinerant traveler in every region—the diffuser of the fragrances of the Love of God—is engaged in travelling into the regions of God, which were concealed from the eyes of the veiled people. Year 1316 Hijra (1898 A.D.)*

Our Lord 'Abdu'l-Bahá revealed a prayer for him in Arabic:

(Prayer for elevation of the soul of late Jamál Effendí, inscribed by Mírzá Munír, in 1316)

He is the Most Glorious

O God, My God! How can my tongue form speech, or my hand move across this page while grief doth billow and surge within me like an ocean? My plight is indeed grievous. Methinks this world is like unto a fathomless abyss, that seeketh to swallow me even as I quaff from the chalice of tribulation, consumed at every moment by the fires of tests and trials. Thou hast given me to drink this day of the cup of bitterness, proffered by the hands of Thine irrevocable decree and irresistible Will, for Thou hast summoned up Thy servant, that Solomon of Knowledge, and called him back to Thy Kingdom. He in turn gave heed and hastened toward Thy call, O Thou the Lord of lords! Thou didst graciously receive him within Thy holy precincts, delivering him from the flames of anguish that well-nigh consumed him in his separation from Thee. But I am immersed in a sea of separation, bereft of all reunion with Thee and wandering in the wilderness of remoteness, far from Thy presence.

O Lord! This is Thy servant who hath believed in Thee and in Thy verses, who hath been illumined by Thy splendors, discovered Thy mysteries, and believed in Thy Exalted Beauty. He took refuge beneath the shade of Thy Heavenly Tree, quaffing his fill from the hands of the bounteous Cupbearer, until he was attracted by the sweet savors of Thy All-Glorious Kingdom. Hastening towards that field of reunion, he presented himself before Thee with utmost humility and submission, trusting in Thy favors, ablaze with the fire of Thy love, enamored and hearkening to Thy call. He heard Thy words, proclaimed Thy truth, and became illumined by the light of ecstasy, quaffing the sweet nectar of reunion and intoxicated by the wine of Thy Beauty beneath the canopy of Thy glory. He hastened far and wide in the southern regions, magnifying Thy Name and speak-

ing Thy praise, calling the people to Thy Faith. He expounded Thy proofs and disseminated Thy Words; he elucidated Thy mysteries, led multitudes to the wellspring of Thy providence and sheltering guidance, illumined their vision with the splendors of Thy bounties and sanctified their hearts through Thy love. Now, he hath returned to the abode of Thy effulgent glory and the dawning place of Thy grandeur. He dwelt beneath Thy luminous pavilion, circling around the point around which circumambulate Thy Concourse on High, kissing the dust of Thy Exalted Threshold and prostrating himself before Thy luminous holy Shrine, until he was summoned to the precincts of Thy forgiveness and entered Thy abode by Thy gracious favor. O God! Admit him within the shelter of Thy might in Thy holy Garden set among the meadows of Thy good pleasure, and grant him leave to attain Thy presence. Let him dwell in Thy nearness and quaff from the chalice of Thy favors. Bestow upon him heavenly sustenance: make him a shining light on Thy luminous Horizon, and exalt his station in Thy highest heaven. Thou, verily, art the Bestower, the Compassionate.

MARBLE SARCOPHAGUS OF THE BÁB

Before the ascension of Jamál Effendi to the Abhá Kingdom, our beloved Master 'Abdu'l-Bahá commanded this humble servant to prepare a casket from Burmese marble for His Holiness the Báb in union with the friends in Mandalay and Rangoon. He sent me the measurements and the design of the inscription of the Greatest Name: Yá Bahá'u'l-Abhá, in the beautiful calligraphy of Jináb-i-Mishkín-Qalam, the well-known Persian Bahá'í calligrapher.

The friends of Rangoon and Mandalay unitedly acted. On the suggestion of our Bahá'í brother of Rangoon, Jináb-i-Áqá Ḥájí Siyyid Mihdí Shírází, the supervision of this unique project was entrusted to his wife's cousin, Áqá 'Abbás-'Alí, to be assisted by the Mandalay friends. A huge block of marble was brought on a raft from the Sagyin mine (a distance of a hundred miles), which naturally contained small rubies in it. Sculptors were engaged and the work was carried on for several months until it was satisfactorily accomplished.

Our Lord 'Abdu'l-Bahá, in a Tablet addressed to this servant, revealed:

> *. . . Thou hast written regarding the Holy Casket, stating that every effort is being exerted in this matter. It is certain that thou who art intoxicated with the wine of love, and all the loved ones of God are wholeheartedly and devotedly working towards this goal. Some friends here have requested permission to travel to that land to assist in the management of this affair, but this Servant, out of his love for thee, hath chosen thee for this service—O thou who art enraptured by the Divine Countenance! This is merely a token of my deep love for thee. Render thanks unto God for this bounty that is the envy of every sincere one. It behooveth you to glory in having been chosen, amongst all who are in heaven and on earth, to accomplish this service. I beseech God to graciously assist you to fulfill your goal, and make of your endeavor a lamp which shall illumine the globe of creation with its bright flame . . .*

The casket was of one solid piece of marble, and the cover was carved from a separate one. The Mandalay friends took a group photograph near their old mosque, carefully packed the casket, and sent it to Rangoon by railway, thence to Port Sa'íd by Bibby Line steamer. Ḥájí Siyyid Mihdí Shírází, his wife Shahrbánú, his son Siyyid Ismá'íl Shírází with his wife Mah Yin and a baby Siyyid 'Abdu'l-Ḥusayn, accompanied the casket on the same steamer to the Holy Land.

Their house on 32nd street was left in the care of a cousin, Áqá Muḥammad Kaẓím. The Bahá'ís held their weekly meetings in this house. After their return, the Beloved Lord addressed Siyyid Mihdí and Siyyid Ismá'íl with the following Tablet:

O ye two favoured servants of the Lord!
Ibn-i Abhar, the glory of the All-Glorious Lord rest upon him, hath arrived and the news of those regions brought much joy and happiness to our hearts. Praise be the Lord that the loved ones of God are in utmost unity, joy and radiance. They have been freed of chains and fetters, attracted wholeheartedly to the Beauty of the All-Glorious, and seek peace and comfort under His all-encompassing shadow. They are occupied with service to the Cause of God, engaged in exalting the word of God and characterized by Bahá'í virtues. This age is the century of the Great Announcement, and the world of creation is the reflection of the celestial effulgence of the Compassionate and Merciful Lord. This is the season of planting and cultivation; this whole earth is a paradise. Now is the season for scattering seeds, the time of sacrifice, for from every grain of corn shall grow seven ears,[2] and from every ear a thousand seeds. Blessed is the farmer who planteth in this divine field, and soweth seeds whose results shall be an abundant harvest in this world and the next . . .

Burmese Bahá'ís gathered in Mandalay with the marble sarcophagus prepared for the sacred remains of the Báb.

A group of early believers in Rangoon. Sitting from right to left are Áqá Muḥammad Ibrahim Shírází, Siyyid Ismá'íl Shírází, Ḥájí Siyyid Mihdí Shírází. Siyyid Muṣṭafá Rúmí is sitting fourth from the left.

- 7 -

ÁQÁ MÍRZÁ MAḤRAM

After my marriage I was involved in commercial business with my two brothers-in-law, Abú-Ẓafar Qurashí and Abú-Naṣr Qurashí. I wrote Jamal Effendi to supplicate the Holy Presence of our Lord 'Abdu'l-Bahá to send a Bahá'í teacher to us who would be suitable for this region. He replied that my supplication was granted and Jináb-i-Áqá Mírzá Maḥram, "who is now in the Holy Presence, is commanded to go to Burma after his visit to India." At the instruction of 'Abdu'l-Bahá, Mírzá Maḥram made two trips to Bombay in 1897 and 1898.

His first visit to Burma was on 19 June 1899. Áqá Siyyid Mihdí Shírází and his family had taken the marble sarcophagus that was in Burma on instructions from 'Abdu'l-Bahá to the Holy Land. As their house was vacant, Mírzá Maḥram and his companion, Mr. Khodadad Jamshíd Ḥakím, were invited to stay there.

Mírzá Maḥram was about thirty-five years old, a very generous and prudent young man. He had good expertise in Persian and to a certain extent in Arabic languages. He was a very good speaker and well versed in the Holy Scriptures—the Qur'án, the Bible, and Zand Avesta of the Parsee religion. But as he could not speak the Indian and Burmese languages or English, I devoted all my time from 6 a.m. to 12 p.m. to his service and as his interpreter.

People of all denominations came to see him and could not defeat him with their religious arguments. One day the teacher of a private Urdu primary school, Siyyid Dánish-'Alí, wrote a long letter and sent it to us by his office bearer who was in the school uniform. All citizens of

Rangoon were well-known to me, and I suspected a mischief. I refused to accept the letter and sent word through the same bearer to him and invited him to come to see us. This was on a Friday morning. In the afternoon, after performance of Friday prayer, hundreds of Madrasa Cholia Sunní Muslims gathered in front of our residence armed with sticks and stones in order to expel us from the house. Mírzá Maḥram, 'Abdu'l-Karím, and I were in the house. Mírzá Maḥram asked Abdu'l-Karím to lock the door leading to the street, but I saw that the head of the mob was the cargo-boat owner who supplied me boats for carrying my paddy[1] from the district to the mills while I was in the paddy trade. I opened the door and greeted them all and invited them to come in. As soon as he saw me, he became calm and peacefully dispersed the mob. Some of the ringleaders came in, and after silently listening to Mírzá Maḥram, quietly went away.

Later we heard that Dáni<u>sh</u>-'Alí, the headmaster of the school, had incited people in the mosque, telling them that "a man with a big mustache has come to stay in the house on 32nd street, openly violating our noble faith of Islam by daring to take the title of God for himself. O people awaken and arise to destroy his abode and expel him from this soil; be careful lest the whole Burma region become affected by his deadly and poisonous teachings." Thus the ignorant mob, unaware of the teachings of the Cause, ran to the house to attack the innocent guests. Our Lord saved us from this fatal calamity.

In the evening when friends came to see Mírzá Maḥram, they unanimously decided to report the incident to the nearest police station for future protection and safety. It was reported to the police instantly, and two European inspectors called upon us to find out about the situation and the place of the incident. Mírzá Maḥram talked to them about the fulfilment of Biblical prophecies and the advent of Lord Jesus Christ in His second coming. They contradicted him and denied the authenticity of the Holy Bible. Mírzá Maḥram with sound arguments tried for hours to prove the truth of the Old and New Testaments. But his efforts were ineffectual.

After the appearance of the police, people became frightened to visit us and for a couple of months we did not have visitors. During his stay in Rangoon, Mírzá Maḥram and his companion were my guests for over a month, and then the Rangoon Bahá'í Assembly took over. When visitors ceased to come to the house the valuable time of the great teacher was wasted and he deemed it proper to leave for Mandalay. I objected to this hasty departure and asked him to stay for another two weeks for me to settle some important personal affairs. About three years prior I had purchased a piece of land in a government auction sale and it was transferred to my name by a registered deed of sale. But the officers in charge were unable to ascertain the exact borders of the land for it to be delivered to me. I appealed the decision of lower courts to the deputy commissioner in charge of the district but was defeated. I then appealed to the divisional commissioner, who disappointed me also. At last I appealed the matter to the financial commissioner, who decided and issued orders to the deputy commissioner of the Hanthawaddy district, Mr. Tadd Naylar, to personally transfer the possession of the land to me. I asked the secretary of the deputy, who was my friend, to expedite the dispatch of the order, so it would take less than a week to be given to the deputy commissioner. I begged and entreated Mírzá Maḥram to stay for another two weeks as I had won the case after three years. The land in question was very valuable and situated just in the proximity of Rangoon town. It was worth at least 10,000 rupees, which when obtained could comfortably defray the expenses of the promulgation of the supreme Cause. But Mírzá Maḥram did not agree and left for Mandalay. I resigned to the Will of God and accompanied him to Mandalay by the same train.

Jamshíd Khodadad Ḥakím had returned to Bombay fifteen days before, and another Parsee Bahá'í friend, Jamshíd Dastúr, who was already in Rangoon, joined us for the trip to Mandalay. We had informed the Mandalay friends about Mírzá Maḥram's arrival. A large gathering of friends, men and women, were waiting at the station platform to welcome him. The thrilling cry of Alláh-u-Abhá filled the air and the shining faces of the believers vivified the spirits. We were taken to a newly built home on the main road of 84th Street that was owned by Mr. Po Tha's eldest son, Moung Po Thin. Mr. Po Tha was the richest Bahá'í in Mandalay. At this time there were about four hundred Bahá'ís in Mandalay.

In those days the well-known Bahá'ís were K͟halífa Muḥammad Yúnis (alias Ko Po Thwe Palitaga); Mr. Moujud (alias U Po Tha); Politaga U Po Choo and his wife Ma Phan Palitaga; 'Abdu'l-Qádir (alias U Po Win); Amu Yan and his son-in-law Muḥammad S͟háfí (alias M Nyo) and his wife Ma Gyi; Sulaymán (alias Ko Po Chit); U Shwe Zin; Moung Moung Gle; Yedwin Taga Ko Asman, his son-in-law Ko Shwe Ban, and Ma Ma Gyi, the said Ko Shwe Ban's wife, who later dedicated her brick built building for the Bahá'í Center. Others included: Saya Byow, Ko Koo of Whoojan, Ma Kyow, Ma May and their families; and G͟hulám-Ḥusayn.

Within a week everything was settled and people gradually started to visit Mírzá Maḥram. Soon after our arrival I received a cablegram from the Deputy Commissioner of Hanthawaddy, Rangoon, to go there within three days to take possession of my piece of land. In consultation with the friends I left for Rangoon immediately by night train and did my level best to expedite the task. At the appointed time the deputy commissioner arrived at the land with surveyors and the police. We all walked over the land and marked the boundary, and the possession paper was given to me. The land was about three and a half acres, and I engaged twenty workmen to fence it with barbed wire. The adjacent landowners on both sides of this land were Indian Muslim brick manufacturers. To create disturbance they erected a small mosque in one night. I did not object to it but put a crossing on both sides of the land outside the fence, and asked them to pray for me also. I built a temporary hut on the land and employed a watchman to guard it. While I was getting ready to return to Mandalay, one of the adjacent landowners offered me 3,000 rupees for my land [which was well below its price]. I closed the transaction and received the amount and transferred the property to the buyer's name. While I was preparing to leave for Mandalay I received an urgent telegram from Mírzá Maḥram to go to him at once.

In Mandalay the friends informed me that for two days the Muslim residents known as Jirbaries, had regularly visited and had discussions with Mírzá Maḥram, making inquiries about me.

Mírzá Maḥram told me that "from two or three days ago our meeting hall has been crowded with different kinds of people; even today a large crowd is expected." He expressed his thankful pleasure for my speedy arrival. Upon entering the meeting hall, we saw it was full with people of all ranks of Sunní Muslim residents. They asked questions on various subjects, which were politely answered. Some of them expressed their dissatisfaction and introduced some irrelevant new subjects. The audience was disgusted with them as they could not find any reason for such irrational controversy. The discourse continued for hours and Mírzá Maḥram, as was his habit, persisted in answering them, although he could not satisfy them.

The previous day, among the crowd in our meeting there was a respectable gentleman, U Po Kyu, who may have been a leader of the Palitana Gunners in Burmese time. Some hot discussion took place between him and Mírzá Maḥram. He impolitely persisted on his irrational arguments and stubbornly resisted Mírzá Maḥram's answers. Finally Mírzá Maḥram asked Jamshíd Dastúr to evict the man from the room. As he was publicly disgraced, the next day he sent his armed staff to create disturbances and attack the Bahá'ís. The Mandalay Bahá'ís had always lived peacefully in town and had never known such commotions. They did not appreciate Mírzá Maḥram's action and told him that the man who was forcibly evicted was a leader of the "Ashe-Amyouktan" of the Gunners, who were known as barbarous ruffians and respected by them. He would not tolerate this insult and as a result Bahá'ís would suffer. They feared that the Muslims of the neighboring villages would attack the handful of Bahá'ís of Mandalay in revenge. Although the danger had passed for the moment, the members of the community were uncomfortable as they were informed that the leading members of the Muslim community had decided to attack them without delay.

The next morning while we were taking breakfast, a man in the garb of an Afghani Dervish appeared in a carriage, accompanied by three other Muslims. He came directly toward our door and sat down quietly on the roadside portico in front of the house. I approached and saluted him and asked him politely in Hindi to come in but he did not answer. I finally asked him in English and told him to please get away from our door. Hearing English, he gazed at me furiously and went to join his companions. I anticipated great trouble for the Bahá'ís and invited the whole community for a meeting. They came immediately. Meanwhile we saw hundreds of carriages coming, with four or five armed men from the Muslim community in each, and stopping on the highway in front of our door. They all gathered in the mosque opposite our house. An English gentleman with four of his companions entered our house and rudely said that he was Mr. Hill, a deputy superintendent of the Mandalay police and had come to arrest the recently arrived violators of the Islamic religion and to take them to court. I replied that he had come on duty without a uniform and could not be recognized as a police officer. Also entering a house without a warrant, he had committed a criminal offence. I also pointed out that he was trying to drag innocent people to court without any reason. Therefore, we refused to pay attention to his lawless demands.

He immediately left and returned in uniform with a European magistrate who removed his hat and asked permission to enter the house. I went to the door and welcomed and received him cordially. He pointed out the mob assembled in the surrounding compound opposite our door and said, "You must have spoken something against the Islamic faith to excite the feelings of its followers as they came in throngs to attack you." Mírzá Maḥram replied, "As the magistrate stated, the mob is outside our residence, where they are not supposed to be, and lawfully we could not be responsible. As to our sacrilegious provoking expressions to excite the Muslim community, God forbid. According to our faith we believe in the oneness of all prophets and the divinity of all religions, thus we never speak and assuredly never could utter any word against any religion. Did the savior Jesus Christ utter discourteously a word against Moses or his Law? Then why did the Jews crucify the Messiah? Our position and circumstances are exactly the same. During our visit here many Muslims have entered this house, uninvited and with intention to create disturbances and breach of peace. They asked insolently various questions and we answered them all calmly and asked the audience to observe peace and keep order. It is the duty of the magistrate to make enquiries as to why this mob have taken the law in their own hands and have unlawfully gathered here." The magistrate was pleased and satisfied and asked permission to go out to make inquiries. The moment he appeared outside, the crowd dispersed and most ran away.

The magistrate posted a police guard to watch our house. He instructed the watchmen to strictly disallow people from entering the house without getting permission from us. Thus the visit of the Muslims to our house was completely curtailed. It was so strict that even the Bahá'ís had to enter by permission as the watchmen changed every few hours and had no opportunity to be acquainted with each and every member of the Bahá'í community. The friends were annoyed and the Cause of God remained silent and its promoters were idly passing time in vain. For fear of further disturbances, the friends of God had to postpone their own businesses and personal affairs for the sake of attending collectively in the meeting hall all day and into the late hours of night.

After due consideration, a general meeting was called and a resolution was unanimously passed that we should change our residence, situated on the public thoroughfare, to the house of our Bahá'í friends—Ko Shwe Ban and his wife, Ma Ma Gyi—who had kindly given their house to us free of charge. We moved to the top floor of the building at no. 9, 34th street, and the owners lived in the lower flat. Ma Ma Gyi, after the passing of her husband, Ko Shwe Ban, dedicated the whole building with all its furniture to the Bahá'í Cause. The Assembly paid off her small debts and the building became known as the Bahá'í Hall. The police also moved to this place but were not as strict as before. After moving to this building everything became quiet and there was no need for the police watchmen anymore. After reporting the particulars to the District Superintendent of police, the guards were removed.

In this place, except for a few Burmese Christian missionaries, nobody visited us, and as they were paid servants they would not accept the Faith. However, to perform our duty and pass time, discussions continued for several days. At last we came to know that the missionaries were sent by their chief, Rev. Dr. Kelly, to learn the method of teaching used by the Bahá'ís. We were cut off from the Mandalay Muslim community, even from the relatives of the Bahá'ís. This was a fatal blow and a severe test for some feeble minded persons who loved their worldly relationships more than their spiritual and eternal connection with the Cause of God and fearfully recanted and returned to their old beliefs.

There were eighty-six mosques in Mandalay that belonged to Sunní Muslims, but disagreements between their leaders had caused great dissension among them, so much so that they had excommunicated each other although they were kinsmen. The Bahá'ís lived among them with love and harmony and all Muslims participated in the memorial ceremony for Jamál Effendi after his passing. As I was known in the Muslim community of Mandalay as a peacemaker, and as I knew about their disagreements, one day I decided to go directly to their grand mullá, Mawláná 'Abdu'l-Halím, a cleric from Afghanistan who had settled in Mandalay since the Burmese sovereignty more than fifty years prior. I expressed the desire of the Bahá'í community for unity, and, after a loving discussion, fixed a Friday morning for a meeting with the condition to bring together leaders of all different parties including K. T. Palitaga, who was said to be my greatest foe.

Accompanied by some of the Bahá'í friends, I went around to see all of the clerics, including K. T. Palitaga, and peacefully received their consent to attend the meeting at an appointed time in the residence of the said grand mullá. Fortunately all of the well-known clerics came in time, including my so called enemy. My wife's cousin Mr. 'Abdu'l-Ghaní Naikwara was appointed as chairman by the grand mullá and thus everything was in our favor. Through divine assistance I delivered a short speech concerning unity, equality, fraternity, and harmony and asked for reconciliation and peace. All of them agreed. First the foe of the grand mullá came forward and asked him for favor and forgiveness. He got up and embraced him and then all those who were present embraced each other and shook hands as a token of peace and amity. Thus peace was established among the Mandalay Muslim community and on the same night all mosques were decorated with illumination. Mr. Swinho, a leading European lawyer, appreciated the occasion and wrote an article in the *Rangoon Times* about it.

On the third day of this unique occasion, a temporary structure made of bamboo was erected on the road to hold about one thousand men. Carpets were spread on the floor and all members of the Mandalay Muslim community were invited. Customary dishes of Persian rice were served from early morning to noon. Before serving the food, the grand mullá stood up and delivered a short speech on unity and brotherhood, and highly commended the noble deeds and dignified activities of the Bahá'í community for the unity and brotherhood of all mankind. "It is hoped," he said, "that this recently established link of unity and fraternity, which is the foundation of all true religions will last forever." I then got up, thanked the grand mullá and the noble audience, and delivered a speech on the same subject with quotations from the verses of the Qur'án and the Bahá'í writings for attainment to this paramount goal. The grand mullá performed the opening prayer and the food was served. After the meal, once more he chanted the concluding prayer of thanksgiving and people dispersed. This was at the beginning of the year 1898 A.D.

Jináb-i-Ḥájí Siyyid Mihdí Shírází of Rangoon returned with his family from their pilgrimage to the Holy Land and came up to see Mírzá Maḥram in Mandalay. A Bahá'í from Jewish background, Mullá Barookh Baba, from Bokhara, (Russian Turkistan) visited Mandalay for the trading of precious stones. He knew Mírzá Maḥram from Bombay. He was well versed in the Bible because of his priestly heritage. To protect himself, however, he traveled in disguise.

'Abdu'l-Bahá, in a Tablet to this humble servant, privately commanded that during my accompaniment of Mírzá Maḥram I should submissively and with absolute resignation gain his good pleasure. In obedience to the holy command of my beloved Master, I always humbly sat in the presence of Mírzá Maḥram respectfully as a loyal servant. Unfortunately, I became sick with a serious attack of fever and had to stay in the house of my brother-in-law, Abu'l-Ḥasan Qura<u>sh</u>í, a leading advocate in Mandalay, for medical treatment. The doctor advised that I should be sent to Rangoon within twenty-four hours as I was suffering from Typhoid fever. I left for Rangoon by the next mail train and was sick in bed for six months. It took over three months after that for me to gain my strength.

The hostility of the Muslims toward the Bahá'ís grew rapidly after my departure. Mírzá Maḥram also left for Bombay. Among the sufferers of this horrible calamity was <u>Kh</u>alífa Muḥammad Yúnis, U Po To Thwe, whose parents were faithful believers. His father was a mullá of the mosque of the Jundan quarter, and after resigning the post, he died of old age and was buried according to Bahá'í rites. They lived in close proximity to the fanatic Muslim hostiles who surrounded their house. They were pelted with stones while walking in the streets at night and lived in great distress for a couple of months and then had to sell their valuable properties by auction, and purchase a house in proximity of the Bahá'í circle to live in comfort.

The Bahá'í residents, to assure their protection, often cordially invited the leading persons of the Muslim community, who were their friends in business, to visit them and peacefully resolve their differences in a public meeting with the presence of government high officials, but it was to no avail. Thus, they resigned to the divine Will with submission, and devoted their time in confirming the believers in their faith and in establishing the principles of unity. After recovery from my long illness I returned to Mandalay, and Mírzá Maḥram also returned from his trip to Bombay.

The first Assembly in Rangoon was formed in 1896 and we called it the Unity Council. We reported it to 'Abdu'l-Bahá and received great praise from Him:

> *. . . For some time, the sweet divine fragrance and gentle dawn breezes have wafted over those regions. Now, their effect should be felt throughout that land. Where the flame of love blazeth and those breezes blow, the conflagration will quickly spread and the light of divine guidance grow strong. But if no breeze wafteth, the blaze will be confined to one spot and eventually be quenched. Therefore, seek thou the zephyr of His loving kindness, and be like unto a gentle breeze of guidance for those souls, so that the smoldering embers may spark to life and the entire region be set swiftly ablaze. This Servant and Jináb-i-Jamál do remember thee at every morn and eve, supplicating on thy behalf at the Holy Shrine. Our hope is that the Divine Lord will answer our prayers.* . . .

In Mandalay also, a sort of Council was formed. And in the year 1898, with the arrival of Mírzá Maḥram, a Council was formed in Bombay. When Hand of the Cause Jináb-i-Adíb visited, a constitution for the Council was written that was used for their working procedure. I translated the constitution into Burmese and from then on the Council was called a Spiritual Assembly and has since been regularly elected and is continuing to function.

Among Áqá Mírzá Maḥram's many accomplishments was assisting the late Professor Áqá Mírzá Muḥammad Riḍá Shírází of Karachi to embrace the Bahá'í Faith. He became an indefatigable and ardent teacher of the Cause in India. He had attended high school in Karachi, and obtained his B.A. in one of the best colleges in Bombay, close to the Bahá'í Hall. During his days in college he became acquainted with Mírzá Maḥram, who guided him to the Cause and deepened him in it. Two of Mírzá Muḥammad Riḍá's colleagues also accepted the Faith: Mr. N. R. Vakil of Nausari, Surat; and, Ḥishmatu'lláh Qurashí of Agra. These three digni-

Hand of the Cause of God Jináb-i-Adíb.

fied souls jointly and separately rendered many remarkable services to the Cause in India after the passing of the revered teacher Mírzá Maḥram. On 12 April 1925, the Bahá'í Community of India and Burma suffered a great loss with the premature passing of our beloved Bahá'í brother Áqá Mírzá Muḥammad Riḍá'-i-Shírází, who ascended to the Abhá Kingdom while taking a swim in the Indus River in Hyderabad, Sindh.

Mírzá Maḥram passed away in 1913 in Bombay. His resting place is in Bahá'í Gulistan at Antop Hill, Wadala, Bombay. His services to the Faith are everlasting.

'Abdu'l-Bahá revealed the following prayer for the elevation of his soul:

He is God
O God, my God! This is Thy servant who hath hearkened unto Thy call, responded to Thy summons, turned his face towards Thee, uttered Thy praises, and invited all who heard him to enter the Realm of Thy Oneness. He hath guided them to the heaven of Thy Singleness, announced unto the righteous the appearance of the tokens of Thy Holiness, and eagerly called them to the Kingdom of Thy Mysteries. He remained firm in Thy Cause until he returned unto Thee, placing his whole trust in Thee. O Lord, purify him from the dross of sinfulness, and cause him to enter the kingdom of Thy forgiveness. Plunge him in the oceans of Thy bounty and loving kindness so that he may be immersed in a sea of light within Thy Kingdom, O Thou the All-Glorious, O Thou the All-Compelling. Thou art, verily, the Most Powerful, the Unrestrained, the Gracious, the Bountiful.

'Abdu'l-Bahá also sent the following to be inscribed on his gravestone: "Mírzá Mahram Wanderer in the path of service to God confident of the boundless favours of God's forgiveness and mercy winged his flight to the heavenly realm."

Group of believers in Rangoon. Sitting from left to right: Ḥájí Siyyid Mihdí Shírází, Mírzá Maḥram, Jináb-i- Adíbu'l-'Ulamá, Siyyid Muṣṭafá Rúmí, Siyyid Ismá'íl Shírází.

Gravesite of Mírzá Maḥram.

- 8 -

FIRST PILGRIMAGE, 1903

I was honored with a holy Tablet from 'Abdu'l-Bahá in 1903, graciously giving me permission to attend His holy presence. The last paragraph read,

> *A reply to thy detailed supplication was previously written and duly dispatched which assuredly has reached thee by this time. Thou hath attained the great blessings of the Blessed Beauty. This privilege is particularly bestowed upon thee for no pilgrims are permitted to come in these days although many people earnestly supplicated for permission. But thou art very fortunate to come to share the calamities of the Great Prison with us. A.A.*[1]

In April 1903 A.D., I boarded the *SS Dalmatia Anchor* from Rangoon to Port Sa'íd. The sea was calm and smooth all along the voyage and it was a very pleasant trip. All the time I was occupied in translating into Burmese the book *The Revelation of Bahaullah in a Sequence of Four Lessons,* compiled by Isabella D. Brittingham and published in 1902. This task was commanded by the Master and it was accomplished before my arrival at Suez. Mírzá 'Ináyatu'lláh and Mírzá 'Abdu'l-Ḥusayn, employees in the shop of Áqá Aḥmad Yazdí in Port Sa'íd, came onboard the ship to receive me. The revered brother, Áqá Aḥmad Yazdí, was waiting for me at the customs and with great kindness took me to his own home. Fortunately I arrived during the sacred days of the Riḍván festivities, and after meeting the friends in the evening I embarked on an Austrian boat that was leaving for Haifa.

This was my preliminary voyage to these countries, and as at that time there were no restrictions, I did not have a passport. Áqá Aḥmad Yazdí kindly acquired a passport for me as a Persian subject that was attested by the Turkish authorities at Port Sa'íd. He warned me to take particular precautions in my actions not to harm the supreme Cause. I confined myself to the cabin, and the next day the lighthouse on Mount Carmel was sighted from a long distance.

Áqá Aḥmad Yazdí told me that he had sent a message to his brother, Mírzá Ḥusayn, to receive me and unless I received a note from him through his Arab boatman intimating his presence on the harbor, I should not disembark. The boatman came but without a note. I sent him back and he returned with a note and only then I disembarked. I passed through customs easily and spent the night in his house. The next morning he engaged an omnibus vehicle for me, and in utmost and eager desire to kiss the feet of my Lord I proceeded toward 'Akká.

The friends who were commanded by our Lord were waiting at the gate to receive and welcome me. They took me with my luggage to Kh͟án-i-'Avámíd, the rest house where the oriental pilgrims were housed. The caretaker, Áqá Muḥammad Ḥasan, kindly arranged everything for my comfort. That same evening I was called to attend the holy presence of my Lord. I followed Áqá Muḥammad Ḥasan eagerly to the house of the Master [House of 'Abdu'lláh Pás͟há] and went up the stone steps until I reached the top. At the door of a visiting hall on the right hand my guide told me to go in, and he left. I entered the hall where my Lord was standing to receive me. I fell on His feet and lost consciousness. He raised me up, embraced, and kissed me according to oriental etiquette and made me sit on a divan near to Him. I felt a new spirit animating me. He then turned His face toward this humble servant and in a loving voice welcomed me and said that for a long time He had an ardent desire to see this servant as Jamál Effendi had favorably commended me to Him.

He compassionately made inquiry about the progress of the holy Cause and welfare of the friends in India and particularly in Burma. I was able to understand His utterances but I was overwhelmed with the power and effulgence of His majestic glory and was unable to utter a word. I only shed tears in silence. I was alone in His presence for about an hour, and then the friends were permitted to come up from the visiting hall situated downstairs. After a prayer was chanted, all were permitted to retire. We returned to our residence. Being an old servant of the Threshold I was known to all friends long before my arrival and we rejoiced to meet each other. As a rule the friends were allowed to visit the holy house every evening.

Our Lord occupied two houses; one was called 'Abdu'lláh Pá<u>sh</u>á's House, where he received the visitors and where the Greatest Holy Leaf lived. The other one was His private residence with His family. Mrs. Lua Getsinger was permitted to live in this house to teach English to the children.

On the second day of my arrival I was summoned to the first house. I had the bounty of attending the holy presence of the Master, and after excessive blessings I was commanded to go with His son-in-law Mírzá Muḥsin Afnán to the Master's private residence. We both went up to see Lua Getsinger and after an exchange of loving greetings, my guide asked me to translate a Persian Tablet into English. In spite of my little knowledge of English, I did so and after review and approval by Mrs. Getsinger, it was taken to the holy presence of the Master.

Jináb-i-Mírzá Yúnis <u>Kh</u>án and Dr. Árástú <u>Kh</u>án were already serving as translators of the holy Tablets and teachers of English in the Bahá'í school established in one of the rooms at the Inn at 'Akká. I was appointed as an additional translator with all my incompetence and incapability. Mrs. Getsinger was authorized to correct all English translations, and after her corrections we wrote fair copies and submitted them to our Lord to be sent abroad. We translated the book *Bahá'í Martyrdom in Persia in 1903* but my name is not credited in the publication. I was given a separate room nearby for my office in the same inn, which was later turned into a Bahá'í clinic when our translation department was closed.

The [Khán-i-'Avámíd], with a clock tower, consisted of many rooms all around and was occupied by married Bahá'ís with their families, and used for oriental pilgrims. To my good fortune I lived close to the great Persian teacher Jináb-i-Áqá Ḥájí Mírzá Ḥaydár 'Alí-i-Iṣfahání, who was ninety years old and lived in a separate room. He was a real lover and admirer of our Lord 'Abdu'l-Bahá.

Upon receiving the sorrowful news of the martyrdoms of Bahá'ís in Yazd and Iṣfahán, our Lord did not take any food, even his usual Persian tea or coffee, for three days. He moved around with such might and majesty in His supreme glory that was never seen before. It was clear that by this mighty power He could put down the entire world system if He willed. All the friends—men, women, and children—were so thunder-struck that they also forsook food and sleep. On the third evening, the Greatest Holy Leaf at last sent for Ḥájí Mírzá Ḥaydár 'Alí and told him to take permission of the Master to enter into His holy presence, as no one was admitted to go to His presence. She also asked him to take me with him to firmly hold the hem of His garment and beg Him to drink a cup of tea to break His fast.

In obedience to her command we went up and stood reverently by the door in full resignation. He felt our presence at the door and permitted both of us to enter into His holy presence. We fell upon His feet holding firmly His hem and wept bitterly like children. I am unable to explain that peculiar moment. We did not leave His hem and His feet until He compassionately consented to take a cup of tea. The holy household gathered together in the adjacent room, weeping and waiting for His command to serve Him a cup of tea. He called out "Bring a cup of tea. It is impossible to disappoint these two devoted servants of the Blessed Beauty." He then expressed His earnest desire to share martyrdom with those sacrificial true believers who were enraptured with the Blessed Beauty. Subsequently the friends were granted admission as before to enter His presence.

Lua Getsinger went on a hunger strike with an American flag in her hand aspiring to saturate it in her blood, weeping and beseeching day and night for the Master's permission to go to Persia and share in the martyrdom of the friends. Although the Master assured her of the bestowal of the exalted station of martyrdom she was not satisfied. At last the Master instructed her that for eighteen days she should say a certain holy verse revealed by the Báb, "Say: God sufficeth all things above all things, and nothing in the heavens or in the earth but God sufficeth. Verily, He is in Himself the Knower, the Sustainer, the Omnipotent," 314 times before dawn. If she succeeded to accomplish this task without interruption then she would be permitted to go to Persia. She requested three of us to also repeat the verse. She failed twice to accomplish this task. Mírzá Yúnis Khán and Dr. Árástú Khán and I failed also. It was then that she realized the mysteries of the divine wisdom explained for her by the Master.

I had arrived in the beginning of May 1903 and had the bounty to remain at the holy presence until the end of October 1903, during which time I observed numerous miracles, although just the daily movements of our beloved Master are miracles in the sight of His admirers.

Dr. Árástú Khán was anxious to see Jerusalem, and after his repeated invitations I consented to go with him. Thus both of us supplicated for permission at the holy presence, which was graciously granted. A Bahá'í friend in 'Akká kindly sent a telegram to his relative in Jaffa to receive us onboard the Italian ship. We were allowed on the ship by showing our passports and reached Jaffa the following morning. We were cordially welcomed and kindly treated. On the same day we left by train and arrived in the afternoon at Jerusalem. On the train we met Dr. Arbela, an elderly Jewish gentleman, who was a very experienced traveler, a linguist, and proficient in oriental and occidental languages. He was a well-known resident of Jaffa. He took us to a well-furnished German Jewish Hostel owned by Mr. Chaminitz.

We took a room for both of us and the next morning took a guide to take us to all sacred places in and out of Jerusalem. Though I could speak Arabic fluently, in several places of worship I spoke in English to escape unpleasantness. We bought some trinkets and after three days returned to Jaffa. Within this short period we visited many historical sites and all the sacred places in Jerusalem. We also met some of the renowned Jewish and Christian religious Rabbis and Patriarchs. We returned to Haifa by land in a high carriage of three horses. It took us forty-two hours to reach Haifa, and we then took another carriage to 'Akká and reached there after sunset.

The next day we both entered into the holy presence of our Lord. Dr. Árástú Khán was questioned by Him about the journey and he submitted the circumstances briefly. Owing to various sorts of troubles continually created by the Turkish authorities in 'Akká, our translation department had to be closed and we the servants were idle. I was called to the holy presence and after the bestowal of boundless blessings and kind encouragement I was commanded to be ready with my passport and all necessary items for travel:

> *Thou hath become a citizen of 'Akká but we are going to banish thee to Burma and India. Do not be disheartened, thou art now newly created by the holy breath of the Blessed Beauty. Today is the day of service. 'Abdu'l Bahá is the exemplary sign of servitude. All should imitate and follow My footsteps. Thou art granted the dignity of a shepherd, ere long thou shalt go to some unfamiliar regions and wilt call out the sheep of God and they will come to thee in flocks, running swiftly. Thou wilt be helped with hosts of innumerable angels of the Supreme Concourse. Be ready for service, energetically, girdle up thy loins, rise up with utmost steadfastness and proclaim the holy Covenant of Bahá'u'lláh freely and fearlessly everywhere thou mayest find it possible to go. The Center of the Covenant is thy guardian and eternal protector at all times.*

It was a very lengthy and majestic talk, but I have written a brief account of what I could absorb. I was commanded to take a young man of about thirty years, Rafatu'lláh, with me to Burma. He had some mental problems and his uncle was employed as the caretaker of the oriental pilgrim house.

About the end of October 1903, I left for Haifa with my companion, assured by our Lord in every respect for my safety. The boat for Port Sa'íd was delayed for about a fortnight. Ḥájí Mírzá Hádí Afnán, the son-in-law of the Master, was my host. I wept for my misfortune of deprivation from the holy presence. The Master comprehended my feeling through His infallible divine wisdom and revealed a holy Tablet in His own hand for this humble servant, showering me with boundless merciful consolation and encouragement:

> *O thou my companion!*
> *It seems that thou hast become a prisoner in the city of Haifa, for whenever the means of travel are delayed, the place becomes like unto a prison for the traveler. This, verily, is a bounty from thy Merciful and Compassionate Lord, inasmuch as this pause in Haifa hath become a means of receiving divine blessings, and an opportunity to inhale the heavenly breezes and the musky fragrances. My prayer during thy sojourn is that the Almighty in His loving kindness will confirm and assist thee, and graciously aid thee to serve this Cause. May thou be triumphant and victorious in resisting the hosts of self and passion, in promoting the divine sweet savours, and uniting the hearts of the beloved of the Lord.*

Finally a boat arrived and we left for Port Sa'íd. On arrival at the port we were met by an employee of Áqá Aḥmad Yazdí, the Persian Consul, who took us to his master's house. We had to wait for a boat bound for Rangoon and were guests of his kind hospitality.

We boarded a German cargo boat, *SS Rosenfeld,* which was bound directly for Rangoon. Except for an Indian Portuguese cook, all the crew were German and there were no passengers but us. I arranged to pay the cook to supply meals for us up to Rangoon. The sea was calm and comfortable up to Aden but thereafter the captain forecasted serious stormy weather with his barometer and ordered the sailors to put my entire luggage in the cabin with us to prevent it being washed away by the waves of the high sea.

My companion had been sent with me in the hope that the sea air might help him. However, to my misfortune, since our departure from Port Sa'íd he had waited to find an opportunity to attack me. We slept in one cabin and I constantly watched his attitude, but also appreciated his presence for he was sent with me by the Master. After the ship passed the Gulf of Aden, one day the cook came in search of his large kitchen knife and during the absence of my companion found it under his pillows. There was an opened sharp razor also near the knife. The cook was an elderly man and at once suspected a murder plot and warned me about it. I was firm in my belief that he would not harm me, as I was assured and promised protection by the Master. One day, before sunset suddenly a violent storm and heavy rain set in. The cook came up and took away my bedding to his cabin. My companion disappeared and we later found out that he had taken shelter in another part of the ship, thus we were peacefully separated by His mighty will. The ship was about 2,000 tons and the waves of the ocean were violently high. The boat seemed to be running under water. The storm continued for days until we approached the Rangoon lighthouse; only then could I go in search of my troubled friend. The cook said he always supplied him with bread and beef and also occasionally tea.

The German cargo boats did not run more than seven or eight knots per hour and thus we arrived in Rangoon after many difficulties on the twenty-seventh day after we had left Port Sa'íd.

Rafatu'lláh declined to go with me and preferred to stay with Mírzá Maḥram. I sent him with his small luggage with my servant who had come with my brother-in-law to receive me for Mírzá Maḥram.

Soon after my arrival, Mírzá Maḥram with Khalífa Muḥammad Yúnis (alias Ko Po Thwe) of Mandalay and Dr. Khabíru'd-Dín and Dr. Siyyid Sajjád Ḥusayn, both of Rangoon, left for the Holy Land via Madras and Bombay. Ḥájí Siyyid Mihdí Shírází also went directly from Rangoon to Port Sa'íd. They soon returned to Burma, but Mirza Maḥram remained in Bombay. Subsequently Ḥájí Siyyid Mihdí Shírází arrived, and he and his son Áqá Siyyid Ismá'íl Shírází moved from 32nd Street to no. 20 Sparks Street, and opened the Bahá'í meeting hall on the ground floor of their house and lived on the top floor. I lived with my wife and her relatives in no. 1 Sparks Street, near the Strand Road.

- 9 -

EVENTS OF 1904–1906

In 1904, Áqá Mírzá Maḥmúd Zarqání came to Burma from India. The following Tablet from our Lord had been received in his honor in Rangoon in October of that year:

> *. . . I am aware that in this trip thou art burdened with troubles and afflictions. However, if thou considereth the results, troubles become mercies and afflictions ease and comfort. The start of events should not be considered, but one should persevere with pure motive in affairs and await the end-results. Comfort and contentment have never yielded fruits. In any age and century achievements have been the results of toil, sacrifice, and tolerance of afflictions.*
>
> *Therefore, whatever adversity and hardship appear in this path should be confronted with utmost joy and perseverance to attain lofty and profound results.*
>
> *Consider how holy ones of bygone ages tolerated hardships, adversities, difficulties and trials. They confronted them with good pleasure until they became signs of divine unity and standards of the Lord All Glorious. It is revealed in the Qur'án: "Do you think you will find your way to paradise even though you have not known what the others before you have gone through? They had suffered affliction and loss . . ."*[1] *Thou also shouldst tolerate all hardships and adversities. . . .*

The Rangoon Bahá'í Assembly exerted its level best to promulgate the divine Cause by reprinting and publishing the American leaflets and pamphlets relating to the holy Cause, even the Seven Valleys and the Hidden Words. Áqá Siyyid Ismá'íl S͟hírází voluntarily defrayed all expenses for this noble task. The management of all these works was carried out by this humble servant. At this time Mr. Amiru'l Islam of Chittagong (Bengal) accepted the Cause.[2]

At the repeated requests of the friends of Mandalay, in 1906 A.D. I went to see them. It was heartening to see that Dr. Siyyid Sajjád Ḥusayn, K͟halífa Muḥammad Yúnis (alias Ko Po Thwe) and Áqá G͟hulám Ḥusayn, with all the Bahá'í friends, had opened an English primary class in the house of Muḥammad S͟háfí (alias U Nyo), under the management of Sulaymán (alias Ko Po Chit), and were active and ardently engaged in educating the Bahá'í children.

We were invited by the Buddhist Society to their gathering in U Pe Si Pagoda. The Tablet revealed by 'Abdu'l-Bahá that I had translated was published for free distribution. In the company of friends, I went there and delivered a speech on the advent of their expected Maitrya, the fifth Buddha of the present cycle, which is called "Maha Bhadra Kalpa." Maitrya means a person who is full of love and kindness. Amitabha—endowed with infinite light and splendor, had now appeared in this gloomy cycle to enlighten and illuminate the world of humanity with divine wisdom. Thus I was able to deliver the great message of Bahá'u'lláh to the Burmese speaking Buddhist audience.[3]

Our Bahá'í brother Safdar 'Alí from Chittagong, who had accepted the Faith in Rangoon, was working as an engineer in one of the flotilla steamers. On his trip to Mandalay he arranged a meeting in the Sunní Muslim mosque and escorted me with about twenty Bahá'ís there. There was a full moon as we walked over, and, after they performed their evening prayers, all of us entered the mosque. A large number of crews and petty officers who worked on the steamers in the Irrawaddy River were there. As we entered, I became rather alarmed. There were no lights except a few small candles on the pulpit, which could easily be extinguished. Their priest was asked to speak on Islam and the Prophet without giving us a chance to speak. Suddenly there was a horrible shouting and the candles were abruptly put out and a fearful commotion ensued. I stood up at once and told the friends to immediately follow me, and walked out. I stood by the police station at the corner of the street, anxiously waiting for my companions. They all safely made it out, and in a procession we marched to our homes. We thanked God for our safe return.

In the year 1909 A.D. I compiled a booklet in Burmese titled *Mizanul-Forghan* (The Four Methods for Acquiring Knowledge). It was immediately printed and widely distributed. I then dictated another booklet in Burmese, as at the time I could not read and write Burmese fluently. It was called *Shajartu'l-Adyan* (Tree of Religions). It was published at Rangoon (2,000 copies) for the benefit of the friends of Daidanow Kalazoo, Kungyangon. All the expenses of publication, which was about 150 rupees, were borne by Áqá Siyyid Ismá'íl Shírází.

During my stay at Mandalay I was informed that the old lady Ma Ma Gyi, widow of Ko Shwe Ban, intended to sell her property, a two-story brick building with a compound at the back, situated at no. 9, 34th street in order to clear her various debts. This building was known as the Bahá'í Hall as weekly meetings were held there. I advised her not to sell it as the small amount of money that would be left for her after clearing her debts could hardly provide for her maintenance during her lifetime. She agreed and asked my advice in order to pass her lonely remaining life free of anxieties with peace and tranquility. I advised her to dedicate the building by a registered deed of trust to the Bahá'í Cause and told her that the Local Spiritual Assembly would pay off all her debts. She could remain in her home as before, serving the Cause and receiving assistance sufficient to live on, which would be decided by the Assembly with her consent. Her noble sacrifice would be highly appreciated by the Master and it would be recorded as a commendable charity for eternity. She accepted the terms of my proposal with joy. A meeting was called and I tendered the proposal with full explanation of terms and conditions. It was unanimously passed, a deed of trust was duly executed by her in the government registration office, and she consented to receive a monthly honorarium.

Our compassionate Master 'Abdu'l-Bahá revealed the following Tablet on her behalf:

> *. . . O thou who art nigh unto His Exalted Threshold! A fortunate fate rendered thee the embodiment of divine favours, making thee the recipient of His guiding light. This is naught but a sign of the loving kindness of the Lord, for faith and certitude are granted by His grace, not His justice. He guideth whomsoever He willeth to the Straight Path. Praise be to God that thou hast faithfully served His Cause. Thou didst desire thy house to be a Mas͟hriqu'l-Ad͟hkár, a center of the propagation of the mysteries of God and a dawning place of His splendours. Praise be to God that thy wish hath been granted; this is, indeed, a token of the grace of thy All-Merciful and Compassionate Lord . . .*

She passed to the Abhá Kingdom at the age of seventy-eight in 1931.

- 10 -

ARRIVAL OF THE FAITH AT DAIDANOW KALAZOO VILLAGE

DAIDANOW KALAZOO VILLAGE, THE VILLAGE OF 'ABDU'L-BAHÁ

Its name is a combination of *Daidanow*—which was the name of a Pagoda built in ancient times by a ruling nation called *Talaing,* situated in the northwest of the village—and *Kala* meaning "foreigners," and *Zoo* meaning a "foreign group."

THE FOUNDING OF THE VILLAGE

Soon after the British government conquered Burma in 1885, a group of outsiders—consisting of Muslims and Buddhists—migrated from the Shwebo district in upper Burma. They were utterly destitute and their poverty compelled them to serve as laborers under Burmese landlords. As they were ignorant of their Islamic principles, they gradually adopted the Burmese customs and manners.

In 1905, a priest named Saya Kauk from their homeland of the Shwebo district, came down and re-established their former faith of Islam. He made material reform and compelled them to erect a mosque and to remain under his control. He collected a large sum of money from this and other villages in lower Burma in the name of reformation, and misappropriated it for his own purposes and only erected one or two small mosques in some isolated quarters. Therefore, most of the Muslims lost their faith in the priest. They appointed a mullá for the small mosque in their village and pretended to follow Islam.

MY VISIT TO DAIDANOW KALAZOO

The year 1907 A.D. was a very remarkable one in the history of the Bahá'í Faith in Burma for fulfillment of the prophecies of 'Abdu'l-Bahá—particularly those on my behalf, while I was honored to be a recipient of boundless blessings in His holy presence.

It was sometime in April 1907 that an old man, U Chit-Tun, a well-known resident of the village of Daidanow Kalazoo, situated in the Township of Kungyangon in the Hanthawaddy district, came to Rangoon to hire a lawyer to defend him in a criminal case brought against him by his younger brother's widow in Kungyangon. On his arrival at Rangoon, he was swindled by a man who pretended to be a lawyer's clerk and lost all his money. One day, he came to the stall of 'Abdu'l-Karím, alias U Ma, a Bahá'í, to buy cigars. In reply to the enquiry of his whereabouts, he related his painful experience and sought help. 'Abdu'l-Karím brought him to me. After full consideration into his affairs, I consented to go with him to the court as well as to his village.

The magistrate before whom the case was pending for final decision was my close friend. The case was to be heard the day after our arrival and I had no time to consult the friends, nor an opportunity for any kind of preparation. The place was quite new to me and the man whom I had employed to help me was not known to me or to the Bahá'í friend who brought him to me. The place where I intended to stay was known to be unsafe. I took all sorts of risks to defend the distressed old man. To our great astonishment, I had met the same magistrate onboard the steam-launch and he had kindly promised to do justice in the case in my presence. The next morning I attended the court with the accused and personally pleaded the case. He was acquitted as the plaintiff had no documentation for her case, which proved to be false. The old man and his co-accused were anxious to sue the plaintiff for false accusation and defamation. After conclusion of the case I went to their village, where about a dozen of the old man's relatives surrounded me. I convinced them not to take any action against their accuser.

People were astonished by my loving expressions and started questioning me about my faith. They said it was known that reward and punishment are the two principle standards in all the religions of the world. Most of the Islamic precepts regarding the punishment of criminals are based on Mosaic laws, such as an eye for an eye, so that criminals are proportionately punished for their crimes. Otherwise the vicious practice of the wicked persons will be increased to their highest level. What was the reason for such tolerance and merciful acts of forgiveness? Was I adhering to any reformed new faith that was more liberal and tolerant than their Islamic faith? Finding a good opportunity to declare our Bahá'í beliefs, I told them about the new Manifestation of God and His divine teachings, which are to be the remedy for the fatal diseases of the present age. They were impressed and I returned to Rangoon with the same old man the next morning.

After returning to his village the old man came back with a group of other villagers to investigate the truth of the Faith in detail. They stayed in my house for a couple of nights and attentively listened to all my explanations. Filled with a joyful spirit they returned to their village. The creative Word of God did not allow them to rest quietly and they discussed the subject together all the time and consulted with their kindred. At last they unanimously decided that the holy Cause should be declared openly in public. They sent U Chit Tung, a member of their community, to invite me to their village. I accepted their invitation, and, accompanied by a Bahá'í friend, 'Abdu'l-Karím, as well as a cook and some necessary provisions, went there.

After our arrival at the village we stayed for three days in a mosque made of bamboo as there was no proper residence in the whole village. On our arrival, the villagers—both Muslim and Buddhist—surrounded me. Like a talking machine I had to speak day and night, sitting on a hard bamboo floor in the Persian fashion (kneeling down) without taking any rest, except after midnight to take a short nap. I quoted from the Qur'án and the traditions of Muḥammad and from the Buddhist scriptures about the time and the place of the appearance of the new Manifestation.

No objection was raised by any individual, nor was any contradictory question put to me by them. The night before my departure about forty souls, men and women, openly and publicly declared their faith in the divine Cause.

Although there was no opposition in this first trip, I was apprehensive in anticipation of some fatal calamity that I would have to suffer on subsequent trips. As the villagers were farmers and laborers in the paddy fields, the best times to meet them in their village occurred twice a year—after their ploughing season in August or September and after their harvest in March or April.

My second trip to Daidanow Kalazoo village was in April 1908 at the invitation of the friends. They came to Kungyangon with their bullock carts to receive me at the mooring of the launch. A large multitude of Muslims and Buddhists were gathered in front of the bamboo mosque to meet me upon my arrival. As in my former trip I had to stay in the same mosque and meet large audiences day and night. I tried very hard on this trip to promulgate the holy Cause, as there was great opposition against the new believers. One of the fanatic villagers, Muḥammad Ḥusayn, alias Saya Maung Po Ni, came to the meeting and angrily shouted that he was going "to call the high priest from the adjacent village, Englon, to argue with this transgressor and impostor, Siyyid Muṣṭafá Rúmí, who has come with false pretentions to violate the true religion of our ancestors and introduce a new faith." He further shouted: "If he fails to prove his claim before the expected high priest, he should be killed on the spot in this mosque." He produced a sharpened dagger and waved it violently as the weapon to be used.

Muḥammad Ḥusayn was twenty-five years old, with great furious zeal, energy, and a haughty temper. He was better off than the other villagers, so they tried their level best to appease him but to no avail. The more humility the villagers showed the more he raged. He immediately went away to fetch the grand mullá, Miya Sat, a native of Patna district,

India. He was an elderly man of about sixty-five years who had lived in that village for thirty-five years and was believed by the villagers to be a great learned sage and a holy man. His word was accepted by all as the word of God, although his sons and daughters were known as notoriously bad characters.

Muḥammad Ḥusayn brought the mullá within half-an-hour and warned him that unless he declared publicly his opponent's truthfulness or falsehood, his authority would not be accepted thereafter.

The grand mullá arrived at the meeting while I was delivering a public speech in Burmese for the Buddhist audience, proving the authenticity of the claim of his Holiness Muḥammad. After the conclusion of my discourse, I greeted the high priest and he expressed his loving sentiments with utmost pleasure. He could understand and speak the Burmese language well and stood up and declared the authenticity of my discourse. He faced the audience and said, "This honorable guest is a great sage and is following the right path of our true religion, a real proclaimer of the unity of God and truthfulness of all holy prophets up to this day. Should any person accuse him of falsehood or contrary belief, such person is considered to be of illegitimate birth and will go directly to hell. This is the final decision of our holy prophet Muḥammad in His sacred tradition. We should honor this divine personage, accept and follow his teachings faithfully. I testify that these teachings are divine and a real means for the progress of humanity . . ."

I replied in suitable words and thanked him for his kind expressions. Muḥammad Ḥusayn took him back in the bullock cart that he had brought him in to our meeting. On his way home, the priest highly commended me and told him that he had comprehended a divine light in this Siyyid and sincerely recommended seeking the companionship of such a noble soul. It was about midnight when this young man returned to the meeting while the audience was still keenly awaiting the consequences. Muḥammad Ḥusayn, to the astonishment of the multitude was completely changed and immediately after his arrival declared his belief in the Bahá'í Faith. He was accompanied by his father, U Son, and his maternal grandfather, Palitagah U Shwe Ngon, a venerable old man who had built the first mosque in the Muslim quarter.

On that marvelous night, which was beyond our expectation, about eighty souls voluntarily accepted the holy Cause and duly registered their names together with their families. Muḥammad Ḥusayn turned out to be a very firm Bahá'í, like a solid rock pillar, and vigorously tolerated all calamities that crossed his path.

The temporary bamboo mosque that we used as our meeting place was blown away by the storm during the rainy season. Villagers gathered the particles together and erected a temporary meeting hall on the same spot. No mosque was built there again.

Gradually the divine Cause became more vigorously confirmed and popular. The number of adherents increased and we had to think about the education of the children. It was proposed that the meeting hall be used for a school, but owing to its instability it could not be done. The village Bahá'ís were poor and unable to construct a decent building to suit the purpose. They appealed to the Rangoon Bahá'ís for help. U Chit Toon called a meeting of the Bahá'í villagers and collected a small sum of about $23. They purchased an old house from a neighboring village, and the Rangoon friends—Ḥájí Siyyid Mihdí Shírází and his son Áqá Siyyid Ismá'íl Shírází, Mr. Muḥammad Yúsuf, Dr. 'Abdu'l-Ḥakím, and Siyyid Muṣṭafá Rúmí—contributed toward the building of a Bahá'í hall. It was built immediately at a cost of about eighty pounds sterling. Many revered foreign teachers, such as Fáḍil-i-Mázandarání, his companion Áqá Siyyid 'Abdu'l-Ḥusayn-i-Ardistání, Howard Struven, Áqá Mírzá Maḥmúd Zarqání, Mr. and Mrs. S. Schopflocher, Mrs. Inez Cook, Mrs. Hagarty and her children, were received in that building. Some stayed for a night or a couple of days and some paid a flying visit. In May 1927, Mírzá Munír Nabíl-Zadeh with his nephew Prof. 'Alí-Muḥammad Nabílí visited this spot and stayed for some days.[1]

I was usually invited by the friends at the yearly visiting season of their harvest time. The moment I arrived, the news would spread everywhere. One day the people of the adjacent mosque came to the Bahá'í elders,

Siyyid Muṣṭafá Rúmí with Inez Cook and the Bahá'ís of Daidanow Kalazoo village. For more details on the visit of Inez Cook, see Appendix I: Visitors to Burma.

Siyyid Muṣṭafá Rúmí with Inez Cook and the children of Daidanow Kalazoo village.

saying that they had made arrangements for holding a public meeting to discuss the authenticity of the Bahá'í Cause so that their grand mullá would make the final decision about this difficult situation. They had invited four grand ulamá from Rangoon, Tawkayan, and Kungyangon towns, who had already arrived at the village mosque. They were offering

Siyyid Muṣṭafá Rúmí with Inez Cook and other guests at Daidanow Kalazoo village.

this opportunity to the Bahá'ís and were willing to allow them to discuss the subject with them in the Bahá'í Hall or host them at the Muslim quarters. After consultation we decided to invite the Muslims to come to us to discuss the subject in the Bahá'í Hall. We assured them of a cordial reception.

The Muslim villagers accompanied the four ulamá and a group of Kungyangon traders, the Muslim policemen of Kungyangon, and many spectators numbering more than forty, in addition to about 100 Muslim villagers who were present. All were armed with sticks and other deadly weapons. As our small hall was filled by these visitors, the Bahá'í friends could not enter and had to be kept away from me. The friends felt that the mob had come with some treacherous plan in order to create problems or to kill me and declare victory. As I was left helplessly alone, the friends surrounded the place and opened the side door to enable them to enter the hall in case of disorder.

After exchanging cordial greetings with the guests, I suggested to the ulamá that as the majority of the audience was Burmese speaking, to safeguard their interest, our conversation should be in the Burmese language only. This was unanimously accepted by all. Then I said that the chief purpose of their coming to this place after sustaining such a tedious journey was for two reasons: First to know the principles of the Bahá'í Cause and that if they proved to be in conformity with their Islamic principles there would be no need for further discussion. Second, if they find it contrary to the Islamic principles, they should prove by sound arguments that I was wrong and to guide me to the right path to save the multitude from such wrong notions. The ulamá and their companions unanimously confirmed my suggestion. They cried out that this was their sole intention for coming to this village.

I declared that I believed in the unity of God with all His sacred names and attributes; in the authenticity and truthfulness of all holy Prophets and divine Manifestations without exception or rejection of any one of them. I declared my belief in the truth of all holy books revealed by the holy Prophets, I declared my belief in the existence of divine angels and the Day of Judgment or resurrection. I explained the day of resurrection according to the Holy Qur'án and the sacred traditions and said that I believed that there are two kinds of resurrections—the minor resurrection, *Qiyámat-Ṣughrá,* and the major resurrection, *Qiyámat-Kubrá.* The minor resurrection is, as universally believed, the period of the corruption of the Islamic Faith, which began 260 years after the Hijra and would last for one thousand years. Then, upon the termination of this period of one thousand years, 1260 years after the Hijra, the second cycle would commence, which is called the major resurrection: Qiyámat-Kubrá. Its greatest signs are the appearance of the Imám Mihdí, the Qá'im, and subsequently the advent of Jesus, the Spirit of God, Who is qualified with all divine attributes, power, glory, and righteousness. I proved for them each subject separately by furnishing strong evidences from the Holy Qur'án, the sacred traditions of His Holiness Muḥammad, and the accepted authorities from the great sages of Islam that are unanimously agreed upon and accepted by the two great sects of Islam—the Sunní and Shí'ih. I said that His Holiness the Báb was the promised Imám

Mihdí and Qá'im, and His Holiness Bahá'u'lláh was the true Manifestation of the divine spirit, the Advent of the Word of God.

Feeling that they were convinced, I concluded the discourse and asked the learned sages, as well as the audience, whether they were ready to accept and believe the holy verses of the Qur'án and the unerring words of His Holiness Muḥammad. They all publicly responded that they believed all of it and found nothing to discuss or dispute. They did not question the authenticity of the Bahá'í Faith but they were not going to believe in the Báb and Bahá'u'lláh as true Promised Ones of all nations. "Where is the Anti-Christ, Dajjál? The Anti-Christ will be known distinctly from the written inscription on his forehead as Káfir, the Infidel. Paradise will be on his right side and hell on his left. Where are the two nations of Gog and Magog? The great multitudes of the ulamá in Mecca, Arabia, Turkey, Egypt, and India, who are universally believed as great authorities in the Islamic world, have not yet given opinions about these two Promised Ones."

They finally decided that the matter was doubtful and mysterious for them and had not at the present time been investigated. But as regards S. M. Rúmí there was no reason to oppose him, for he may have believed after scrutinizing this particular subject in depth.

I tried my best to clear their doubts by showing them the real meanings of Anti-Christ and the nations of Gog and Magog from their own holy books, but to no avail. They promised to come again to learn more if they found an opportunity to do so. They expressed their gratitude, and peacefully retired to their mosque with their followers.

Soon after they left, there was a wonderful large gathering in the evening with a remarkable result. About one hundred souls accepted the Bahá'í Cause and their names were duly registered in the book. The people of the mosque were much annoyed and blamed their ulamá for their weakness of opinion and irrational decision, causing obvious victory of the Bahá'ís and progress of their Cause. The Bahá'ís were filled with utmost enthusiasm and energy for they had observed the wonderful effect of divine confirmation, glory, and power.

Group of believers at Daidanow Kalazoo village. People in the photograph are labeled as follows: A. Mr. Árástú; B. Ghulám-Ḥusayn; C. Maung Po Ni, schoolmaster of the Bahá'í school; 1. Ko Hlun Gywe, president of the Bahá'í Assembly of Daidanow; 2. Howard Struven; 3. Charles Mason Remey; 4. Siyyid Muṣṭafá Rúmí; 5. Siyyid Ismá'íl Shírází; 6. Siyyid 'Abdu'l-Ḥusayn, the son of Siyyid Ismá'íl Shírází.

Witnessing the rapid establishment of the Bahá'í Cause in Daidanow Kalazoo and the Tan-Bim-Gyoung village in the jungle, situated at a distance of three miles from this village, the friends were induced to build a small structure of about twenty by forty feet for a school of a temporary, but durable, nature. The friends were unable to contribute even a small sum of money to buy new timber, but every one of them brought whatever they could in planks and other materials. The required amount in cash to buy roofing etc. was contributed by this humble servant in the name of the beloved Master, 'Abdu'l-Bahá. After the completion of the building the report of all activities was submitted with supplication to the holy presence and the following Tablet was revealed in answer:

> *. . . Praised be to God that all these events have occurred in a timely fashion, for this is an evidence of the bounty and confirmations bestowed*

upon thee. Thou hast done thine utmost to convene a gathering: now, divine blessings are needed to achieve the rest. With respect to travel and lack of stability, it is indeed as thou hast written. Teachers of the Faith should not remain or rest in one place, but rather be constantly on the move. They should forge ahead with the utmost detachment, joy and radiance, ablaze with the fire of the love of God, and disseminate the divine fragrances, breathing the breaths of holiness far and wide. Otherwise, it would be impossible to achieve the desired effect. . . .

As regards the Kunjangun school, this school is extremely important and hath been inaugurated in the name of this humble servant. It must be run with the utmost order and regularity, and all the friends in India must lend it their support . . .

In the beginning, teaching in this primary school was in the Burmese vernacular with a few unqualified village teachers. In 1914 it was organized under two qualified Bahá'í teachers, father and son—Saya U Po U and Saya Ko Ba Sein—from Mandalay, and was registered in the Government Education Department as a government aided school. In 1928 the friends tried their best to open an English language school, but owing to lack of funds it was suspended. Mr. G. E. Desilva from Ceylon, a student of Cambridge University, is still in the village, supported by the Bahá'ís and teaches English to some of the Bahá'í children.

Our present Bahá'í village has 250 houses and about 800 inhabitants—men, women, and children. It is bounded on the west by a Muslim village consisting of about fifteen houses and fifty inhabitants—men, women, and children—with a little mosque. Daidanow Pagoda and Burmese Daidanow village are located further up toward the west. About two and a half miles from the Bahá'í village is the town of Kungyangon with its large number of inhabitants of all nationalities, shops, a market, a post office, civil and criminal courts, a hospital, and a jail. It also has a mooring station for the steam launches and a rest-house, Dak Banglow, for government officials.

On the east, which is the termination of the Bahá'í village, the Bahá'í cemetery is located. On the north some paddy fields, and on the south a navigable creek with flux and reflux of the sea tides and a number of paddy fields that belong to the Bahá'í Assembly, some of the friends, and Burmese and Karen people. A public paved road runs through the center of the village leading on one end to Kungyangon town and on the other end to the town of Twantay, which is a halting station for all cargo and passenger steam launches to and from Rangoon. It has a regular motor-car service to and from Kungyangon town. From Rangoon one can take a boat in the morning and arrive at Twantay, engage a car for going to the Bahá'í village, and return by the same route to Rangoon in the same evening. These wonderful facilities are due to divine bestowals upon the Bahá'ís. For formerly we had to go by a direct ferry boat from Rangoon to Kungyangon, which used to take about ten or eleven hours, arriving at its mooring sometimes before sunset, and generally after sunset, and then by a bullock cart to Daidanow Kalazoo, the Bahá'í village.

We had a glorious feast and gathering at the village of our Lord 'Abdu'l-Bahá. Eight hundred friends—male, female, aged and underage children—were in the meeting during our stay there. By day and by night, continually the hall was full of friends. We felt that the blessing of the Holy Spirit was pouring down from our Heavenly Father. Indeed it was a vivifying gathering of pure sincere Bahá'í souls.

I received the following Tablet in answer to our supplication:

> *. . . Thy services have been remembered in the Abhá Kingdom, and thy tireless efforts in diffusing the divine fragrances deemed praiseworthy and acceptable. Praise be to God that thou hast, in recent years, arisen to serve wholeheartedly, and achieved remarkable results. Indeed, the current state of India can in no way be compared to its condition in the past, for at present the name and fame of the Faith hath been noised abroad in many of its regions, and the call of the chosen ones of God heard by every discerning heart. My fervent hope is that all India*

shall be transformed into a celestial paradise through the outpourings of the sweet savours of the All-Merciful, and that the breezes of the Abhá Kingdom may waft therefrom unto the far reaches of China and Japan. The hosts of the Abhá Kingdom are in truth most powerful, and shall conquer the hearts of every people. The cry of Yá Rabíya'l-A'alá may be heard in the East, and the call of Yá Bahá'u'l-Abhá in the West. It is my hope, O thou faithful servant, that through the everlasting bounty of the Compassionate Lord, thou shalt achieve great victories, and become the first among teachers. This, verily, is not beyond the loving providence of thy Lord and His confirming power. . . . [May 1909]

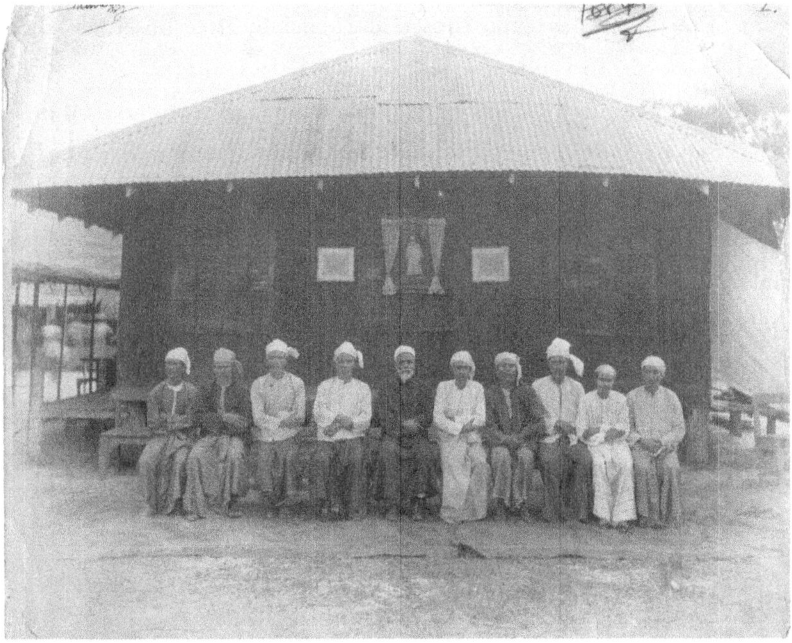

The Spiritual Assembly of Daidanow Kalazoo village with Siyyid Muṣṭafá Rúmí.

- 11 -

THE YEARS 1909–13

In September 1909 I was invited by the Chigon villagers who had accepted the Bahá'í Cause in Daidanow Kalazoo. U Chit Toon, the first believer in Daidanow Kalazoo, accompanied by Ko Po Kyaw, another Bahá'í, came to me in Rangoon and requested that I make a trip to Chigon village in the Shwebo District, which was their native home. I gladly accepted their invitation and left Rangoon in their company for Mandalay.

My wife was confined to bed with heart disease; however, she urged me to go. We stayed in the Bahá'í Hall of Mandalay for about a week to consult with the friends. They proposed to send our Bahá'í friend Saya Bwin with his wife Má Gyi to assist us. Saya Bwin was well-versed in the Buddhist scripture and was a good speaker.

We left Mandalay, and, after crossing the Irrawaddy River by ferry and railway, arrived at Tan Tabin (or Zigon) station, where we were met by Ko Chantha, the son-in-law of a retired police officer. He took us in his two bullock carts to Kyigon (Chigon) village, to his father-in-law's house, situated near the mosque. I stayed there for three or four days and met hundreds of people, Buddhists and Muslims, from early morning to the late hours of night. People sat peacefully listening attentively to my discourse. No one, except an Indian from Punjab asked questions. He was a contractor in the public works.

He announced that he would pay me 200 rupees if I could read a book that he had brought with him. He stepped into the hall and took a seat without being asked. I received him cordially in a Bahá'í manner, and apologized and asked him to wait until I had finished my discussion with a young Buddhist man, who was a Muslim by birth. I was speaking to him about the oneness of all religions and cited a verse from the holy Qur'án. As soon as I recited the verse, the Indian man shouted that it was "fabricated and falsehood." Again, I had to urge him to be silent. After finishing my talk with the young man, I asked my opponent to express freely all that he wanted. He said "there is no such verse, that you quoted from the holy Qur'án, and the expression of the truth of seven main religions is absolutely false." A well-known Burmese Buddhist schoolmaster was present. I wrote the Arabic verse in Burmese characters and read it before the public and asked the Burmese gentleman to read it aloud. I then produced the same verse in the Qur'án and asked my opponent to read it aloud. He said he could not read without his glasses. As a jeweler, I had half-a-dozen spectacles in my bag. He tried several of them, and finally one suited him. He read the verse in Arabic and shamefully accepted the truth and did not speak anymore. I asked him to show me the book he had brought for me to examine, but he left.

On this trip, many relatives of my companion, U Chit Toon, accepted the Bahá'í Faith and openly declared it. People of all adjacent villages—such as Myedoo, Booji, Wetto, Nayanai, Youngbin Zeik, Chitma chin, and Kabo—came to see me during my short stay. On the morning of the fifth day of our arrival, we returned home. Expenses for this trip were partly defrayed by this humble servant and partly by the Rangoon and Mandalay Assemblies.

My next trip to Kyigon (Chigon) was with U Chit Toon, Ko Po Kyon, and Saya Kha, a Bahá'í of Mandalay who lived in Rangoon. We were invited again by Ko Chan Tha of Kyigon to go there after their harvest. In May 1910 we left via Mandalay. Ko Chan Tha came to the railway station with several bullock carts to receive us and took us to his house. The gathering there was much larger than the previous trip. I had to talk from morning until the late hours of night during my stay there. The subjects of my talks consisted of proof of the time of the appearance of the divine

Manifestation according to the revealed prophecies of the holy Qur'án and the traditions of His Holiness Muḥammad, as expected by Muslims.

Group of believers in Mandalay in the winter of 1910.
Howard Struven and Siyyid Muṣṭafá Rúmí are seated to the left of center.

The news of my arrival spread, and a learned mullá, Saya Hla, from another village of the same district came for a discussion with me. He stayed in the adjacent mosque close to our residence and invited us to go to the mosque. Expecting problems for the Bahá'ís of this village, as well as of Daidanow Kalazoo, I made a plan. Through my companion U Chit Toon, I sent a message to the mullá in which I cited a tradition of the holy Prophet stating that "the guest should not go to visit any of the citizens, but they should call on him." I mentioned that he would be cordially received if he would come to our home. Thousands of people gathered in the mosque, and hearing that the mullá had refused my invitation they surrounded the mosque. Our house was also full of people. Our host, Ko Chautha, seeing the uncontrollable rush of people, stood up armed with a sword and spear to prevent any kind of violence. I talked loudly so that my words were heard by all. Thus, the divine Message was delivered to all those who were present. The mob did not dare to commit any criminal acts or violence because our host was a retired police officer and the village head was present among our audience. This dangerous incident was over at a very late hour when the crowd was dispersed, and we passed the remaining hours of night peacefully.

I did not go to the mosque to meet the mullá because I knew their intention was to announce in the whole province that the Bahá'í teacher Siyyid Muṣṭafá had personally entered their mosque and had publicly denounced the Bahá'í Cause. It might have affected the feelings of the new believers of Daidanow Kalazoo and might have even caused their recantation.

I stayed there for about a week to uproot all doubts that were created by the mullá. Before our departure, many souls accepted the Bahá'í Cause. As the Islamic month of Ramaḍán had begun, we left for Mandalay. To our misfortune there was a serious breakage of the railway line between Mandalay and Rangoon and we had to return by Irrawaddy Flotilla boat to Prome, and thence by railway to Rangoon.

On my return I found my wife in a critical condition. She was under treatment by two doctors of the Rangoon General Hospital. On 23

Group of believers in Rangoon, 1910. Siyyid Muṣṭafá Rúmí and Howard Struven are seated from right to left.

November 1910, she ascended to the Abhá Kingdom. We had been married in peace and harmony for twenty-three years.

Immediately after her funeral ceremony, I conveyed my mournful situation to the holy threshold of my beloved Lord, imploring for His merciful grace on behalf of the departed soul of my wife, and for His divine guidance concerning my future life in the service of the holy Cause. The following holy Tablet and a prayer were revealed, which I received on 3 February 1911:

> *. . . The ascension of the maidservant of God, thine esteemed wife, saddened Our heart. Thou must not grieve, however, but remain patient and grateful, for that moth hath soared upwards towards the bright flame of the Concourse on High, and that bird winged its flight on the dawn breeze to reach the rose garden of the Abhá Kingdom. . . .*
>
> *Prayer for the elevation of the soul of the late spouse of Aqá Siyyid Mustafá, upon her rest the glory of God, the Most Glorious*
>
> *O my Lord, my heart's desire! Thy pure-hearted and saintly maidservant hath, verily, abandoned this transitory realm, returning unto Thee in the eternal world. O Lord! She is Thy faithful maidservant, Thy true handmaid who hath approached Thy most glorious Threshold and the court of Thy sanctified Name, seeking out Thy bounties and beseeching Thy pardon for her sins. O Lord! Make her a token of Thy mercy amongst Thy creatures, submerged in the oceans of Thy forgiveness. O Lord! Welcome her unto Thine abode, grant her heart's desire, delight her soul in the midmost point of Thy paradise, and bestow upon her reunion with Thee through Thy loving providence. Thou art the Benevolent, the Merciful; Thou art the Ever-Forgiving, the Beneficent.*

I left for India as a Bahá'í delegate to the second All-Religions Convention, held in Allahabad, the united provinces of Agra and Oudh, on 9, 10, and 11 January 1911. I took one thousand printed copies of a booklet entitled "A short thesis of the Bahá'í Cause" for distribution at the Convention. Religious leaders of all existing religions in India, such as different branches of Hinduism, Buddhism, Jainism, Sikhism, Arya Semaj, Brahmanism, Deva Dharma, Radha Swami, Theosophists with all different schools of Vedanta, Christianity with its different sects, Islam with its sects and schools of thought, Judaism, and Zoroastrianism were present. As my voice was hoarse due to my constant talks in Burma, I asked Mírzá Maḥram to send Mr. N. R. Vakil to read my thesis.

I left Rangoon with Mr. 'Abbás-'Alí Butt, then a new Bahá'í. After arriving in Calcutta Mr. Butt was unable to accompany me, and instead Mr. Muḥammad Árástú of Chapra, Bihar traveled with me. After our arrival at Allahabad, we went to find Mr. N. R. Vakil at the great exhibition held there. I saw him at the entrance and recognized him without any previous acquaintance. As a Hindu, he was staying in a Hindu hotel and we were guests of a Rangoon friend of mine, Mr. 'Abdu'l-Shakúr, a timber merchant.

My voice was better but I asked the secretary of the Convention to register Mr. N. R. Vakil's name for reading my thesis. However, I was asked to chant the opening prayer. Although in the program it was listed as a Muslim prayer, I chanted the Prayer for America revealed by our Lord 'Abdu'l-Bahá for their Assemblies.

On the final day, to our astonishment, Mr. Shrish Basu, Judge of the Civil Court of Benares, Mr. C. D. Ross, Inspector of Allahabad Railways, and Mr. A. Ramaswami Ayer, publicly declared that they had accepted the Bahá'í Faith. Mr. N. R Vakil left for Bombay and after a couple of days we left for Badayun to visit two former Bahá'í friends who had accepted the Cause through Jamál Effendi when he visited Burma.

On our arrival in Lucknow city railway station, a Hindu young man with his young wife stepped into our reserved compartment and sat at the end of our berth near the door. My Bahá'í friend, Mr. Árástú, vacated his berth for the couple. The young man was surprised at our kindness toward two strangers. His name was Suraj Narayan and he was working as a clerk in the office of the postmaster general in Lucknow. He asked about our whereabouts and faith. I told him about the Cause and that we served the world of humanity. I gave him my thesis and other Bahá'í literature with the address of our Bahá'í brother Mr. N. R. Vakil, and asked him to write him for more information. The educated couple promised to contact Mr. Vakil. After four hours' continual conversation, we separated from each other at Barreilly railway station, the couple went to their parents, and we changed to another train going to Badayun.

Our young friends became Bahá'ís and after a few years when Mr. Vakil visited them in Lucknow, there were about seventy more Hindu young men who had accepted the Bahá'í Cause.

After arriving at Badayun we met our Bahá'í brother Shahwali Khand on the platform as he had kindly agreed to receive us. We stayed with him as his guests for three days and went around to all the well-known sages and dignified personages to deliver the divine message.

From there we went directly to Bombay, to the Bahá'í Hall in Forbes Street. We were welcomed by Mírzá Maḥram, the revered teacher. Owing to some material disputes and discord, and personal differences between the friends, the Spiritual Assembly had been discontinued for more than two years, which was not known to me. After consultation with Mírzá Maḥram, I proposed that Bombay should become the Bahá'í central place for promulgation of the divine Cause in India. Three competent teachers should be sent to all the centers defined in a plan to be drawn. Each teacher would start from Bombay a fortnight after the previous teacher's departure for the same spot, and each of them would stay in every place, according to the instructions which would be provided upon submittal of their weekly report. The report would be read and considered by an organized body of deepened persons and registered in minutes and submitted to the holy threshold. Thus the Cause would be widely promulgated in all centers in India and would be firmly established and speedily comprehended all over India. Mírzá Maḥram supported this proposal and encouraged me to submit this suggestion to the holy presence of our Lord 'Abdu'l-Bahá.

We left Bombay for Chapra, the native place of my companion, Mr. Muḥammad Árástú. His elder brother, Mahboub, was strongly against the Cause and endeavored his level best to turn his two younger brothers, Árástú and 'Abbás-'Alí, who had become Bahá'ís in Rangoon, against the Cause. Árástú had been taught by Ḥájí Mírzá Muḥammad Taqí Ṭabasí, a well-known Persian merchant of Bombay, while coming to Rangoon from the Holy Land onboard the Bibby Line ship, *SS Warwickshire.* 'Abbás-'Alí was taught the Cause by me. 'Abbás-'Alí turned out to be a very powerful Bahá'í and delivered the divine message to the Governor of Bengal. He also gave the message to many Indian shop owners. All of them accepted the holy Cause through his magnetic power of speech. 'Abbás-'Alí met 'Abdu'l-Bahá while our Lord was in London. Árástú had the blessing of going to the Holy Land to the presence of our Lord before the great war of 1914. There were only these two Bahá'í households in Rawzeh. 'Abbás-'Alí was on his usual voyage to Europe during my visit at their village.

Mahboub, who was an opponent of the Cause, invited two learned ulamá from the city of Arah, Mawlawí Sháh 'Aynu'l-Ḥaq and Mawlawí 'Abdu'l-Núr, to talk to me. They wrote a letter in Arabic to ascertain my capability in Arabic literature. Mahboub, who had brought the letter, demanded a reply, but I refused to answer it as it was not a polite note. Finally Mawlawí 'Abdu'l-Núr came to my place with a dozen of his followers. They entered the house without permission or salutation and vulgarly sat and began to ask my name, my qualification, and where I had come from. I answered their questions politely but when I asked his name, he replied "what do you have to do with my name?" I said "Are you not Mawlawí 'Abdu'l-Núr"? He was startled and immediately went out and told the people that I was a sorcerer. His followers blamed him for his cowardly retreat. He shamefully tried to come back from the back door, but the landlord, Mr. Árástú, refused to grant him admission. They then arranged for two meetings. In Mahboub's house they convened a general meeting and asked me to go there. I sent Mr. Árástú instead. He silenced them by his sound arguments. They convened another general meeting at night in the open place behind our residence, under Árástú's supervision, with a clear understanding that I would deliver my talk in Urdu on the Bahá'í Cause.

Believing their treacherous announcement to be in good faith, I went to the meeting before time, and sat in the Persian fashion on the floor. Nearly two thousand gathered to hear my speech, but I was not allowed to talk. I got up twice with the permission of the chairman that they had appointed, but I was made to sit down. The Hindu community of the village were considerably annoyed and intended to attack the leaders. I returned to my cottage and silenced them. The audience dispersed unsatisfied and the next morning, to our surprise, bubonic plague spread and overwhelmed the whole district. Meanwhile I received a telegram from Mírzá Maḥram saying "Don't go to Calcutta, urgently come."

I felt that there must be some good tidings and left by the first available train. On the train I delivered the sacred message to the travelers I found to be interested. From the junction of Moghul Sarai I telegraphed Mírzá Maḥram to meet me at the railway station. The next morning I arrived in Bombay, and in the company of Mírzá Maḥram went to the Bahá'í Hall.

A Tablet was received from our Lord 'Abdu'l-Bahá, through Jamshíd Khodadad, addressed to this humble servant, dated March 1911. The first part contained commendations bestowed upon me with reference to my services performed in the Allahabad Religious Convention, and upon Mr. Shrish Chandra Bose the Judge of the Benares court for his declaration of belief in the Bahá'í Cause, His merciful grace and greetings, to Mr. 'Abbás-'Alí Butt, Mr. M. Árástú, Mr. N. R. Vakil, and Mr. Pritam Singh: In this Tablet 'Abdu'l-Bahá instructed that the Bombay Assembly should be appointed a National Center:

> *. . . regarding Bombay being the centre, that which thou hast written is acceptable. Thou shouldst return to Bombay. Jináb-i Mírzá Mahram, Jináb-i Aqá Mírzá Asadu'lláh, and Aqá Mírzá 'Abdu'l-Husayn are already there. You should together establish a central committee for your*

activities, so that its members may manage the affairs of the Faith and communicate with other regions, making and implementing the necessary decisions regarding all matters. Thou shouldst rest assured that God will assist and confirm your efforts, and that this work, undertaken with utmost steadfastness in collaboration with Jináb-i Aqá Mírzá Mahram, Jináb-i Aqá Mírzá Asadu'lláh, Jináb-i Aqá Mírzá 'Abdu'l-Husayn, as well as Jamshíd Khudádád, Jináb-i Mihr 'Alí, Jináb-i Aqá Khusruw and others, will make of Bombay a focal point for unity. Boundless divine favours and unstinting assistance will no doubt surround you, and the foundations of harmony, compassion, and love will be established among the friends. My earnest hope is that you may be blessed in this great endeavour.

O thou who art firm in the Covenant! India has become a vast arena of service, and it has great capacity. Were the friends to be united, travel and engage in visiting the surrounding areas, they would in a short time stir up and invigorate the whole country; conversely, remaining dispirited and disheartened will never bring good results. Once the Local Spiritual Assembly of Bombay is formed through the due participation of all in its election, my hope is that it will become the means for the promulgation of the Faith of God. Upon thee be the Glory of the Most Glorious.

In another Tablet He instructed:

. . . The teachers of the Cause must not remain in one place. They should be constantly on the move, abide in absolute detachment, joy and radiance, and burn with the fire of the love of God as they diffuse the divine fragrances. This is the only manner in which their efforts will be effective; otherwise, success is impossible.

This Holy Tablet was read by Mírzá 'Abdu'l-Ḥusayn Ardistání in the weekly general meeting. The friends were urged to exert every effort for its early implementation. The election was completed and the Spiritual

Assembly was once more established. Jináb-i-Faḍíl, Mírzá 'Abdu'l-Ḥusayn Ardistání, and this humble servant jointly submitted our report with utmost gratitude to the Holy Threshold of our beloved Lord, the Master.

There were many good opportunities in Bombay and its suburbs for successful promulgation of the holy Cause, but unfortunately, I was deprived of such blessings as the Spiritual Assembly of Bombay did not extend their help. I submitted another report, imploring for guidance. My Lord sent me a cablegram, accompanied by a generous gift of 200 rupees for traveling expenses, and commanded me to proceed to Calcutta with Mírzá Asadu'lláh Faḍíl and Áqá Mírzá 'Abdu'l-Ḥusayn Ardistání.

These venerable personages had been sent by our beloved Master to see the great celebrated mujtahid of the Shí'is in Najaf. There they were mercilessly tortured and persecuted by the ulamá and sent back to Tehran in chains and shackles by the Persian Consulate. After their release they had gone to the Holy Land, and, after having healed their afflicted and wounded hearts in the holy presence of our Lord, were commanded by Him to go back to Bombay and were instructed to live among the Persian non-Bahá'ís without publicly contacting the Bombay Bahá'í friends. In obedience to the supreme command they did their best to proclaim the Cause with wisdom. After a few months, they came across a fanatic mullá from Najaf who knew them well and had witnessed the oppressive events. He made them known to everyone and enticed the mob to harm them. They submitted the report of the situation to the holy threshold and in reply they were commanded to live under the safe protection of the Bahá'í friends of Bombay. They engaged a small room close to some Bahá'í friends.

We left for Calcutta on 2 June 1911 and there engaged a house in the area of the Bahá'í Center, which turned out to be unhealthy for us and we had to move to the Taltalla neighborhood near the Islamic College, called Madrasa-i-'Alíyah, with a high rent for several days. We had some good gatherings and meanwhile Ḥájí Mírzá Muḥammad Taqí Ṭabasí arrived from Persia to open a branch office for Messrs. Ommid and Co.

of 'Is͟hqábád, Russian Turkistan, in Calcutta. Through my best efforts, he opened an office in the business center and equipped it with all necessary furnishings.

On 22 August 1911, my revered friends, Mírzá Asadu'lláh Faḍíl and Mírzá 'Abdu'l-Ḥusayn Ardistání left for Burma, as we could not do any commendable service to the holy Cause in Calcutta. Our funds were spent on the house rent, servants' wages, food, carriage fare, and doctor's bills as both of the revered teachers were still feeling the effect of the severe malaria that they had suffered from in Bombay. We submitted our report to the holy threshold and in reply we were commanded to go to Burma. In this holy Tablet our Lord revealed that I should stay in Burma, and that both revered teachers, after visiting Burma, should return to Persia.

I accomplished my services for the Ommid and Co., and left for Rangoon on 27 August. After a few days we left for Mandalay and Daidanow Kalazoo, Kungyangon, for a couple of days to see the Bahá'í friends. Our two friends then left for Persia via Calcutta and Bombay. I went to Mandalay to settle and resume my religious duties.

I used to visit Rangoon and Daidanow Kalazoo twice a year, once in August or September and once again in April. In one visit I met Jináb-i-Áqá Mírzá Mihdí Ras͟htí, a tea merchant of Shanghai, who was once a managing partner of Messrs. Ommid and Co. of 'Is͟hqábád in Shanghai, and was going to Persia via Rangoon, to Port Sa'íd and Egypt to attain the presence of our Lord. He visited our Bahá'í Hall and suggested that in the interest of the Cause it would be advantageous if I were to go to Shanghai and work together with him in his office for a year. I could assist him in his business and promulgate the divine Cause. I replied that as a humble servant of the holy threshold it made no difference to me whether I was in Burma or China. I sked him to supplicate on my behalf while he was in the presence of 'Abdu'l-Bahá. He promised to do so. I also asked for His guidance in my own letter. I received a Tablet from 'Abdu'l-Bahá and was permitted to go to Shanghai.

It is the intention of Áqá Mírzá Mihdíy-i-Rashtí to impel thee China-wards—to travel thither in thy company, that is; should ye then be able to establish yourselves in the tea trade and at the same time to spread the divine fragrances throughout the territory of China, it would be an eminently satisfactory arrangement. When Jináb-i-Mírzá Mihdíy-i-Rashtí returns from Egypt, I will discuss this matter with him.

Mírzá Mihdí Ra<u>sh</u>tí also wrote to me about it and urged me to reach Shanghai before 15 May at the start of the tea season.

I left Burma on 25 April 1912 and arrived in Shanghai on 12 May. I went directly to my old Bahá'í friend from Bombay, Mírzá 'Abdu'l-Báqí, the manager of the firm of Messrs. Ommid and Co. He treated me very kindly until Mírzá Mihdí Ra<u>sh</u>tí's arrival on 19 May 1912. Our business as "Commission Agent" started in June, and as a linguist I wrote several letters to the partners everywhere in Arabic, Persian, Urdu, Hindi, and English. Up to the middle of July no replies came in and no orders for purchase and shipment were received. My boss was annoyed and upset. He questioned me about what I had written. I had copies, which I had to translate for him in Persian. Yet he was dissatisfied. All my life I had managed my own business without serving under a boss and I was unable to bear ill-treatment and reproach patiently. As a Bahá'í I did not speak a word to him and quietly went to the manager of Messrs. Ommid and Co. and asked him to sell my ruby ring surrounded with small diamonds for me to pay for my passage to Burma. It was sold for 75 Chinese dollars. I bought all that was necessary for the voyage and prepared to leave. My boss noticed my actions and told me that he owed me my passage to and from China and also for the services I had rendered. He gave me a check for 140 Tiles, on Russian Asiatic Bank of Shanghai, and I cashed it and remitted the amount I had borrowed for my traveling expenses (200 rupees) to the Mandalay Bahá'í Assembly. I embarked on a French mail-boat on 27 July 1912 via Sigon Port (French Possession).

I arrived on 5 August at Singapore and left by a B. I. boat on 8 August 1912, arriving at Rangoon on 13 August 1912. I went to see the friends of Daidanow Kalazoo, Kungyangon, and after a short visit went to Mandalay. I had to decide about the matter of the inheritance of our Bahá'í friend Dr. Siyyid Sajjád Ḥusayn according to Bahá'í law, and submitted it to the holy threshold. The Master commanded the payment of Ḥuqúqu'lláh and instructed that the remaining funds should be spent on the education of his three young daughters and two sons.

After accomplishing this urgent matter I went to Daidanow Kalazoo again. Áqá Muḥammad Ibrahim S͟hírází, a member of the Rangoon Bahá'í Assembly, purchased two plots of land in close proximity to the Bahá'í Hall building, extended from the public road to the creek on the north and south, and donated them to the Cause.

The longstanding need of the Bahá'ís of this village was to establish a local charity fund. Although I exerted my level best to introduce this very important system, yet in absence of the means for its development, it was unfortunately left for a more favorable time. A few Bahá'í youth had secretly formed a small group of five or six as an association and had collected thirty rupees, equal to $10, as a subscription for membership fees. Hearing this, I brought the matter to the general body of Bahá'í friends and asked them to lay the foundation of a charity fund.

I mentioned that as Bahá'ís we are enjoined to earnestly work for the interest of the general public, and lead any material action for a spiritual end. These few youth were confirmed to feel and anticipate the need of such a great and important matter that was not yet perceived by the elders. I urged the community to jointly endeavor to establish a local charity fund. I offered to make a program and help them to organize such a fund. I explained that I knew perfectly well that they were poor and unable to contribute a large amount, but I suggested that they make it very easy so that it could be equally suitable to the poor and the rich.

A charitable association was duly formed. Registration of the names of the contributors and the account were opened. In a period of three years the fund increased to two thousand rupees. On the third year a great famine struck the whole district and the village went into fearful distress. I visited the friends and witnessed their lamentable condition and consoled them with utmost sympathy. I told them that I would recite the Long Healing Prayer revealed by Bahá'u'lláh for such a time of distress and agony and surely they would have a good harvest next year with high prices of paddy. I asked all of them to promise to make full repayment of their debt to the charity fund that had helped them in their need. All of them unitedly agreed and promised to make full payment of principle and interest to the charity fund.

I recited the prayer with devotion and resignation. The audience, numbering about 600 Bahá'ís, was filled with the Holy Spirit, and after sojourning for a couple of days I returned to my home in Mandalay.

To our great astonishment miraculously the next harvest was the most splendid ever seen during the last fifty years; the price of paddy reached higher and higher from 80/- rupees per 100 Bushels to 200/- and 250/-. Every one of the friends cleared his debt as it was promised and our charity fund reached to about 3,000 rupees.

The following Tablet of my beloved Lord gladdened my humble heart:

> *. . . It hath been some time since news of your dear self reached us here, or a fresh breeze wafted from that direction. Our longing hearts anticipate the receipt of a message or letter from our dearly beloved ones. By this is meant that, despite every test, preoccupation, trial and tribulation we suffer here, we constantly remember thee and keep thee close to our hearts, beseeching the True One to assist thee in the affairs of the Kingdom and aid thee in thy services to the threshold of the Desired One. All other matters are like unto a mirage in the desert, for they are mere suppositions and not substantial, reflections and not reality.*
>
> *Praise be the Lord that thou dost possess the faculties of eloquent speech and a detached soul, lofty belief and a sincere heart, and that thou art a luminous being and a shining presence. These capacities and bounties have been ordained for thee in the divine kingdom. A little*

effort is needed and a slight service is necessary. Glory be upon thee and all those who are firm and steadfast . . .

Group of Rangoon Bahá'ís at a picnic party in the garden of Siyyid Ismá'íl Shírází. The following people are identified by hand-drawn numbers: 1. (standing to the left) Siyyid Ismá'íl Shírází; 2. Ḥájí Siyyid Mihdí Shírází; 3. Siyyid Muṣṭafá Rúmí; 4. Mírzá Maḥram; 5. Jináb-i- Adíbu'l-'Ulamá; 6. Hippolyte Dreyfus; 7. Sydney Sprague.

- 12 -

SECOND PILGRIMAGE TO THE HOLY LAND

It was in early 1914 in Bombay that I saw a Tablet revealed by 'Abdu'l-Bahá to Persia after His European and American trips, expressing distinctly that He had already accomplished all His duties for the holy Cause and now ardently wished to ascend to the Abhá Kingdom.

> *Hasten, O my God the days of my ascension unto Thee, and of my coming before Thee, and of my entry into Thy presence, that I may be delivered from the darkness of the cruelty inflicted by them upon me, and may enter the luminous atmosphere of Thy nearness, O my Lord, the All-Glorious, and may rest under the shadow of Thy most great mercy.*[1]

After reading the Tablet, I felt utterly restless and submitted a supplication imploring for permission to attend to His presence as He had promised me. My prayer was heard and accepted and in response the following telegram, dated 21 February 1914, arrived for me: "NOT ADVISABLE YOUNG MOHAMADAN KHOJA GOING AMERICA. ANDALIB, MUSTAFA, VAKIL, SHIRAZI COME BEFORE BARASAT ABBAS."[2]

I sent cablegrams to Mr. Vakil in Surat and Prof. Shírází in Karachi to expedite their departure. Prof. Shírází replied that he would meet us in Haifa. Jináb-i-'Andalíb,[3] Shaykh 'Alí-Akbar Qúchání, Mr. Vakil, and I, with six Persian Parsee friends who also had permission, sailed on 10 March and arrived at Port Sa'íd on 21 March. Aziz Effendi and Yúsuf

Afs͟hár were sent by Áqá Aḥmad Effendi Yazdí to receive us. They put our luggage in a small boat for a night to carry to the Khedivial Steamer leaving the next day for Haifa. We were the guests of Mírzá Yúsuf Afs͟hár for the night, and, after having our morning tea, left for Haifa. We arrived at about 5:00 p.m., before sunset. We were taken to the Oriental Pilgrim House on top of Mount Carmel near the sacred Shrine of the Báb. The next morning on 24 March, we had the bounty of attaining the Holy Presence of our beloved Lord 'Abdu'l-Bahá. I am unable to express my feelings in that moment. I would have swooned had not 'Abdu'l-Bahá embraced me. We had the bounty to be in His presence in mornings and evenings. Boundless blessings were showered upon us each time.

My beloved friend Mr. N. R. Vakil submitted to the Master that he was an orthodox Hindu by birth and followed the inherited religion of his forefathers blindly as his coreligionists do. But since he became enlightened by the divine teachings of the Cause, he had given up the wrong dogmatic beliefs of his ancestors and firmly believed that the principles of all divine religions are one. However, he had some beliefs of his former faith that still remained unsolved for him.

The Master with fatherly love asked him to write down all those problems and bring them with him the next day. Mr. Vakil was a scholar of Hindu scriptures in Sanskrit, and a graduate in English literature. He wrote down several pages full of facts and theories.

The next morning the Master asked Mr. Vakil to proceed with his written questions. Mr. Vakil searched in his coat pockets but he could not find his notes, only a few blank sheets of paper that he had brought to note down the answers. He whispered to me quietly to go and fetch his notes. Our Lord noticed this and kindly told him to write down His answers one by one and see if all his questions were satisfactorily cleared and his problems entirely solved. I was commended to interpret the holy utterances. Mr. Vakil wrote down all the answers and brought them back to the Pilgrim House. He compared these answers with the series of his questions, and found them to match exactly. He was truly astonished; his face was shining brilliantly with boundless joy. That evening when we entered into the holy presence of the Master, Mr. Vakil thankfully submitted his loyal obedience and prostrated and humbly begged forgiveness for his doubts. He said that he was perfectly satisfied and confirmed in the holy Cause and the divine Covenant.

Our Lord was very pleased with Mr. Vakil. He was the first Hindu gentleman to have the bounty of visiting the Holy Land and entering into the holy presence.

During the time of our stay in the Holy Land we had the honor of visiting the holy Shrine of the Blessed Beauty, Bahá'u'lláh, several times in the company of 'Abdu'l-Bahá, Who chanted the Tablet of Visitation. We also visited all the sacred places accessible in those days of the Turkish regime. We were very fortunate to have the blessing of staying in the Holy Presence of our beloved Lord from 23 March until 19 April 1914, during which time Prof. Shírází also arrived.

The Master told me that a great World War in Europe was imminent within a few months, and it would affect the whole world. Therefore, I should remain in Burma and protect the friends during that time without going to any other regions. Áqá Muḥammad Ḥasan, the caretaker of the Eastern Pilgrim House, told us that all the pilgrims were commanded by the Master to prepare for our return the next morning. Dr. Luṭfu'lláh Ḥakím kindly attended to all that was necessary for our voyage and we were booked for Port Sa'íd. Jináb-i-'Andalíb was given permission by our Lord to remain. Two Parsee friends went to see their relatives at 'Adasíyyih. With grieving hearts we were all ready to leave, but the Master, through His supreme grace, conferred two additional days upon His humble servants to remain in His holy presence.

The night before our departure, all of us were summoned to His holy presence. He imparted loving advice that every Bahá'í needs to attain a higher degree of perfection through discipline and acquiring superhuman spiritual qualities such as morality and divine attributes and characters. He told us that human beings are created in the likeness of God, meaning that God's divine characteristics and attributes are innately deposited into human beings. There is no defect in God's creation, for

He is perfect. From the beginning humankind entered into a spiritual covenant with the Creator that he will not misuse or misappropriate this trust. However, he subsequently neglected and consequently violated that dignified position of divine virtues. The same covenant is renewed in every age by respective prophets and Manifestations of God as is seen in this great cycle. Thus the Bahá'ís should exert their level best to attain the highest degree of perfection, to which they are entitled, to significantly assume the title of a real perfect human being; otherwise, man is yet to surpass the animal kingdom which is naturally inherent in him.

Finally the Master rose from his seat to bid goodbye to the pilgrims and to embrace them in the Persian fashion. I was seated next to my spiritual patron Ḥájí Mírzá Ḥaydar-'Alí. The Master embraced me first and squeezed me so hard that I felt my ribs being twisted. Ḥájí Mírzá Ḥaydar-'Alí clung to the Master's robe, thrice beseeching Him to bestow special divine blessings upon this faithful servant. He did not leave the sacred hem until our Lord graciously assured him by saying, "Ḥájí, special and particularly more special blessings at thy request, Ḥájí leave my garment and be satisfied." All of us wept bitterly. He kissed me several times and breathed a new life into me. He then left me and went forward to embrace the other pilgrims. The audience was over and we went back to the Pilgrim House. In our grief of separation from our beloved Lord, we were unable to sleep and passed the whole night in prayer and meditation.

As the steamer was going to sail the next evening, we had the bounty once more to be in the holy presence in the morning. The Master affectionately consoled my afflicted heart with loving expressions that I would be summoned again to have the honor of His holy presence. With this graceful promise I was comforted and happy.

That evening we embarked aboard the ship sailing for Port Sa'íd and arrived there on the morning of 21 April 1914. We had the privilege of joining the congregation of the first day of Riḍván Feast in the house of Dr. Ba<u>sh</u>ír, as well as that of the ninth day of Riḍván. After these meetings, accompanied by Mr. Azíz, Mr. Yúsuf Af<u>sh</u>ár, and Mr. Muḥammad 'Abdu'l-Ghaní, I boarded the *SS Marianbad,* an Austrian-Indian mail-boat, and sailed for Bombay. In addition to us there were a number of Bahá'ís onboard, including: Mr. N. R. Vakil, Kaykhusraw Furúd, Shahríár Boman, Rashíd Bahrám, Bahman Miḥráb-i-Kirmání, and Keumers Furúd with his wife Fírúzih.

We arrived in Bombay on 10 May 1914. Lua and Dr. Getsinger were still there. We were warmly welcomed by the Bombay friends, and, after lovingly encouraging the friends, I left for Calcutta by a mail-train. I was the guest of Ḥájí Mírzá Muḥammad Taqí Ṭabasí, the manager of the Messrs. Ommid Co. of 'Ishqábád. After loving talks with friends in their meetings, I embarked on the mail-boat *SS Arunda* for Rangoon on 24 May, arriving there on 26 May. On 28 May I left for Daidanow Kalazoo, Kungyangon, and as usual stayed there for three days delivering the Tablets revealed by our beloved Lord 'Abdu'l-Bahá for them. I shared loving discourses day and night, exhorting and encouraging them to remain steadfast in the divine Covenant.

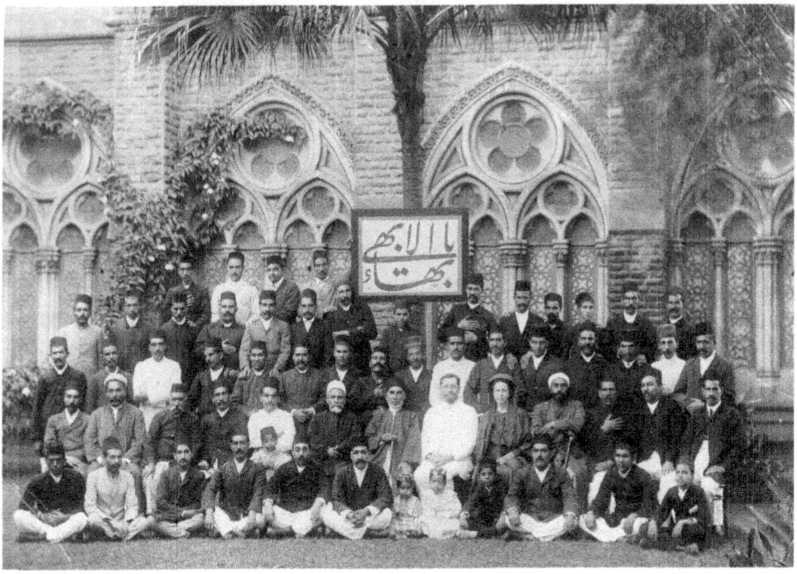

Group of Bahá'ís in Bombay, likely 1914. Seated in the middle row, fifth from the right are Lua and Dr. Getsinger. Siyyid Muṣṭafá Rúmí is sixth from the left in the same row. For more information about the Getsingers' visit, see Appendix I: Visitors to Burma.

On 1 June I left for Rangoon and arrived the same evening. On 3 June, an Indian physician that claimed to be of the Qadiani sect, accompanied by a wealthy Bombay merchant, Ḥájí Muḥammad Jamál, came to our Bahá'í Hall at no. 20 Sparks Street, the home of our revered philanthropist brother Ḥájí Siyyid Mihdí Shírází and his son Áqá Siyyid Ismá'íl Shírází. He came to inquire about the authenticity of the Bahá'í Cause. I had a lengthy discussion with him in proving the time, the place, and the person of the promised Manifestations. As they were Sunní Muslims, I quoted from the divine verses of the holy Qur'án and the authenticated traditions of Prophet Muḥammad. I established the facts, from undeniable authorities, but it was very hard to convince them. They promised to come again, and went away. I had little hope as they were not genuine true seekers.

On 5 June, the Bombay merchant Ḥájí Muḥammad Jamál visited again without his Qadiani companion, and I had a quiet and peaceful talk with him. He was very interested but could not leave the religion of his ancestors. Now when I see him, he inquiries about the progress of the Bahá'í Cause. His son has been to America and has met the Bahá'ís in New York.

On 27 June 1914, I left by noon express train for Mandalay. I was warmly received by the friends, and in the evening in our regular Sunday meeting I read the usual prayers and explained and translated into Burmese all the Tablets revealed for the Mandalay friends, and after making true copies handed them over to them.

- 13 -

EVENTS OF 1914–1920

In obedience to our beloved Master, 'Abdu'l-Bahá, I had to stay in Burma without going to India or elsewhere. Since I was addicted to work and detested inactivity, after a long period in prayer and meditation seeking guidance on how to serve the Burma Bahá'í community, I felt I should compile and translate the holy writings. Thus I devoted myself to writing books needed for the enlightenment and guidance of the Burma Bahá'ís.

A young lady, Ma Ma (Marzieh), who had studied English, was brought to me by her parents, who were devoted Bahá'ís, to teach her Persian. She was a very bright girl and learnt the Persian language within a few months and was able to read and write beautifully. I taught her the Kitáb-i-Íqán, the Book of Certitude, which I had translated into Burmese. She made a copy of my Burmese translation, and after a year it was completed. The manuscript is kept by the Mandalay Bahá'í Assembly.

[The following Tablet of 'Abdu'l-Bahá makes reference to Siyyid Muṣṭafá's translation work:]

> *Thy sorrow and despair brought much sadness to 'Abdu'l-Bahá's heart. Thou shouldst not, regardless of events or circumstances, be dispirited or disheartened by any matter, for—praised be the Lord!—the flame of the love of God is ablaze in thy heart, and the glad tidings of His bounty shall prevail. Why be dejected and disconsolate when thou hast a friend in 'Abdu'l-Bahá? Rest thou assured that He will be faithful.*

Thou hast written regarding the translation into Burmese of a number of literary works by the American friends. This is a very meritorious undertaking; in consequence, some new works will be sent to you to be translated into the Indian languages. Disseminate them widely, so that they may increase the enkindlement of the friends and become the means of guidance to others . . .

The great European war started on 4 August 1914.[1] The Bahá'ís of Burma anxiously prayed for peace and protection of the holy family in the Holy Land. The friends devoted their time in prayer and meditation, longing to hear good news from the Holy Land, as well as that of the friends in every part of the Bahá'í world.

On 28 September, I left by noon train for Rangoon, and after arriving the next day I telegraphed the friends in Daidanow to expect me on 1 October. I was warmly received by a great multitude of friends, in many bullock-carts. A large group of friends were also waiting at our Bahá'í Hall. The fanatic Muslim community of the adjacent village, who were bitter enemies of the Cause, had tried to prevent members of their community from attending the Bahá'í meetings, particularly during my upcoming stay in the village. Their mullá had called me a sorcerer and magician. However, it is impossible to prevent the real truth-seeker from heavenly blessings. The magnetic power of 'Abdu'l-Bahá was so great that those who had once attended our meetings could not be prevented from returning again and again until they accepted the Faith. On the fourth day of my arrival about thirty men, women, and children publicly accepted the Bahá'í Cause.

The friends of God were constantly endeavoring to increase the number of the adherents to the Cause and aid its progress. On the eve of 7 October 1914, a brilliant young man came to our meeting and after a short discussion accepted the Bahá'í Cause with his family. After midnight, I left to catch the launch leaving for Rangoon early the next morning. Many friends kindly came to see me off.

[The following communication was received from 'Abdu'l-Bahá during this period:]

. . . This is the season to stride undaunted into the arena of service, of steadfastness and faithfulness to the Covenant. At this time when a most mighty calamity hath befallen these prisoners, the loved ones of God must show forth strength and confidence, and quicken their hearts and souls by inhaling the sweet scents and divine dawn breezes. There is no time to give details, for most avenues of communication have been blocked, though we did find a means to send this missive to you. Sorrow not in the event of the interruption of news, rather redouble your efforts and strive harder, so that it may become clear that in the most darksome night, the friends of God shine even as candles, growing all the more bright. I have no further time to speak now. Convey My fervent greetings to the loved ones of God. For diverse reasons, Jináb-i Manshádí hath been dispatched to Egypt, and I seized the chance to pen this letter. Upon thee be praise and salutation . . .

On 18 May 1915, I was in Rangoon when our Bahá'í sister Miss Martha Root arrived there. On 19 and 21 May 1915 she delivered lectures in the Theosophical Hall in Rangoon. On 23 May I accompanied her to Mandalay. She was warmly received by the Mandalay friends and my late wife's cousin, Mr. 'Abdu'l-Ghaní Naikwara, invited her to stay in his house during her stay in Mandalay. Although he was not a Bahá'í, his wife and daughters treated Miss Root with respectful love. As she was the guest of the Bahá'í Assembly of Mandalay I persuaded the host to receive all her expenses from me. Their house was close to the Bahá'í quarter. On the evening of 23 May we celebrated the Feast of the Declaration of the Báb, and on the twenty-fourth, the birth of our beloved Master 'Abdu'l-Bahá. On 25 May she gave a beautiful lecture in the Lotus Lodge of the Theosophies in Mandalay. On 29 May we commemorated the Ascension of Bahá'u'lláh, as according to a Tablet of 'Abdu'l-Bahá revealed for the

Persian Bahá'ís, the day of the Ascension was on the seventieth day from Naw-Rúz.

Group of Bahá'ís in Mandaly on 23 May 1915. Martha Root is standing centrally beside Siyyid Muṣṭafá Rúmí.

On 1 June 1915, I accompanied Martha Root to Rangoon. The friends had come to the railway station to greet her. On 4 June she sailed for Singapore by the *SS Lightning,* and on 8 June I left for Mandalay to attend to my duties.

On 18 June 1915, I received a registered letter containing a Tablet for Martha Root, a copy of a Tablet revealed for Áqá Aḥmad Yazdí, and a letter from Mírzá Maḥmúd Zarqání from Bombay that contained the good news of the health of 'Abdu'l-Bahá and the holy household in Haifa. I communicated the glad tidings to all the Bahá'ís of Burma and sent the holy Tablet revealed for Martha Root to her address in America.

On 1 July, in our general meeting the question of the promise of 'Abdu'l-Bahá for coming to India and Burma after the Great War was raised and we unanimously agreed to build a large timber hall in His name. The present site was purchased in 1901. We thus decided to construct a new building in the exalted name of our Lord 'Abdu'l-Bahá, hoping it would be blessed by His feet. After collecting sufficient funds to start the building, an agreement was drawn on 13 October with a carpenter to build a two-story building.

After 9 July and the commemoration of the Martyrdom of the Báb, we received the heart-rending news of the serious illness of our dearly loved philanthropist Bahá'í brother Áqá Siyyid Ismá'íl Shírází in Rangoon. He had sent his son, Siyyid 'Abdu'l-Ḥusayn Shírází, to me for education. We received a telegram from his grandfather, the revered first Bahá'í in Rangoon, Ḥájí Siyyid Mihdí Shírází, informing him that his father was seriously ill. I sent the young man to Rangoon, but alas on 14 August I received another wire with the sorrowful news of his untimely passing to the Abhá Kingdom, and urging my immediate presence.

I immediately left for Rangoon and went to the house of the bereaved family and consoled their hearts by chanting the prayer for the departed. On 16 and 17 August 1915, I accompanied the Bahá'í friends to the Bahá'í Cemetery and chanted the prayer of forgiveness. On 18 August, about thirty friends, male and female, came from Daidanow Kalazoo offering condolences to the bereaved family on behalf of the friends in both the Daidanow Kalazoo and Htanbingyoung villages. The next day they went to visit the grave with all Rangoon Bahá'ís and spent the whole day in prayers and meditation and then returned to their village.

To ascertain the assets and liabilities of the deceased, his father entrusted it to the long-retired partner of the deceased, known as Áqá Muḥammad Báqir-i-Khurásání, who was not a Bahá'í, together with our Bahá'í brother Siyyid Jináb-i-'Alí, a court lawyer. In the presence of all the Rangoon Bahá'í friends, all his assets—consisting of legal documents, title deeds of properties, cash, and diamond jewelry—were made over to the wife of the deceased.

I stayed the whole month in Rangoon, and on 1 September returned by train to Mandalay. On the day of my arrival I received a letter from

Port Sa'íd containing the glad tidings of the excellent health of 'Abdu'l-Bahá and the holy household.

At the repeated invitation from the friends of Daidanow Kalazoo, I left again via Rangoon for the Bahá'í Village on 18 October, arriving on 20 October, and returned back to Rangoon on 27 October after performing my dutiful services. A letter of invitation from the Mandalay Theosophical Society was there urging me to join in their annual Convention. I left for Mandalay on 29 October. At the end of this year, 1915, construction of the building for the visit of 'Abdu'l-Bahá was started by the carpenters.

On 18 March 1916, I was in Daidanow Kalazoo. Owing to the increasing number of the students, the building of the school needed to be extended. All village Bahá'ís gathered and built a large structure with timber and corrugated iron roofing within a few days.

Some Bahá'í friends arrived from Calcutta, Rangoon, and Mandalay to visit the friends, and left after a few days. As always, I checked the account books of the Assembly and left for Mandalay via Rangoon. Once again on 10 October I left for Daidanow Kalazoo via Rangoon and returned on 21 October, arriving at Mandalay on 26 October 1916.

To join the feast of the first day of Riḍván, I left Mandalay on 30 March 1917, and, after performing the usual duties, started back on 23 April and arrived in Mandalay on 28 April 1917. I went to Daidanow again on 1 October and returned to Rangoon a few days later. I had to stay until 24 November in Rangoon to conduct some urgent affairs of my relatives. After arriving in Mandalay I received an urgent telegram from them and had to return to Rangoon again on 27 November and had to stay there for some personal affairs of my relatives until February 1918.

After returning to Mandalay I was engaged in encouraging the friends to contribute funds for the building of the Chicago Mashriqu'l-Adhkár, and writing letters to other centers in Burma. I left for this sacred purpose for Rangoon and Daidanow Kalazoo on 30 March 1918 and was able to collect: 423/- from Mandalay friends; 200/- from the friends in

Daidanow; 100/- from Siyyid Javád 'Alí in Rangoon; 27/- from my late wife's relatives; 9/- from Dr. Ma Ngme Nyun; for a total of 760 rupees. I handed the funds to my beloved spiritual son, Siyyid Javád 'Alí, to remit through Chartered Mercantile Bank in Rangoon to America. I returned to Mandalay on 23 May 1918 on the day of the Declaration the Báb and joined the Mandalay Bahá'í friends for the feast.

[The following communication was received from 'Abdu'l-Baha:]

> *. . . The glad tidings of the unity and harmony, friendship, fellowship, and righteousness of the loved ones of God brought us much joy. The friends must sacrifice themselves for each other, serve and be devoted to one another. This, verily, leads to everlasting honour and spiritual ascendency. That is the divine bestowal of this Dispensation: that this great bounty and infinite mercy should embrace all; that the friends should associate with all the members of the human race beneath the tabernacle of His bounties. The loved ones of God must consider strangers as acquaintances, enemies as friends, the remote as near, and the spiteful as members of their own families.*
>
> *The sum that was contributed for the American Mashriqu'l-Adhkár was received in the Holy Land, and sent on to Chicago. The receipt for those funds from Chicago will be forwarded to you when received. . . .*
>
> *Focus your thoughts on teaching, night and day. . . .*

I received information from the Rangoon Bahá'í friends that the revered teacher Mírzá Maḥmúd Zarqání had arrived on 13 June 1918 from Bombay at the request of our revered Bahá'í brother, Ḥájí Siyyid Mihdí Shírází, a very generous philanthropist, to settle the inheritance affairs between himself and the survivors of his lamented deceased son, Siyyid Ismá'íl Shírází. However, he passed away on 13 July 1918 and was buried in the Rangoon Bahá'í Cemetery. He had appointed Mírzá Maḥmúd Zarqání as his executor.

Siyyid Mihdí's family were from Shíráz, Iran. He came to India as a youth to join his brother in Madras and then moved to Rangoon to start a trading business. As his brother was married to the daughter of a well-known family in Madras, Siyyid Mihdí was welcomed in Rangoon and married the daughter of a well-established merchant there and started to work in his father-in-law's establishment. He had only one child, Siyyid Ismá'íl. He was five years old when Jamál Effendi arrived in Rangoon. As Jamál Effendi did not openly teach the Cause, Siyyid Mihdí at this time did not become aware of the teachings of Bahá'u'lláh.

During the commotion and the incident of the mosque [see pp. 30–31] Siyyid Mihdí became aware of the Cause and visited Jamál Effendi to declare his acceptance of the Cause. He then openly declared everywhere that the Qá'im had appeared and that everyone should go to the home of Jamál Effendi to find out more.

His open declaration caused great opposition to him. All his friends and relatives left him and pressured his wife to divorce him. He remained steadfast and the sons of his wife's aunt came to his assistance. He was forced to move house to a new location. He started a new business with the inheritance of his wife and opened his house for Bahá'í meetings. In spite of his small income, he hosted everyone who attended the meetings with great hospitality.

After receiving a Tablet from 'Abdu'l-Bahá, his business as a cloth merchant became profitable and he was established as a well-known merchant. When 'Abdu'l-Bahá instructed the Bahá'ís of Rangoon to prepare the marble casket for the Báb, Siyyid Mihdí paid all its expenses and accompanied the casket with his family to the presence of 'Abdu'l-Bahá. The following is the Tablet of our Lord addressed to him and his son:

O ye two favoured servants of the Lord!

Ibn-i Abhar, the glory of the All-Glorious Lord rest upon him, hath arrived and the news of those regions brought much joy and happiness to our hearts. Praise be the Lord that the loved ones of God are in utmost unity, joy and radiance. They have been freed of chains and fetters, attracted wholeheartedly to the Beauty of the All-Glorious, and seek peace and comfort under His all-encompassing shadow. They are occupied with service to the Cause of God, engaged in exalting the word of God and characterized by Bahá'í virtues. This age is the century of the Great Announcement, and the world of creation is the reflection of the celestial effulgence of the Compassionate and Merciful Lord. This is the season of planting and cultivation; this whole earth is a paradise. Now is the season for scattering seeds, the time of sacrifice, for from every grain of corn shall grow seven ears,[2] *and from every ear a thousand seeds. Blessed is the farmer who planteth in this divine field, and soweth seeds whose results shall be an abundant harvest in this world and the next . . .*

The tombstone for the departed Shírází father and son and his mother were inscribed in my handwriting and sculptured in Mandalay under my supervision.

On 11 September, Mírzá Maḥmúd Zarqání arrived at Mandalay and was warmly received by us at the railway station. I accompanied him to Rangoon and Kungyangon. We left Rangoon with some friends to go to Daidanow Kalazoo on 26 September and returned to Rangoon four days later. Mr. Zarqání left Rangoon by Calcutta mail-steamer on 8 October for Bombay.

Jináb-i-Áqá Mírzá Mahmúd Zarqání and other friends of God
O ye beloved of the Lord and faithful friends of 'Abdu'l-Bahá!

Your missive was the choice wine that bestowed spiritual ecstasy and abundant joy, for it bore witness to your faith and certitude, and was a testament to your firmness in the Covenant. Blessed are ye that ye have received this great bounty, and tidings of joy be upon you, for ye have followed this lofty guidance. I beseech the Lord of hidden bestowals to assist you, so that ye may all abide under the protection of His providence and goodwill, and be shielded from every sorrow and despon-

dency. May ye all drink your fill of the cup of His overflowing bounty, and disseminate the sweet savours of divine mysteries as ye breathe deep of those musk-scented fragrances, immersing your faces in that shining Light.

In this Day, East and West alike cry out: "O Thou Glory of the Most-Glorious," while the call of the leviathan of love is: "O Thou Most Exalted above all." This melody hath been sung the world over, and the name and fame of the Cause of God recognized by perceptive souls on five continents. The divine teachings have been diffused, and the teachers of the Cause rendered victorious. Their tongues are as keen blades of steel, their hearts rejoiced and their souls enraptured. The prominent leaders of the multitudes stand "as though they were uprooted palm stumps.[3] *The cry of the nations is: "O Thou the Glory of the Most-Glorious!"; the lovers' song the tokens of the beauty and perfection of the Daystar of the world. Now is the time for deeds and action, for destroying the foundations of heedlessness, despair, and torpor. Act in accordance with the teachings of the Blessed Beauty, and ye shall become signs of divine guidance. . . .*

The Daidanow Kalazoo Bahá'í friends did not have a burial ground of their own. The existing cemetery situated at the end of the Bahá'í Village was a narrow strip of land used by Muslims, Chinese, Burmese, Karens,[4] Hindus, and other religions and nationalities. The soil was very bad. I advised them to search for a decent plot, and, after having found it, to apply to the government office for a grant. I went round with them and at last we found a plot of government wasteland situated about 500 feet from the existing cemetery, near a Buddhist monastery. It measured about fourteen acres. I took two certified plans from the government surveyor and advised the friends how to apply with it to the township officer at Kungyangon.

Their application was rejected by the authorities on the grounds that, if approved, every other nationality also would apply for a separate cemetery. They stated: "The Bahá'ís are small in number, living in insignificant huts." We appealed the decision to the deputy commissioner of Hanthawaddy, whose office was located in Rangoon. Being a Burmese Buddhist, he dismissed the appeal on the same grounds. While I was in Rangoon I personally went to the deputy commissioner's office and copied all necessary documents and appealed through my spiritual son Mr. Sajjád 'Alí, a lawyer, to the commissioner of Pegu, Mr. Graham, who was personally known to me from Mandalay. After due investigation into the matter, he directed a grant for four acres be issued and the remaining portion be preserved for further extension whenever we required it. The sub-divisional officer was instructed to deal with the matter personally and to visit the village to inspect and measure the site and to hand it over to the Bahá'ís. I went to see the officer, U Ba Tin, in person. He was a very good young man and promised to do all that was necessary.

He came with his surveyors to the site to see the spot and the Bahá'ís on the Bahá'í Feast day. He saw that a bamboo-made monastery, occupied by a blind Buddhist monk with a layman on a portion of this land, was set on fire through the carelessness of the occupants. Without any delay he gave possession of the site to the Bahá'ís. This was considered a miracle by the friends, for the said monk had occupied the site a couple of months ago as a trespasser simply to create dissension, obstruction, and animosity between the Bahá'ís and the Buddhist villagers. He was enticed and supported by the female donor of the adjacent large monastery. They did not openly object when the proclamation for objections was posted on the land. As the government officer had seen and witnessed the incident personally, they could not bring a charge of arson against the Bahá'ís.

After 27 November 1918, the means of communication between India and the Holy Land opened and we were able to receive good news regularly.

The All-India Bahá'í Convention was to be held for three days in the Bombay Bahá'í Hall from 30 December 1919 to 1 January 1920, but it was postponed by the command of the beloved Master by a telegram dated 23 December 1919.

I regularly made trips to Daidanow Kalazoo and Rangoon during this year to uplift the spirits of the friends.

I received a letter from Mírzá Maḥmúd Zarqání from Bombay stating that he was going to the Holy Land. The friends of Mandalay, Rangoon, Daidanow Kalazoo, Kungyangon, and Bombay prepared a supplication and signed their names and sent it to Mr. Zarqání to submit to our beloved Lord 'Abdu'l-Bahá, imploring Him to bless the soil of India and Burma by His holy feet, as He had promised to pilgrims and had revealed a Tablet in reply to our former supplication. Also some insignificant amount was presented from His humble servants in Burma.

1920

The year 1920 was devoted to the organization of our first All-India Bahá'í Convention to be held at the end of December 1920. It was a very successful year. A Central Fund Committee for India and Burma was established and a Bahá'í Publishing Committee formed in Bombay. A Bahá'í Magazine was started in Persian and English to be edited by Mírzá Maḥmúd Zarqání for its Persian section and Prof. Shírází of Karachi and Prof. Pritam Singh of Lahore for the English section. The united efforts of the following friends made this glorious first Bahá'í Convention very successful: Mr. S. Ḥishmatu'lláh of Agra, Mr. N. R. Vakil of Surat, Mr. Khusraw Boman and his son Rustam of Poona.

There were delegates from every part of India and Burma, including Mr. A. Rangaswami Aya from Madras; Mr. Siávash Rustam from Tehran, Persia, as a visiting representative of the Persian Bahá'ís; Dr. S. Mazher 'Alí and Mr. 'Abbás 'Alí Butt Kashmiri from the Rangoon Bahá'í Assembly; Khalífa Muḥammad Yúnis (alias U Po Thwe); Mr. Moung Ba Kin and Mr. Moung Ba Tin from the Mandalay Bahá'í Assembly; and this humble servant, S.M. Roumie, representative for the Bahá'ís of Burma, and particularly the Daidanow Kalazoo, Kungyangon Bahá'í Assembly.

Of the various resolutions that passed in this Convention, the first was that the Bahá'ís of India and Burma, through their delegates, should sub-

Delegates at the first All-India Bahá'í Convention. Siyyid Muṣṭafá is seated third from the right.

mit a second supplication to the holy presence of 'Abdu'l-Bahá, signed by all the delegates, begging for the bestowal of His visit to India and Burma. The delegates in the first All-India Bahá'í Convention had made the same supplication and 'Abdu'l-Bahá replied as follows:

> *He is God!*
> *. . . Your missives, supplicating 'Abdu'l-Bahá to travel to those regions have been received. I, too, am, eager to be with you. There is no greater joy in the world of creation than seeing the countenances of the friends of God: this is that which gratifieth the heart and the soul. At the present moment, however, there are too many obstacles to undertaking such an endeavour. It is hoped that in future, with the grace and aid of Bahá'u'lláh, a means will be found to make this journey. As soon as that happens, I will immediately travel to India. This undertaking would be conditional on finding the ways and means; for it is a lengthy voyage, and the Holy Land is a centre of communications. Letters*

arrive constantly from different parts of the world, and at least one in ten should be answered. Pilgrims to the Abode of the Beloved also arrive unceasingly, and they should be met and served, for 'Abdu'l-Bahá is the Servant of the beloved of God, and honoured by this glorious task. How can I forsake this bounty? In addition, various other difficulties present themselves.

Nevertheless, My hope is to one day make this journey. While I am present in my heart and soul at the gatherings of the beloved of God, and partake in their devotions and fervent supplications, My eyes too would have their share of this bounty.

Even so, India is stirring up and roaring aloud, with tidings arriving to Us from many of its regions. I fervently and joyfully supplicate the Abhá Kingdom, therefore, to bestow divine bounties and confirmations upon the loved ones of God, imploring the Luminous Kingdom with utmost humility to grant everlasting glory to His devoted followers. Bahá'u'lláh, may My life be a sacrifice to His servants, hath adorned the temples of His loved ones with the crown of everlasting glory, a crown whose radiant gems shall shine from the realms on high throughout the ages and centuries. This Cause is so great that even utter abasement met in the path of God resulteth in glory. Consider, there is no greater abasement than loss of life, confiscation of property and the enslavement of one's children and kindred on the plain of Karbala. Now, reflect on the fact that this abasement of the Siyyidu'sh-Shuhadá, may the souls of all beings be a sacrifice unto him, was transmuted into eternal glory. Yazíd and Valíd, though they seemed outwardly powerful and seated on mighty thrones, were in reality eternally abased. . . .

Our second supplication remained unanswered until 21 September 1921, when a reply was given to this humble servant while on my sacred pilgrimage, to carry it and convey its message to the Bombay friends.

BAHÁ'Í MOVEMENT PUBLIC LECTURES

December 27th to 29th 1920, 5:30 p.m. to 7:30 p.m. Daily.
Under the auspices of the 1st All-India Bahá'í Convention,
At the Bahá'í Hall, 29, Forbes Street, Fort, Bombay.

27th December 1920, 5:30 p.m. to 7:30 p.m. President Dr. Muzhar 'Alí

LECTURES:

"The need of divine educator" Prof. Shírází
"Universal Religion" Mr. N. R. Vakil, B.A. LLB
"The fulfillment of Zoroastrian prophecies in the Manifestation of his Holiness the Báb, Bahá'u'lláh, and 'Abdu'l Bahá" Mr. Shiravax Rustam & Mr. Jamshíd Khodadad
"The New Dispensation. Its proofs from the Jewish and Christian Scriptures" Áqá Siyyid Muṣṭafá Rúmí

28th December 1920, 5:30 p.m. to 7:30 p.m. President, Prof. Shírází

LECTURES:

"The Kalanki Avtar" Mr. A. Rangswami Ayar and Mr. N. R. Vakil
"The immortality of the soul" Áqá Siyyid Muṣṭafá Rúmí
"Equality of Men and Women" Mr. Ḥashmatu'láh, B.A. B.I.
"The proofs of Bahaism from the Muhammadan standpoint" Mr. Mírzá Maḥmúd

29th December 1920, 6.30 p.m. to 7.30 p.m. President, Mr. Ḥas͟hmatu'láh

LECTURES:

"Universal Peace" Mr. Mírzá Maḥmúd
"Universal Language" Áqá Siyyid Muṣṭafá Rúmí
"Life after death" Mr. N. R. Vakil
"The Solution of the Economic and Industrial problem" Prof. S͟hírází
"The Promised One of all the religions has come" Mr. A, Rangswami Ayar.

All are cordially invited to attend the lectures
Mírzá Maḥmúd
Secretary
1st All-India Bahá'í Convention

- 14 -

THIRD PILGRIMAGE TO HOLY LAND IN 1921

It was the greatest blessing that our Lord 'Abdu'l-Bahá—in a holy Tablet dated 13 October 1919, in reply to my supplication of 19 August 1919—graciously permitted me to attain His holy presence, with some of the Bahá'í friends from Burma at the end of winter.

I was asked by the Bahá'í Assembly of Bombay to attend and help the first Bahá'í Convention with other delegates in December 1920. Again, in a holy Tablet written by His secretary Áqá Maḥmúd Zarqání, dated 26 October 1920, 'Abdu'l-Bahá extended His boundless favors upon this humble servant and expressed: *"Jináb-i-Siyyid Muṣṭafá is already permitted to attain the Holy presence, inform him, we are eagerly desirous to see him."* These holy utterances made me hastily put all my affairs in order to enable me to proceed at once toward the beloved of my heart.

As a Persian subject I first had to get the necessary permits from the vice consul of Persia in Rangoon, with a visa from the secretary of the British Foreign Office, which I obtained after my return to Burma from the convention. I visited the Bahá'í friends in Rangoon, Mandalay, and Daidanow Kalazoo, Kungyangon, and then booked my passage in a Bibby Line, and left for Port Sa'íd on 13 April 1921. On 1 May 1921 I arrived at Port Sa'íd. Siyyid Effendi Núshabadí of Port Sa'íd with his Arab assistants kindly came onboard to receive me. After custom clearance we went to his house, which was not far from the customs office. The next day, being the last day of the Riḍván Festival, the Port Sa'id Bahá'í friends, consisting of Persians and Arabs, gathered together in Mr.

Nú<u>sh</u>abadí's house. I considered myself very fortunate to join this glorious congregation as I had passed the first and second days of the Feast alone onboard the ship at sea. A couple of years ago, this house had been raided by a vulgar mob of fanatic Arab Muslims, who committed great mischief against the noble Mr. Nú<u>sh</u>abadí. Now the front doors facing the street were completely blocked and the Bahá'ís entered the house through a side door leading to the staircase of the two upper stories, one occupied by a non-Bahá'í tenant and the other by the landlord, Mr. Nú<u>sh</u>abadí. The friends were full of zeal and loving spirit.

On 3 May 1921, I embarked onboard the vessel of a Khedivial Line and sailed for the Holy Land. On 4 May 1921 at about 10:00 a.m. we arrived at Jaffa, but owing to some horrible confrontation between Muslims and Jews, the ship was ordered to proceed directly to Haifa. We arrived in Haifa at 4:00 p.m. of the same day. We were taken to quarantine and all passengers passed the night like prisoners. At 4:00 p.m. of the next day, first we were taken to the health office at the harbor. They returned our passports and ordered us to appear before a medical officer in town. We were released and passed through customs and went to the Oriental Pilgrim House near the holy Shrine of the Báb.

'Abdu'l-Bahá was in 'Akká and I was told that He would arrive the next day in Haifa. On 6 May 1921, our beloved Lord arrived and I had the bounty of entering into His holy presence alone in His private chamber. I am unable to explain my feelings and my excessive delight in His holy presence. He greeted me with cheerful and loving words. The beloved Master narrated the history of the holy house in Ba<u>gh</u>dád in detail, from the beginning to the present time and said that He "had already accomplished all that was to be done." I humbly said, "my Lord there is yet much to be done for the Supreme Cause." Smilingly He replied, "the outstanding minor duties will be carried out by the selfless Bahá'ís who are earnestly aspiring to serve the holy Cause most devotedly, even thyself, through the divine Confirmation." This heavenly glorious meeting ended with utmost pleasure and happiness which was already apparent from the blessed countenance of my Lord.

At the holy feet of my Lord I presented six different group photographs of the Bahá'ís of Daidanow Kalazoo, Kungyangon and other articles entrusted to me by the Rangoon and Mandalay Bahá'í friends, which were highly appreciated by our Lord Who blessed all of them through His merciful grace and generosity.

On 12 June 1921, I was commanded by our Lord to proceed to Alexandria to distribute three hundred Egyptian gold coins among the surviving heirs of the late Shaykh 'Abdu'l-Jawád Iṣfahání, who had passed away there. They were given to me by our Lord without any explanation. Áqá Aḥmad Yazdí, the son-in-law of 'Abdu'l-Bahá, furnished me with all the details and also advised me to go with Áqá Muḥammad Taqíy-i-Iṣfahání from Cairo, Egypt. After preparing my passport, I left by train on 13 June for Port Sa'íd. After meeting the Bahá'í friends at Port Sa'íd on 17 June I left by train for Cairo. I had informed Áqá Muḥammad Taqíy-i-Iṣfahání by telegraph but no one came to receive me on my arrival at the platform of the railway station. Later I was told that he had left for the districts on private business before the arrival of my telegram. Fortunately, the younger son of Ibrahim Effendi of Port Sa'íd, was traveling in the same train. He kindly took me to the Baháu'd-Dín Street where most of the Bahá'ís lived. As soon as Jináb-i-Shaykh Faraju'lláh Kurdí, a celebrated publisher of the holy books in Egypt, saw me on the carriage, he came down with delighted heart and open arms and took me to his house. I was his guest during my stay in Egypt, and both he and his wife treated me very kindly as their own kinsman. On the night of 18 June, I had the honor to join in the Bahá'í meeting held in the house of Mírzá Zaynu'l-'Ábidín, who was the husband of my host's sister-in-law. There I met all the friends, consisting of Persians, Arabs, Turks, and Armenians.

The next day, on 19 June, accompanied by my host, I went to see our revered Bahá'í sister Mrs. J. Stannard. She was very pleased to see me after many years.

I had to wait for Áqá Muḥammad Taqíy-i-Iṣfahání's return from the districts. He arrived on 26 June, and, on 27 June 1921, we went together by train to Alexandria. On our arrival we were welcomed by

Mírzá 'Abdu'l-Ḥusayn, the son-in-law of the late Shaykh 'Abdu'l-Jawád Iṣfahání, and 'Abdu'l-Wahháb, his son. We were taken to their residence. 'Abdu'l-Bahá had authorized this humble servant to divide the inheritance according to their choice, as the widow—the mother of the children—was Arab. She and all surviving heirs agreed that the inheritance should be divided among them according to Bahá'í law. Thus the amount of 300 gold coins was divided between them after deducting fifty-one coins for Ḥuqúqu'lláh. The four children each received fifty-one coins and the widow received thirty-seven coins and six piasters. The balance of 300 coins was spent for court stamp fee, according to the local government law to draw six indentures and agreements and five separate documents for acknowledgement of receipts. 'Abdu'l-Raḥmán Effendi Rushdí and 'Abdu'l-Futúh Muhammad Al-Bettah Effendi, both Arab Bahá'ís and employees in the Egyptian civil courts, assisted in accomplishment of this affair, which was concluded peacefully.

On 28 June I had the honor of meeting his highness Ottoman Murtaza Páshá, a retired high official of the Egyptian government. After lunch we returned to the railway station at 6:00 p.m. and said good-bye to the dear friends and thanked them for their loving kindness and left for Cairo.

On 1 July 1921, I went to the Persian and the British Consulates to prepare my passport accompanied by Shaykh Faraju'lláh. We had lunch and then proceeded to visit the tomb of our revered Bahá'í, the great Áqá Mírzá Abu'l-Faḍl. On 5 July, I left by night train for the Holy Land. In Ismailiyah, Maḥmúd Effendi Núshabadí very kindly had come to meet me and to give me a sealed package to submit to the holy presence of the Master. In Kantera we had to change trains after crossing the Canal. I arrived in Haifa on 6 July and had the bounty of going to the holy presence immediately. I presented all articles that were entrusted to me by friends and also the documents about the matter of inheritance with the sum of fifty-seven Egyptian gold coins given for Ḥuqúqu'lláh. The Master gave the gold coins to me and commanded me to send them back to Áqá Muḥammad Taqíy-i-Iṣfahání in Egypt with full instructions to distribute the sum to the respective heirs—ten gold coins each to the daughter and three sons, ten to their mother, and seven to the sister of Mírzá 'Abdu'l-Ḥusayn Yazdí. These were sent the next day with the help of our Bahá'í brother Dr. Luṭfu'lláh [Ḥakím] at business hours with a detailed letter concerning the instructions of the beloved Master.

'Abdu'l-Bahá was very pleased with my insignificant services and highly commended me in the public meetings that were held every evening, after which all pilgrims were honored to partake of dinner in His holy presence.

During the time of my pilgrimage, 5 May 1921 to 21 September 1921, often I had the honor of visiting, in the glorious company of my Lord, the holy Shrine at Bahjí and the holy Tomb of the Báb, and the sacred spots where Bahá'u'lláh occasionally pitched His tent on the top of Mount Carmel near the old residence of the German consul. I also had the bounty several times to visit all the sacred places in 'Akká, including the Riḍván and Firdaws Gardens, by the Master's command in the company of the youth pilgrims, such as Jináb-i-Faḍíl-i-Mázindarání; Jináb-i-Shaykh Muḥammad-'Alí Qá'iní of 'Ishqábád; Mrs. Watson; Dr. Luṭfu'lláh [Ḥakím]; Áqá Zaynu'l-'Ábidín Bálázadeh; Áqá Muḥammad-'Alí Shalchí of Tabríz; Shaykh Faraju'lláh Kurdí; Shaykh Muḥammad-el-Khirashí from Egypt; the students from the Beirut American College; Mírzá 'Alí-Muḥammad Khán, Mírzá Maḥmúd Khán, and their younger brother from Shíráz; the sons of Áqá Muḥammad Báhir Khán; Áqá Mírzá Faḍlu'lláh Mílání; Áqá Ḥusayn Maẓlún; 'Alí Effendi of Balabek from Jaffa, and others. Several group photos were taken in His holy presence with the Master's consent, in which this humble servant also was included.

One day the beloved Master entered the room with a glowing face and happily said, "The sun of those of the past has set and our shining orb is lighting the whole world and will never set." On another occasion He smiled, looked at this humble servant and said, "what a great excitement has Siyyid Muṣṭafá started." He then said a few verses of the poem revealed by Him: *"Sham`e Shabestan-i Haq Núr be áfáq bakhsh,"* meaning, "O though candle of God's inner sanctum, spread your light to the whole world."[1]

Several marriage ceremonies took place in the holy presence of the beloved Master, among them the marriage of our Burmese representative in the service of the holy house, K͟husraw (alias Po Min, son of Ma Tok of Rangoon, Burma) with the daughter of an old servant of the holy household since the time of Bahá'u'lláh, the late Áqá Faraj Áqá. It took place in the Master's House in the holy presence of the beloved Master. Our Lord kindly revealed a special sermon and a prayer for this unique occasion as customary in the Orient.[2] K͟husraw had been brought by Jamál Effendi to the Holy Land when he was eight years old.

The divine bestowals extended toward this humble servant on this pilgrimage were so boundless that I am unable to describe them in detail. I was usually alone with my Lord and was commanded to follow Him while He walked from the House up to the Persian Colony and seashore. Sometimes He used His carriage and motor car. His loving kindness toward me was so boundless that I would wish to sacrifice my life in His path.

On 16 September 1921, the beloved Master instructed me to get ready to return with Him from 'Akká to Haifa and then for my return to Burma.

He said "All pilgrims have returned to their homes, thou art the last to depart, with Jináb-i-S͟hayk͟h Muḥammad-'Alí Qá'iní and his son Baháu'd-Dín via Bombay. The S͟hayk͟h will go from Bombay via Sístán and K͟hurásán to his home." In obedience to the holy command, we were ready the next day, but through the clemency of our Lord, Who had seen my distress due to the effect of sudden separation from Him after a long stay, our departure was delayed until 20 September 1921.

The night before my departure I was half-dead when we were summoned to attend at the holy presence, to submit our faithful expression of loyalty, obedience, and servitude. My beloved Lord revived me by embracing me. We retired to the pilgrim house with a broken heart after submitting our due homage to our beloved Lord.

The last group photograph, taken in the Holy presence of our Lord, shows that the condition of the Master's health was deteriorating to a great extent. He told me that He was advised by the doctor who treated him, to abandon all kinds of writing—even a single line. During His walks He would halt at every fifty or one hundred feet on the roadside and sometimes would sit on a chair in the Persian Colony offered by the ladies or little children of that quarter in front of their houses, who were His admirers, and came to kiss His hands or the hem of His holy garment.

On 21 September, we bid farewell to all friends and left by train for Port Sa'íd. We arrived at 11:30 p.m. at our destination and were received by Arab and Persian Bahá'í friends. After waiting about seven days for the steamer, we embarked on an Italian boat, *SS Favignana,* on 29 September 1921. The passengers onboard consisted of a group of Arab Jews of Yemen and Baghdád, and Persians of Hamadan, four Japanese, three Indians from Sindh, Karachi, and a Marathi of Poona. We reached Aden on 8 October 1921, where hundreds of new Indian passengers embarked onboard the ship, mostly Hindus and a few Muslims and a group of Hadharamaut Arabs and a Shí'ih Indian cleric. I had been instructed by the Master to be with Shaykh Muḥammad-'Alí Qá'iní. With his permission I delivered the Bahá'í message to most of the interested souls without mentioning the name Bahá'í. I could speak their language and gave several public lectures to the Hindu community of Bombay, who were ardent followers of Mahatma Gandhi. My talks about the twelve Bahá'í principles were effective to a certain extent. After all endeavors, a young man from Poona, Maratha nation, who was a shopkeeper in the African coasts of Port Sudan and was returning home, accepted the Faith and accompanied us to the Bombay Bahá'í Hall.

On 18 October 1921, we arrived in Bombay and were cordially received by Bahá'í friends at the harbor. They took us to the Bahá'í Hall to meet the friends. On 30 October 1921, I left by mail-train for Calcutta and arrived on 1 November 1921 and boarded the British Indian Steamer *SS Alenga* on 4 November, arriving in Rangoon on the afternoon of 7 November.

On 11 November 1921, I went to Kungyangon with Saya Ko Po Ni, who was sent by the Daidanow Kalazoo Assembly to accompany me, for the celebration of the anniversary of the sacred birthday feast of Bahá'u'lláh and the Báb. On 16 November I returned to Rangoon and on 19 November 1921, left by evening mail-train to my permanent abode, Mandalay, and arrived there the next day at noon and met with all the friends who had come to see me in the Bahá'í Hall.

'Abdu'l-Bahá with a group of believers on the steps of the Master's House in Haifa on 7 August 1921. Siyyid Muṣṭafá is standing to the Master's left.

In the Ashraf Garden in 'Akká, August 1921.

- 15 -

EVENTS OF 1921–29

THE ASCENSION OF 'ABDU'L-BAHÁ

The National Spiritual Assembly of the Bahá'ís of India and Burma announced that a second National Convention would be held on 29–31 December 1921, and invited me to visit earlier for consultation and in the meantime represent the Bahá'ís of Burma. I left for Rangoon without staying very long in Mandalay and arrived in Bombay on 21 December 1921. On my arrival at the Bahá'í Hall in Bombay on 22 December 1921, I heard the heartrending news of the Ascension of our beloved Master. The Bombay Bahá'í Assembly had received a telegram from the Greatest Holy Leaf from Haifa in Arabic saying: "Verily 'Abdu'l-Bahá ascended to Abhá Kingdom. Greatest Holy Leaf." The Assembly's members, including Mírzá Maḥmúd Zarqání, at first doubted the authenticity of the message, and to ascertain the truth wired to Haifa, and the reply came just before my arrival in Bombay. Therefore, they had delayed the publication of the mournful announcement to all Assemblies in India and Burma. We also received a wire from Tehran, Persia, saying, "The Light of Covenant is transferred from material eyes to the heart."

I had been exceedingly uneasy and disturbed since my departure from Haifa. I felt that some sort of fatal calamity was destined and would erelong descend upon the Bahá'í world. To avoid such great misfortune, I was constantly taking refuge unto my Lord, praying and meditating. I also asked the Assemblies in Burma to chant the special prayer revealed by Bahá'u'lláh. The Ascension of our beloved Master was a fatal blow and a great trial for the Bahá'ís of the world. I had no fear of any kind of trial and temptation for the Bahá'ís of Burma and was certain that nobody ever could mislead them. Since my return from the first pilgrimage in 1904, I always told them that after the Ascension of the Center of the Covenant our Lord 'Abdu'l-Bahá, assuredly Shoghi Effendi Rabbani will be His successor, leader of the Bahá'í world and Guardian of the divine Cause.

After our second Bahá'í Convention I left Bombay on 11 January 1922 via Nagpore for Calcutta and Burma. On 13 January I arrived in Calcutta, and by *SS Aronda* left for Rangoon, and arrived on 17 January 1922. On 28 January I left for Mandalay, and the next day on 29 January, arrived at my destination.

MY FOURTH PILGRIMAGE TO THE HOLY LAND, 1922

On 11 February 1922, I had the bounty to receive a telegram from our beloved Guardian saying "IMMEDIATE PRESENCE NECESSARY IF POSSIBLE ANSWER SHOGHI." Without delay, I informed the Bombay Bahá'í Assembly by telegram with a copy of the telegram that I had received. On 12 February I received a reply saying "PATRIOT MANDALAY SIYYED MUSTAFA LEAVE IMMEDIATELY FOR HOLY PRESENCE." On 13 February 1922 I telegraphed the Holy Land, submitting the following: "IMMEDIATELY STARTING PREPARING MUSTAFA." After complete preparation on 15 February, I went to the railway station to reserve a berth for myself for Rangoon.

On 10 March 1922, after preparation of our passports, Mr. 'Abbás-'Alí Butt of Kashmir, Siyyid 'Abdu'l-Ḥusayn Shírází, and Áqá Siyyid Maḥmúd Shírází and I secured our passage on the Bibby Line, which sailed on the evening of 15 March 1922.

We arrived in Colombo on 22 March, and on 2 April we reached Suez. We arrived at Port Sa'íd on 3 April. Maḥmúd Effendi Núshabadí came onboard the ship and cordially received all of us.

We left for Haifa in a Trieste Lloyd boat but landed for a while again to meet the Bahá'í friends who were eagerly waiting for us in the Bahá'í Hall. After chanting some prayers and bidding farewell to the dear friends we returned to our ship and left at night.

In the afternoon of 4 April we reached Jaffa. On 5 April at about 9:00 p.m. the boat left for Haifa and at 5:00 a.m. arrived there. The port health officer came aboard the ship and permitted us to land. We then left for the Oriental Pilgrim House. To our great misfortune our beloved Guardian, Shoghi Effendi Rabbani, had left by train via Egypt for Europe a few hours before our arrival.[1] Our fellow pilgrim from Burma, Mr. 'Abbás-'Alí Butt of Kashmir, had been indisposed since the second day of our leaving Rangoon and still was unwell. I had attended to him throughout the voyage and also served the other two young men, as it was their first voyage.

The Greatest Holy Leaf, the Holy Mother, and all those in the Holy House, were very kind to all of us, consoling everyone for our disappointment and deprivation of not meeting our beloved Guardian.

As Mr. 'Abbás-'Alí Butt was a teacher in the Christian High School in Rangoon, and Siyyid Maḥmúd Shírází was a student of the government college in Rangoon, they were unable to remain any longer and supplicated the Greatest Holy Leaf for leave to return to Burma, which was granted. I was to accompany them to Egypt and on their return there do all that was necessary for their safe embarkation onboard the first Bibby Line boat leaving for Burma.[2] We left on 20 April for Egypt by train and on 27 April left Cairo for Port Sa'íd. Fortunately, we found a Bibby Boat on arrival at Port Sa'íd and they left for Rangoon on 28 April 1922.

After their departure I stayed for a few days in Port Sa'íd, and on 3 May left by train for Haifa. I stayed in the Holy Land until 24 July 1922, and during this blessed period I was elected as a member of the Haifa Bahá'í Spiritual Assembly, established temporarily during the absence of the beloved Guardian. For the guidance of the Bahá'ís of India and Burma and the protection of the divine Cause, I asked Mírzá Munír Zayn[3] to provide me with copies of the Kitáb-i-'Ahd, the Will and Testament of Bahá'u'lláh, and the Will and Testament of 'Abdu'l-Bahá, which were authenticated with His sacred seal.

In addition to the various misfortunes I had undergone during my lifetime, including being deprived of the bounty of meeting the beloved

Guardian on his return from Europe, I had to sustain one more in the Holy Land on 14 July 1922. I received a telegram from one of the relatives of my first wife in Rangoon that the youngest brother of my wife, Abu Ṭaráb Qurashí, had died on 10 July.

Before leaving Burma, in consideration of all circumstances in case I might not return to Burma, I had transferred my business and a small paddy field unconditionally to my brother-in-law. I brought my awkward situation to the Greatest Holy Leaf and the Haifa Spiritual Assembly for consultation and asked for their advice and guidance. They unanimously resolved that with the approval of the Greatest Holy Leaf I should immediately leave for Burma. Before leaving, with permission of the Greatest Holy Leaf, I visited the holy Shrine of Bahá'u'lláh and other sacred places in the company of Mr. and Mrs. Frank Durban Clack of Lompoc, California. The Greatest Holy Leaf and the Holy Mother gave me several presents and the Greatest Holy Leaf even provided me with new garments.

With a sorrowful heart I left for Port Sa'íd by train on 25 July 1922, after paying respectful homage to the holy household and bidding farewell to the beloved friends. On 26 July I arrived at Port Sa'íd. Many friends had kindly come to the station to receive me. They took me to the Bahá'í Hall to meet the gathered friends. On 8 August, together with Ḥájí 'Alí Naqí Shírází, we booked places for Bombay and embarked on 9 August 1922. We reached Aden on 14 August, and on 21 August we arrived at Bombay. Many friends cordially received us on our arrival at the harbor and took me to the Bahá'í Hall. Áqá Mírzá Maḥmúd Zarqání was also there.

I left for Burma via Calcutta by mail train on 28 August 1922. Meanwhile Jináb-i-Zarqání, at the request of Mr. Ibrahim Isa Bhoy, a new Bohra Bahá'í of Bombay, decided to go by the same train to Burhanpore, a small town on the way to Calcutta. He asked me to accompany him to that town in order to have discussions with some of the ulamá of the Ismá'íliyyih sect of the Bohra community to inform them about the manifestation of their long-expected Imám with the divine names of the "Báb" and "Bahá'u'lláh."

I accompanied him to Burhanpore. We were directed by our guide, Ibrahim Isa Bhoy, to the Coronation High School. This school was dedicated to the benefit of the Dawoodi Bohra Community and was attended by their boarder students from all parts of India. It was well organized and supported with graduate teachers. As I had already purchased a direct railway ticket and was allowed to halt at any station for one day only after the journey of 100 miles, I could not stay any longer. We had a very short discourse on the main subject. I left Mírzá Maḥmúd Zarqání there and the next day left via Bhusawal junction for Calcutta. On 1 September, I arrived at Calcutta and on 3 September 1922 embarked onboard the ship leaving for Rangoon. On 5 September I arrived at Rangoon. After settling my material affairs there, on 15 October I left for Daidanow Kalazoo, the Bahá'í village of 'Abdu'l-Bahá, and stayed there until 25 October 1922. I devoted my time to teaching and uplifting the spirits of the Bahá'í friends. At this time they were usually free after ploughing, thus there were good gatherings at all times during the day up to the late hours of night. On 26 October I returned to Rangoon by a ferry steam launch; and left by train for Mandalay on 1 November 1922.

I was cordially welcomed by the friends on the platform of the railway station and was conducted to the Bahá'í Hall, which was my permanent residence since I had become a homeless widower after the death of my wife in 1910. During my stay in Mandalay I did not waste my time and was occupied in compiling booklets and translating the holy writing into Burmese for the benefit of the Burmese Bahá'ís and true seekers.

On 3 March 1923 I left for Rangoon. Then on 14 March left for Daidanow Kalazoo, Kungyangon. I stayed there until 3 April 1923 and devoted all my time to writing the yearly accounts of the Bahá'í Spiritual Assembly and their yearly diary and minutes. On 4 April 1923 I returned to Rangoon. During my absence, Siyyid Jináb-i-'Alí had returned from England via Haifa. After passing the barrister law examination in England he had the honor of meeting the beloved Guardian and receiving instructions for uplifting the divine Cause through his service.

He stayed for a few days in Rangoon and left for Calcutta, his native home. On 14 April I received his letter from Calcutta, dated 8 April 1923, and also his previously written letter from Haifa. He stated in his Calcutta letter that he was instructed by the Guardian to consult with me regarding many important matters relating to the Cause, such as the establishment of Local Spiritual Assemblies, a National Spiritual Assembly for Burma with a view to the ultimate establishment of the International House of Justice at Haifa as contemplated in the Master's Will, and publication of a Bahá'í organ from Burma in English, Persian, and Burmese. He wrote: "The Guardian of the Cause has spoken to me in detail about the importance of these matters and particularly ordered me to take immediate steps regarding them in consultation with you. . . . God willing, I shall leave Calcutta on 24 April and reach Rangoon on 27 April . . ."

At this time all Bahá'í Spiritual Assemblies were newly organized, and with great enthusiasm and steadfastness each and every sincere soul exerted his level best to promote the divine Cause and thereby attain the good pleasure of the beloved Guardian, Shoghi Effendi.

Though, in obedience to the command of the beloved Guardian, the preliminary issue of our Burma Bahá'í magazine, *The Dawn,* was immediately ready for publication, owing to the rarity of Persian types and trained compositors, the matter was delayed until September 1923. Through divine confirmations, we overcame all those difficulties and achieved our purpose. Our editorial board was composed of six members but none of them came forward to extend a helping hand. The whole burden of editing, proofreading, publishing and dispatching of the magazine was laid upon my shoulders. I organized this task diligently and singlehandedly and discharged my services sincerely and honestly from September 1923 until 9 January 1928. I received from the Spiritual Assembly under whose auspices the magazine was issued, a sort of monthly honorarium to cover the petty expenses from October 1923 up

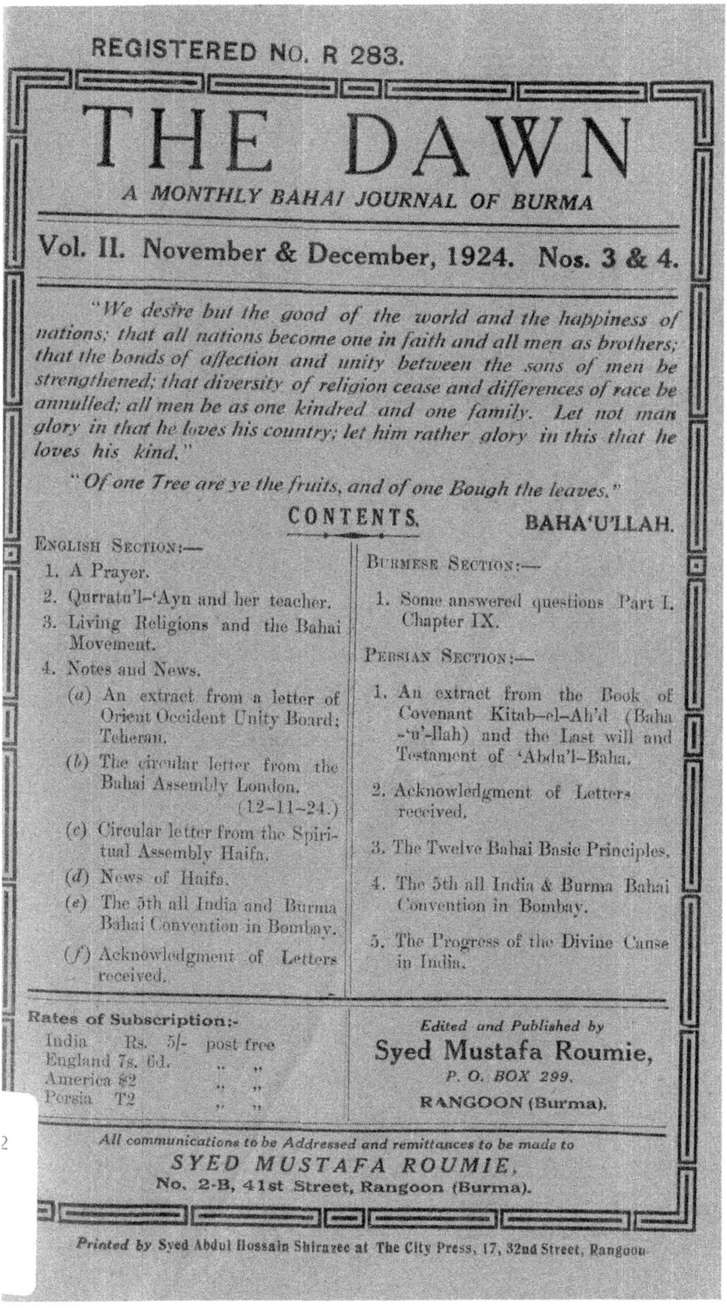

REGISTERED NO. R 283.

THE DAWN

A MONTHLY BAHAI JOURNAL OF BURMA

Vol. II. November & December, 1924. Nos. 3 & 4.

"We desire but the good of the world and the happiness of nations; that all nations become one in faith and all men as brothers; that the bonds of affection and unity between the sons of men be strengthened; that diversity of religion cease and differences of race be annulled; all men be as one kindred and one family. Let not man glory in that he loves his country; let him rather glory in this that he loves his kind."

"Of one Tree are ye the fruits, and of one Bough the leaves."

BAHA'U'LLAH.

CONTENTS.

English Section:—

1. A Prayer.
2. Qurratu'l-'Ayn and her teacher.
3. Living Religions and the Bahai Movement.
4. Notes and News.
   - (*a*) An extract from a letter of Orient Occident Unity Board; Teheran.
   - (*b*) The circular letter from the Bahai Assembly London. (12-11-24.)
   - (*c*) Circular letter from the Spiritual Assembly Haifa.
   - (*d*) News of Haifa.
   - (*e*) The 5th all India and Burma Bahai Convention in Bombay.
   - (*f*) Acknowledgment of Letters received.

Burmese Section:—

1. Some answered questions Part I. Chapter IX.

Persian Section:—

1. An extract from the Book of Covenant Kitab-el-Ah'd (Baha-'u'-llah) and the Last will and Testament of 'Abdu'l-Baha.
2. Acknowledgment of Letters received.
3. The Twelve Bahai Basic Principles.
4. The 5th all India & Burma Bahai Convention in Bombay.
5. The Progress of the Divine Cause in India.

Rates of Subscription:-

India	Rs. 5/-	post free
England	7s. 6d.	" "
America	$2	" "
Persia	T2	" "

Edited and Published by

Syed Mustafa Roumie,

P. O. BOX 299.

RANGOON (Burma).

All communications to be Addressed and remittances to be made to

SYED MUSTAFA ROUMIE,

No. 2-B, 41st Street, Rangoon (Burma).

Printed by Syed Abdul Hossain Shirazee at The City Press, 17, 32nd Street, Rangoon.

Front page of the English edition of The Dawn, the monthly Burmese Bahá'í journal.

to January 1926. For the remaining period up to 9 January 1928, I served absolutely gratis.

The journal received the kind appreciation of the beloved Guardian of the Cause of God, and in several epistles he expressed his loving sentiments and kind blessings. In a letter dated 7 February 1925, he wrote:

To my honoured friends, the editors and publishers of "The Dawn"
Loyal and steadfast workers in the Cause of God! I have read the recent issues of the Dawn which you have been so kind to send me with feelings of heartfelt admiration and gratitude. This valuable organ of the Bahá'í Community in Burma has displayed magnificent efforts in the past, has earned the satisfaction and esteem of its readers, and is steadily and determinedly, exerting itself to establish its claim of providing for a long-standing need and fulfilling a vital function.

Burma, that beloved and picturesque country, standing sentinel on the eastern confines of the Bahá'í world, with its vast number of modest yet ardent followers of the faith, should pursue diligently its work of extending further and further into the very heart of the far-east the sphere of its healing mission of life.

While maintaining the closest and most cordial co-operation with the body of friends in India, as a sign of the growing solidarity of the Cause of God, it should concentrate its energies on the consolidation of its work in its own particular field. It is the privilege of the Burmese friends to re-adjust and stimulate their own activities, lay down their own programme for an intensive and systematic campaign of teaching and with an unshakable resolve arise to carry it to a successful conclusion.

May your cherished and promising journal eloquently recount the tale of your deeds; acquaint your fellow labourers in distant fields with your hopes, your plan and your achievements; reflect the spirit of your selfless endeavours and stand as witness of growing vitality of the noble work you are destined to achieve.

May He, who loves you and watches over you, guide your steps, cheer your hearts, reinforce your efforts, and richly reward you for your loyalty, your perseverance and courage. I assure you of my affectionate sentiments, my deep appreciation and my prayers for you all.

Your brother and fellow worker
Shoghi
Haifa, Palestine
February 7th 1925[4]

Many epistles were received from the beloved Guardian during my editorship of *The Dawn* and all indicated his kind appreciation and loving kindness, which were published from time to time in that journal.

I am indebted to the kindness of my late spiritual son, Siyyid Jináb-i-'Alí, who extended his helping hand for the English edition, from the beginning to the end, due to my deficiency in the English language. I edited the other two sections, the Persian and Burmese editions, without the help of any member of the editorial board, who were nominated prior to the existence of the journal, each one from a different town and Assembly.

Mírzá Maḥmúd Zarqání tried to train the new believers, and exhorted every Bahá'í Spiritual Assembly to assist the editors and promote the publication of the journal. Thus the Cause widely spread in India through this organ, especially among the Urdu readers.

In January 1928, in obedience to the official instruction of the Rangoon Local Spiritual Assembly, under whose auspices the journal was issued, I was asked to resign from my duties. I immediately went to the deputy commissioner of the Rangoon town with the usual application and released myself from the responsibility of the editorship. After a year the publication of *The Dawn* stopped for reasons unknown to me.

FOURTH CONVENTION, 1924

From 30 April 1924 to 2 May 1924, the All-India and Burma Bahá'í Convention was held in Poona (India). Our dear Bahá'í brother Shaykh 'Abdu'l-Raḥmán, who had recently arrived from the Holy Land, joined the Convention. He is Indian by birth, but was naturalized in Damascus, Syria, at the time of the Turkish regime.

The learned teachers <u>Sh</u>ay<u>kh</u> Muhyi'd-Din Sabrí of Egypt and Mírzá Maḥmúd Zarqání visited India in August and September 1924, after visiting the Holy Land, to promulgate the holy Cause. Unfortunately, <u>Sh</u>ay<u>kh</u> Muhyi'd-Din Sabrí could not tolerate the Indian climate, fell ill, and was compelled by the doctors to return to Egypt. Mírzá Maḥmúd Zarqání remained in India for teaching the Cause. During this time he came in contact with three leading and well-educated Arabic and Persian scholars, followers of the late Mírzá <u>Gh</u>ulám Aḥmad Qádíání. As a result of their own independent investigation, without any kind of persuasion from any Bahá'í teacher, they accepted that the teachings of Bahá'u'lláh are divine in origin and provide the only remedy for the cure of the maladies from which the world of humanity is suffering in this age. Consequently they were referred to by the Qádíání chief in his various sermons as outcasts. He stopped his congregation from speaking or shaking hands with them or even responding to their greetings. Although they were harassed severely in various ways, their steadfastness defeated their opponents.

As distorted and incorrect historical accounts had appeared in some of the newspapers, at the suggestion of the friends at the Convention of 1924, a weekly newspaper in Urdu, *Kaukabi Hind* (Star of India) with Agra as its headquarter was established. It is now a monthly journal and widely circulated throughout India, Burma, and the Bahá'í world under the auspices of the National Spiritual Assembly of India and Burma, with its headquarters at Karol Bagh, Delhi.

Mírzá Maḥmúd Zarqání endeavored to train the new believers, and exhorted every Bahá'í Spiritual Assembly to assist the editors and promote the publication of their journal. The Cause widely spread in India through this organ, especially among the Urdu readers.

The Bahá'í community of India and Burma suffered a great loss with the premature passing of our beloved Bahá'í brother Professor Mírzá Muḥammad Riḍá <u>Sh</u>írází of Karachi (India), who ascended to the Abhá Kingdom on 12 April 1925 while taking a swim in the river in Hyderabad, Sindh. He was an indefatigable and ardent teacher of the Cause in India.

He attended high school in Karachi and obtained his B.A. degree in one of the best colleges in Bombay, close to the Bahá'í Hall. During his days in college he became acquainted with Mírzá Maḥram, the great learned Bahá'í teacher, and through his eloquent discourses Mírzá Muḥammad Riḍá embraced the Bahá'í Cause. Two of Mírzá Muḥammad Riḍá's colleagues, Mr. N. R. Vakil and Mr. Ḥishmatu'lláh Quraṣhí of Agra, also accepted the Faith. These three dignified souls jointly and separately rendered many remarkable services to the Cause in India after the passing of the revered teacher Mírzá Maḥram. Professor Ṣhírází went on a teaching tour in European countries, America, and around India. Though small in stature, he had a powerful, penetrating, and magnetic voice. He was the founder of the Local Spiritual Assembly of Karachi, and left behind many steadfast and noble souls, who exemplify his undying attributes of unselfish love and service. Mr. 'Abbásí and Mr. Isfandíyár Baḵhtíyárí are now examples of his sacrifice and devotion, and give their life and wealth for the promotion of the Cause in Karachi, Sindh (currently in Pakistan), which is a well-known port for all foreign steamers.

Professor Ṣhírází was loved by all as he endeavored to be a humble follower of the beloved Master by helping the weak, comforting the sorrowful, and radiating an atmosphere of love around him.

1925

The last trip of Mírzá Maḥmúd Zarqání to India was in 1925. He arrived in Rangoon on 23 February and left for Mandalay on 2 April returning on the seventh. He left Rangoon for the Holy Land via Calcutta and Bombay on 14 April 1925.

1926

The Bahá'í Spiritual Assembly of Mandalay decided to send a teaching party from 28 August to 7 September 1926 for spreading the Cause at Kyigon village, in the Shweb District of upper Burma. Most of the villagers in this area were the relatives of the Bahá'ís of Daidanow Kalazoo, Kungyangon. I had been there twice in 1909 and 1910. A few souls had accepted the Faith through the Daidanow Bahá'ís during their yearly trips there for their cattle.

Khalífa Muḥammad Yúnis, alias Dowshin U Mya, and three other Bahá'ís of Mandalay were sent to this village and stayed in the houses of Bahá'ís. Khalífa Muḥammad Yúnis visited there several more times during the year, and reported that he was able to deliver the message to no less than 155 interested souls, and the latest fruit of his labor in the field of service was that ten young men of that village accepted the Cause and joined the band of the faithful servants of Bahá'u'lláh in this province. He passed away in November 1928.

In India, Siyyid Maḥfúẓ'ul Ḥaq Ilmí and Mihr Muḥammad Khán Shiháb worked hard to deliver the message in various communities, and successfully worked on the journal *Kaukabi Hind*.

JINÁB-I-ÁQÁ MÍRZÁ MAḤMÚD ZARQÁNÍ

While touring in India, Mírzá Maḥmúd challenged Ghulám Aḥmad Qádíání, the founder of the Aḥmadíyyih movement, through a widely circulated daily paper *Paisa-Akhbar*. The only response from Qádíání was that he was unable to accept his challenge at the time as he was very busy with certain litigation in law courts. Mírzá Maḥmúd insisted through the same paper that if he had no time at that moment he would be glad to meet him at any later suitable date. At the request of the Bahá'í Assembly of Rangoon, I translated Mírzá Maḥmúd's article into Urdu with the title "A Refutation of the Lecture of Jináb-i-Qádíání," and it was published twice in India as a booklet with some additions by me. The last publication of one thousand copies was in 1908, which formed an important landmark in the history of the Bahá'í Cause in India. After the widespread publication of that booklet, Mírzá Maḥmúd remained in Lahore for a considerable time, publishing three thousand copies of the "Episode of the Báb" in Urdu, translated by this humble servant, the expenses of which were generously covered by our beloved Bahá'í brother of Rangoon, Áqá Siyyid Ismá'íl Shírází. This led many of the staunch and well-educated members of the Qádíání sect to come into the Bahá'í fold; the most prominent among whom are Jináb-i-Mawlawí Faḍil Siyyid Maḥfúẓ'ul Ḥaq Ilmí and Mihr Muḥammad Khán Shiháb and two others, who became the editors of the Bahá'í Urdu journal *Kaukabi Hind.*

During his last visit to India in 1924–25, Mírzá Maḥmúd was delighted with the wonderful interest that *Kaukabi Hind* had attracted to the Bahá'í Cause throughout India and Burma. He then concentrated all his efforts to secure the permanence of this paper and spared no effort in encouraging one and all to assist this valuable journal in every possible way.

Mírzá Maḥmúd is prominent in the Bahá'í world for his famous book *Badáyi'u'l-Áthár,* in which he faithfully recorded the account of 'Abdu'l-Bahá's travels in Europe and America in 1911–12. The choice of the beloved Master fell upon him to act as a secretary during this important tour. He edited and published a monthly journal from Bombay called "Al-Bishárát" in Persian, and "Bahá'í News" in English from 1921 to 1922. After the Ascension of the Master, it was Mírzá Maḥmúd's privilege to enjoy the confidence of beloved Shoghi Effendi, the Guardian of the Cause, whom he most devotedly and loyally served as a secretary.

After settling down in Haifa in the presence of the beloved Guardian, he was sent to Persia via Baghdád. He went to Qazvín and Rasht, and while returning to the Holy Land with some pilgrims, Mírzá Maḥmúd ascended to the Abhá Kingdom at the age of fifty-five. The beloved Guardian in the following telegram announced "PROFOUNDLY DEPLORE ZARQANI PASSING HIS OUTSTANDING SERVICE ADORN ENRICH ANNALS OF CAUSE. INSTRUCT FRIENDS HOLD BEFITTING MEMORIAL. SHOGHI"

The National Spiritual Assembly of India and Burma, in obedience to the telegram of the beloved Guardian, arranged for memorial meetings on 10 and 11 November 1927. May God immerse him in the ocean of His divine grace and mercy.

KHALÍFA MUḤAMMAD YÚNIS

Khalífa Muḥammad Yúnis, alias Ko Po Thwai of Mandalay, ascended to the Abhá Kingdom at his home on Sunday 11 November 1928 at the age of sixty-seven. He was buried at the Bahá'í Cemetery in Mandalay.

Our beloved Guardian by a telegram conveyed his heartfelt condolences to his surviving relatives.

Khalífa Muḥammad Yúnis was the son of Ḥájí Shaykh Muḥammad Muṣṭafá, a Muslim divine and hereditary chief of the Sunní mosque of the Gyundan Quarter, Mandalay. His great-grandfather had come to Burma from Delhi a century ago at the time of the great sovereignty of the Burmese King Bodowpra (circa 1784). The mother of Khalífa Muḥammad Yúnis was patronized by the Queen of King Thebow, the last King of Burma, to supply silk cloths and precious stones. Khalífa and his mother joined the Cause in 1895 when Jamál Effendi and I visited Mandalay for the first time. Jamál Effendi gave him the title of Khalífa. His honorable father, Ḥájí Shaykh Muḥammad Muṣṭafá, also resigned his office and joined the Bahá'í fold after the arrival of Áqá Mírzá Maḥram at Mandalay. Both of his parents were buried as Bahá'ís in our cemetery.

Khalífa Muḥammad Yúnis went as a pilgrim to the Holy Land after my return from there with Mírzá Maḥram. The beloved Master addressed him in a Tablet as *"O Thou Spiritual son of Jamál Effendi."* On his return from the pilgrimage, Khalífa served the Cause ardently, being of particular service to Mírzá Maḥram and Mírzá Maḥmúd Zarqání.

At the death of Khalífa's beloved father, the Muslim mob of the Gyundan Quarter where he lived, brought the police to take hold of the dead body and bury it according to Islam. The police did not allow the mob to touch it. We attended the funeral house and at every visit bricks and stones were thrown on us by the enemies of the Cause. Eventually he was buried honorably in the old Bahá'í cemetery and I performed the service peacefully. After a couple of months of suffering, Khalífa was advised by Mírzá Maḥram to sell his houses and to live with his family and children in the vicinity of the Bahá'í quarters in Kungyangon, Gondan, and Letsaifan.

Khalífa visited many towns and villages to give the message. His last trip was in 1927 in the company of Mrs. Schopflocher of Canada and other Mandalay Bahá'í friends.

The beloved Guardian sent the following telegram conveying his heartfelt condolences to the bereaved family of Khalífa Muḥammad Yúnis after his passing: "ASSURE DEEP-FELT CONGRATULATION MAHFOOZAL HUQUE ON BRILLIANT SERVICES AND HEARTFELT CONDOLENCE RELATIVES MUHAMMAD YUNIS"

Khalífa Muḥammad Yúnis was survived by his wife, Daw Shiu, who passed away in Mandalay on 5 October 1929 and was buried in the Bahá'í cemetery. His three sons—Ko Nyun, Ko Eusoof, Ko Baik Ko—and two daughters, Mariam and Ma Lay Tin, are firm Bahá'ís and walk in the footsteps of their late parents.

CONFERENCES

On 16 February 1929, our dear Bahá'í sister Miss Hla Hla spoke at the Theosophical Hall, Mandalay, as part of a group of invited representatives of various religions. The subject was "how to attain salvation." There were many speakers, and every one spoke according to their own religious standpoint. But Miss Hla Hla surpassed them all with a speech composed of the Bahá'í holy writings that was inclusive of all holy books of the past ages.

At a religious conference held under the auspices of the Arya Semaj in Delhi on 28 January 1929 the question that came up for discussions was "Can unity be accomplished among the existing religions? If yes, how? If not, why not?"

There was a gathering of about 3,000 people of almost every race and religion. There were representatives of all sects of Hindus, Christians, Mohammedans, and others. The Bahá'ís were represented by Siyyid Maḥfúẓ'ul Ḥaq Ilmí, the editor of the Bahá'í journal in Urdu, *Kaukabi Hind*. He spoke for about an hour on the subject in Urdu. In the course of his speech he endeavored to prove that unity among the existing forms of religions was an impossibility unless and until the dogmas and prejudices in diverse shapes shared by their respective followers were abandoned and the fundamental reality underlying each religion was strictly adhered to. He then impressed upon the audience that religious unity was only practicable through the teachings of Bahá'u'lláh. He next explained some of the basic principles of the Bahá'í religion: oneness of humanity, oneness of the divine revelation, and so forth.

Siyyid Muṣṭafá Rúmí

- 16 -

MY SECOND MARRIAGE, 1929

I remained a widower from 1910 to 18 April 1929. I was born and brought up as a motherless infant from the seventh day of my birth, and had no children and no relatives at the time of my advanced age. The Mandalay Bahá'í Spiritual Assembly members, who are my spiritual children, lovingly suggested a second union for me with a lady of advanced age, Ḥalímih Khánum, alias Poluama'ma'Myaing, who was a widow and without children and relatives. A Bahá'í lady was asked to explain the feeling of the Local Spiritual Assembly to me, and some members of the Local Assembly talked to Ḥalímih Khánum. After receiving our consent, the date was fixed and all the Bahá'ís of Mandalay were invited for the marriage ceremony. After the marriage vows, all the guests were invited to the Bahá'í Hall to partake in a festive dinner at which we served a delicious Burmese dish called Kyazan.

On the same evening I left the Bahá'í Hall, which had been my permanent residence, and went to live in my wife's house, no. 115, 84th street Koonjan, corner of 35th street.

She was formerly married to our Bahá'í brother 'Abdu'l-Qádir, known as Palitafa M Po Win. He was known by the surname Palitafa because he had built and dedicated a mosque for his Muslim friends in Amarapura, the ancient capital of the kings of Burma, situated at a distance of about four miles from Mandalay. He was a wholesale merchant of raw silk yarn, imported mainly from China, but due to his advanced age his office was run by his wife Ḥalímih Khánum. After the ascension of Bahá'u'lláh, he and his mother, Ma Fáṭimih, were honored by Tablets revealed by the beloved Master. 'Abdu'l-Qádir passed away in October 1920.

My wife was prosperous on her own and did not claim any inheritance from her husband. They agreed to give all that belonged to him to his sister's children during his lifetime.

Siyyid Muṣṭafá Rúmí with his wife, Ḥalímih Khánum

My wife had to close her business long before our union, owing to fluctuation of the silk market. She treated her debtors with utmost benevolence and clemency when she discovered their distressful condition of destitution and poverty. Her exemplary and unique dealings with utmost love and clemency, her liberal charity and generosity as a Bahá'í were talked about by one and all. In 1928, one year before our marriage, she compiled and published a booklet in Burmese titled *Hoququ'l-Insanieh,* "The Duties of Humankind," which made her more widely known in the circle of Buddhists and Muslims.

When she became a member of the Bahá'í Faith, her generous activities grew in all directions, particularly the Holy Land, The Chicago Bahá'í Temple, and the Mandalay Bahá'í Assembly. She was honored with several holy Tablets revealed by the beloved Master as well as letters from the Guardian of the Cause of God, Shoghi Effendi Rabbani.

After our marriage she expressed her ardent desire to transfer our dwelling houses and properties, which were in her own name, to that of Shoghi Effendi Rabbani as endowments for the benefit of the Cause of Bahá'u'lláh. She said: "We both are advanced in age, our life is uncertain, we have no legal heirs to inherit our property after our death, our death is assuredly certain. We are not going to live in this transitory abode forever, which is full of temptation, distress, misery, and affliction. Let us do what we are willing to do immediately. Please expedite the task." I agreed that her desire was the main goal of our lives and was a noble sacrifice and magnificent service in the path of our Lord God. I told her, "Your devotional discourse testifies and denotes that you exactly know the supreme divine Manifestation, and His exalted Station. Your steadfastness upon His Covenant is with assured firm faith. His unfading love, the love of the Center of His Covenant and your perpetual, successive, sincere loyalty to Their designated Guardian of the Holy Cause are the reason persuading you to perform this glorious service to our dearly beloved Cause. Such is the heartfelt desire of every true Bahá'í. As it is revealed by the Supreme Pen in the Persian Hidden Word":

O My Friends!
Walk ye in the ways of the good pleasure of the Friend, and know that His pleasure is in the pleasure of His creatures. That is: no man should enter the house of his friend save at his friend's pleasure, nor lay hands upon his treasures nor prefer his own will to his friend's, and in no wise seek an advantage over him. Ponder this, ye that have insight![1]

As it was a legal matter, I had to consult a competent lawyer friend, asking him to draw a deed of trust or endowment and send it to the chairman of our National Spiritual Assembly for his legal opinion. Then we would have to execute and register the document in court. While I was attending to this task, on the morning of 27 November 1929 at about 8:00 a.m., after performing ablutions for her morning prayer, my wife fainted. We lived on the corner of 35th and 84th street at the Koonjan quarter, which is far from other Bahá'í houses. We were surrounded by Muslims who were bitter enemies of the Cause. No help could be expected from them. We had an elderly female Muslim servant who helped us during the day and I was quite new to the people of this locality and was completely helpless.

Through the confirmation of the Kingdom of Abhá I acted personally. I applied eucalyptus oil, which I had brought from Rangoon, to her whole body while repeating the Greatest Name and used hot water bags and covered her with woolen blankets. After a couple of hours, she opened her eyes and felt better. She miraculously recovered within a few days from this attack, but the convalescence lasted for several months.

With submissiveness and full resignation, I constantly chanted the holy healing prayer for her. All the friends individually and also in the Assembly meetings constantly prayed on her behalf. It is a great mystery to comprehend the divine wisdom. To my great grief, on the same date of 27 November 1929, my spiritual son Mr. Siyyid Jináb-i-'Alí was struck with the same fatal and dreadful disease as my wife while he was onboard a ship going to Calcutta, his native home, for treatment of an old sickness. In Calcutta he was under the treatment of many great and famous doctors, but he did not recover. My wife was treated by a Burmese physician for a few days and by applying some Burmese home medicines she fully recovered within a couple of months.

Alas my spiritual beloved son passed to the Kingdom of Abhá on 2 January 1930. This was a great loss for me and all the friends in Burma. As weak and helpless human beings we are unable to comprehend the divine wisdom and we are bound to submit to His Supreme Will in full resignation. On receiving the news of his passing, the beloved Guardian sent the following missive:

> . . . He was very sorry to learn of the illness of Syed Jenab Ali and since the receipt of your letter, he has been extremely grieved to learn of his passing. His sudden departure throws a shadow of gloom upon all of us here and in India and while Burma loses a distinguished and truly earnest Bahá'í leader, it must be especially unfortunate to you that just at a time when you were considering and preparing the ground for Government Recognition and a temporary consideration of Bahá'í laws, you were deprived of his valued cooperation. The Cause in India is as yet in such a tender age that we can ill afford the loss of those few that keep the torch aflame.
>
> *The news of the passing of our dear and able friend and collaborator Syed Jenab Ali has brought profound sorrow to our hearts. He leaves a great gap behind him. I hope that the friends far from feeling disheartened and discouraged at such a great loss will arise and redouble their efforts in order to compensate for the loss which they have sustained. Kindly assure his relatives of my deep grief, and my prayers for his departed soul . . .*[2]

In a humble supplication to the beloved Guardian, dated 14 April 1930, I wrote about my situation and begged for permission to draw a deed of trust in his name for our properties and execute it legally in the Court. I received the following answer:

> . . . I am now directed by the Guardian to thank you for your letter of April 14th with the comprehensive report of the Bahá'í Census which you were so good to send him.
>
> He appreciates this work immensely and it will be a very valuable data for consideration of the Cause in Burma. He hopes to make good use of it.
>
> Regarding the most generous wish of your dear wife and yourself to leave some property after yourselves for the progress of the Faith and in the name of our Guardian, I will say nothing as I am sure he will wish to append a few words himself. But I am sure he wants me to express his grateful appreciation of the spirit that animates your offer. The life of both of you has been rich in services rendered to the Cause of Bahá'u'lláh and what a happy blessing that even after you, you may leave your little share for the progress of the Faith. . . .
>
> *My dear and precious co-worker:*
> *I deeply appreciate your noble sentiments, your self-sacrificing efforts, your pioneer services and your glorious steadfastness in the path. I wish to congratulate you on your union with the hand-maid of God Halimeh, who I trust will in close collaboration with you render inestimable services to the Faith.*
>
> *The packages you sent me have all arrived and will be preserved in your name in the archives of the Holy Land.*
>
> *As to your desire to offer your property to the Cause and to transfer it to my name as a trust, I deeply appreciate your generous offer, but wish you and your dear wife to benefit from its rent so long as you are living and to transfer it in later years.*
>
> *I will supplicate for both of you from the depth of my heart at His Holy Shrine. Rest assured.*
>
> *Shoghi*[3]

After my wife's full recovery, I personally drafted a deed of endowment and sent it by registered mail to Mr. N. R. Vakil, Chairman of our National Spiritual Assembly of India and Burma, for his direction and opinion. He consulted a notary public and asked him to draw a deed of trust. He sent me a typed copy by return mail. I altered a paragraph of that deed which was against our wish and inserted a new paragraph. I was directed by the beloved Guardian in his epistle of 7 May 1930: "But wish you and your dear wife to benefit from its rent so long as you are living." I consulted with some of my lawyer friends and after due amendments, attached a certified copy to the deed and both of us signed them in the presence of the chairman and the vice chairman and the secretary of the Mandalay Bahá'í Spiritual Assembly. All of us then went to the registration office on 7 November 1930 and transferred all our rights to the title and interest in that property as trust in the exalted name of Shoghi Effendi Rabbani, the beloved Guardian of the Cause of Bahá'u'lláh, and executed the document before the registrar.

The deed of trust was duly received back from the registration office on 22 November 1930. I applied for two more certified copies of the same, and meanwhile took our photograph. On 11 December 1930 everything was ready and I submitted the original deed of trust together with our photograph and a short supplication at the holy feet of the beloved Guardian, and on the same day sent a certified copy of the same to Mr. N. R. Vakil. I kept another certified copy for future reference.

My wife is a true and sacrificial Bahá'í. She has been the treasurer of the Local Spiritual Assembly since its inception. She humbly serves the friends with absolute humility. She chants Arabic prayers and is an expert writer in the Burmese language. Now in the year 1933 she is the vice chairman of the Local Spiritual Assembly of Mandalay. She is seventy-three years old and still serves the friends.

The house that we have registered in the name of the beloved Guardian is composed of four buildings located in a wide road. There are some other houses around them. We are now advanced in age and do not work anymore. Whatever is our income we spend for our meager needs and the repair of the buildings.

The previous price of these buildings was about fifty thousand rupees. Now the market is lower, but because these buildings are in a wide road and close to the electric tram in the corner of a large square, I believe the price will not reduce further. Whatever is the Will of God we obey. Its address is: 115 84th Street, Kunjan, Mandalay.

Persian Colony
Haifa, Palestine
3-1-31
Mr Sayed Mustafa Rumie
115, 84th street, Kunjan, Mandalay, Burma
Dear friends,
Shoghi Effendi wishes me to acknowledge the receipt of your joint letter dated December 15th 1930 as well as the Trust Deed for the property you have transferred to his name. He is deeply appreciative of the services you have been constantly rendering to the Cause and the sacrifices you are doing in furthering its interests. May God in His infinite bounty fully repay your endevours.

Shoghi Effendi is quite well and as usual busy in performing his many duties. The successes that are being constantly achieved in spreading the Cause and furthering its interests, however are fully repaying his labours promising wonderful results for the near future. In these days the place where the greatest amount of work is being achieved is Persia, where the government is liberal and accords to the friends all the freedom they desire to spread the message.

In closing may I assure you of Shoghi Effendi's loving greetings and best wishes for the success of your work in serving the Faith.

My dear and precious Co-worker:
The deed has reached safely the Holy Land and stands as a further evidence of your exemplary devotion to the Cause of God. I will continue to pray for you, your dear wife and the precious friends in Burma from all my heart. You are often in my thoughts and your distinguished services past and present cheer and heartens me in my task. Rest assured and be happy, and always remember that my prayers will continue to be offered in your behalf at the holy shrines.
Your true brother
Shoghi[4]

Siyyid Muṣṭafá Rúmí and his wife Ḥalímih Khánum standing outside their home in 1930, having registered it in the name of Shoghi Effendi as a trust.

GLORIOUS SECOND VISIT TO BURMA OF OUR REVERED BAHÁ'Í SISTER MARTHA L. ROOT AND HER DIGNIFIED COMPANION FROM INDIA MR. ISFANDÍYÁR BAKHTÍYÁRÍ OF KARACHI

During the year 1930, on Saturday morning, 26 July, our dearly beloved revered Bahá'í sister Miss Martha L. Root and Jináb-i-Isfandíyár Bakhtíyárí, chairman of the Bahá'í Spiritual Assembly of Karachi (India) arrived in Mandalay. As previously arranged, she and her honorable companion were put up in two separate rooms in the magnificent building, which was dedicated in 1917 during the world war in the exalted name of our beloved Lord and Master 'Abdu'l-Bahá, for His promised sacred visit after the war. It is situated in a large compound adjacent to the house of the chairman of the Mandalay Bahá'í Spiritual Assembly. We were unfortunately deprived of that glorious visit and blessing and thus gave it for rent to a Bahá'í family.

Our dear revered sister was comfortable there. They were the guests of this humble servant and Mrs. Roumie during their stay in Mandalay. The friends devotedly appreciated her blessed presence and arranged for several meetings. She delivered a lecture on the Bahá'í Cause at 6:30 p.m. in the Theosophical Society "Lotus Lodge" on 83rd street. The meeting was presided over by Dr. N. B. Meullan, the retired health officer of Mandalay. There was a large audience and they acclaimed and cheered her joyfully. Her second lecture was in the public library in China Street, opposite the Sikh community's temple. It was again chaired by Dr. Meullan. More than 200 were present. Most of them were highly interested. The subject was "Life after Death" according to Bahá'í views. All were deeply interested. The Rangoon Bahá'í friends had arranged to send her to Mandalay immediately after her arrival, and had arranged her lectures during her absence. Miss Root did not stay in Mandalay very long, and left for Rangoon on the third day of her arrival on 29 July 1930.

The Rangoon Bahá'í friends had arranged several lectures for her. She wrote about them in detail in her booklet "Bahá'í Letters about India and Burma from Martha L. Root" on pages 14–19.

Miss Root and Mr. Ba<u>kh</u>tíyárí also visited the village of 'Abdu'l-Bahá—Daidanow Kalazoo, Kungyangon—on 31 July and returned to Rangoon the same evening.

Mr. Ba<u>kh</u>tíyárí returned to Karachi but Miss Martha Root remained lecturing in Rangoon up to 7 August 1930, when the boat for China via Singapore was available.[5]

- 17 -

THE ASCENSION OF BAHÍYYIH KHÁNUM, THE GREATEST HOLY LEAF

On 15 July 1932, the National Spiritual Assembly of the Bahá'ís of India and Burma, through its Chairman, Mr. N. R. Vakil, received the following cablegram from the beloved Guardian, which was communicated to all Local Spiritual Assemblies in India and Burma:

> JULY 14, 1932
>
> GREATEST HOLY LEAF ASCENDED ABHA KINGDOM OUR GRIEF IMMENSE OUR LOSS IRREPARABLE INFORM LOCAL ASSEMBLIES COMMEMORATE BEFITTINGLY SACRED EXPERIENCES SO RICH SO SUBLIME SO EVENTFUL A LIFE. MAGNITUDE OF OUR SORROW DEMANDS COMPLETE SUSPENSION FOR 9 MONTHS THROUGHOUT BAHÁ'Í WORLD EVERY FORM RELIGIOUS FESTIVITY. HER MORTAL REMAINS LAID VICINITY HOLY SHRINES.
>
> SHOGHI[1]

On that same day, the Assembly and this humble servant dispatched cablegrams to the beloved Guardian: "MANDALAY ASSEMBLY WITH MUSTAFA IMMENSELY GRIEVED SUBMITTING CONDOLENCE TO HOLY HOUSEHOLD. INSTRUCTIONS CARRIED OUT."

On the evening of the same day, a memorial service was held in the Bahá'í Hall of Mandalay, and I, with profound grief and heartrending lamentation, chanted a holy Tablet revealed by Bahá'u'lláh. I also submitted a supplication on behalf of all the Local Assemblies of Burma and myself to the Holy Land on 18 July 1932.

The beloved Guardian kindly replied:

> JULY 27, 1932
>
> RANGOON ASSEMBLY CARE VAKIL
>
> MY SORROW LADEN HEART RELIEVED YOUR VALUED SYMPATHY
>
> SHOGHI

> "Siyyid Mustafa Mandalay Assembly care Vakil Havadia Chakla Surat"
> "Deepest loving appreciation noble sympathy" Shoghi

The Greatest Holy Leaf, Bahíyyih Khánum, our beloved heavenly mother and the beloved sister of 'Abbás Effendi, 'Abdu'l-Bahá, according to "The Dawn-Breakers" accompanied her beloved Father and Brother to Baghdád in 1269 H.E, 1853 A.D., at the age of seven; thus she was born in 1846 and ascended to the Abhá Kingdom when she was eighty-six years old.

Her ascension to the Supreme Kingdom of Abhá on 15 July 1932 cast a gloom over the Bahá'í world and filled every heart with profound sorrow and grief. The beloved Guardian, in his cablegram to the National Spiritual Assembly of the United States of America, said:

> . . . OUR BELOVED FAITH WELL-NIGH CRUSHED BY DEVASTATING BLOW OF 'ABDU'L-BAHÁ'S UNEXPECTED ASCENSION, NOW LAMENTS PASSING OF LAST REMNANT OF BAHA'U'LLAH ITS MOST EXALTED MEMBER. HOLY FAMILY CRUELLY DIVESTED OF ITS MOST PRECIOUS GREAT ADORNING. . . .[2]

Memorial services were held as commanded by the Guardian by every Local Spiritual Assembly in India as well as in Burma, and messages of condolence were sent to the bereaved Holy Family. On 14 September 1932, I received the reply to my supplication of condolence dated 18 July 1932:

August 25, 1932

Beloved co-worker in the Faith,

Your message of condolence and sympathy dated July 18th, 1932 . . . was received and its perusal greatly comforted the bleeding heart of the Guardian. He wishes me to thank you from the very depth of his heart and assure you of his abiding appreciation of your continued and precious services to the Faith.

The ascension of the Greatest Holy Leaf has grieved his heart beyond words and had it not been for his assurance that in this calamitous event the friends are experiencing a profound spiritual awakening he would have remained utterly disconsolate.

His thoughts, in this terrible hour, are with you who are toiling so faithfully for the greater extension and consolidation of the Faith. I need not assure you how deeply appreciative he is of your work and he hopes that you will be enabled to serve the Cause with still greater zeal and success.

The memory of the beloved Khánum will, assuredly, prove to be your great comfort in your moments of sufferings and anxiety and will guide your steps and strengthen your spiritual power and insight. . . .[3]

The Ḥaẓíratu'l-Quds in Rangoon, constructed in 1932 through the efforts of Siyyid Maḥmúd Shírází.

- 18 -

EXTRACTS FROM CORRESPONDENCE, 1931–41

The memoirs of Siyyid Muṣṭafá Rúmí extend no further than 1932; however, details of the remaining years of his life have been gleaned from the following extracts of his correspondence, which include letters of the Guardian that indicate the breadth of his services.

1931

The news of the progress of the Faith in Karachi delighted my heart. These are all bounties of our Lord. Hearing this news I remembered the time that I was in the presence of 'Abdu'l-Bahá in 1921. He entered the room of the pilgrims with great happiness. He looked at me and said, "Áqá Siyyid Muṣṭafá is really winning." He repeated it several times. He then repeated a poem that said, light is shining in the West and East.[1]

1933

Although weakness prevents me from service, I have finished the translation of *Bahá'u'lláh and the New Era* into the Burmese language. May it be acceptable by the beloved Guardian. The Guardian has graciously sent nine pounds toward the cost of its publication. The Burmese friends also have contributed according to their capacity. Our beloved Guardian has written that when the book is ready, if I write him the cost of publication he will send the funds for it.[2]

September 10, 1933

I have been requested by Shoghi Effendi to acknowledge the receipt of your letter dated August 14th, 1933 and to renew the expression of his abiding appreciation of the pioneering services you have been, and are so increasingly rendering to the Faith in Mandalay. I wish to thank you particularly on his behalf for the admirable way in which you have carried out his wishes and instructions in connection with the translation and publication of Dr. Esslemont's book into Burmese. Such a highly difficult task has, undoubtedly, cost you a good deal of self-sacrifice and of hard and continued effort. But you can be assured that the result obtained is of such a high significance and importance to the progress of the Cause in Mandalay that it will not only add a fresh lustre to the immense work that you have been doing for so many long years, but will constitute a challenge to every thoughtful and loyal believer to follow the example you have set before him. Our beloved Master is surely looking down upon you from the Realm above with eyes full of admiration and praise, and is looking still forward to see you more active and more ardent than ever in His Divine Covenant.

Assuring you once more of our Guardian's best wishes and of his fervent prayers on your behalf, so that the Almighty may guide your steps, cheer your heart and keep you firm and constant in His Faith . . .

Dearly beloved co-worker:

What you have accomplished with such zeal, courage, ability and love fills me with joy, thankfulness and admiration for the sterling qualities that have characterized your long and distinguished career of service to the Cause of God. You have added fresh laurels to an already brilliant record of service. The fifty volumes you have sent will be placed on your behalf and in your name in the international Bahá'í library within the holy Mansion at Bahjí adjoining the Shrine of Bahá'u'lláh. I will ever be reminded of your glorious and exemplary services to the Abhá Revelation. I will continue to pray for you from all my heart. Your true brother,

Shoghi[3]

I have written about 600 pages on the history of the progress of the Faith in India and Burma in Persian at the request of the National Spiritual Assembly of Iran. My hope is to send it to Iran when the difficulties of sending Bahá'í materials to that country is solved. Some parts of the English version is published in *Star of the West.*

The translation of New Era is, praise be God, completed and is being printed. I hope it will be ready soon.

On 24 August 1933, at the instruction of the beloved Guardian I mailed fifty-four copies of the New Era book in the Burmese language to his presence. The Bengali translation is sent to me for review and hopefully I will attend to it.[4]

October 5, 1933

I have been requested by the Guardian to thank you for your letter dated September 2nd, 1933, and to express his heartfelt appreciation of your efforts in connection with the writing of the history of the Cause in India and Burma. Your valuable studies on the subject which have appeared in the form of a series of articles in the "Bahá'í Magazine" have greatly interested both the Bahá'ís and the non-Bahá'ís. It is hoped that the history you have been asked to write in Persian will produce similar results. You should try to make it as detailed as possible, giving all the facts you can gather, together with any document or photograph which can illustrate the work and give it a scholarly and scientific character.

In closing, let me assure you once more of Shoghi Effendi's fervent prayers on your behalf and on behalf of all our friends in Burma.

Dear and most prized co-worker:

What you will place on record regarding the history of the Faith in India and Burma will acquire tremendous significance and influence in the days to come. It will serve to instruct, inspire, and cheer countless souls among the rising generation, and will add fresh laurels to those you have so deservedly won in the service of God's immortal Faith. No words can adequately convey the gratitude I feel in my heart for your continued and inestimable services. Your true and affectionate brother,

Shoghi[5]

1934

I am now eighty-two years old and am still trying to offer my meager services to the threshold of the beloved Guardian.[6]

The Bahá'í school in Daidanow is very important. Until now none of the friends in India have helped, although the beloved Master 'Abdu'l-Bahá in 1923 in a Tablet instructed this humble servant: "As regards the Kunjangon school, this school is extremely important, and hath been inaugurated in the name of this humble servant. It must be run with the utmost order and regularity, and all the friends in India must lend it their support."[7]

February 19, 1934
Dear Bahá'í Friend,

I wish to thank you most warmly on behalf of the Guardian for your letter of February 5th which was so full of the news of the progress of the Cause in Mandalay. He was particularly gratified to learn that through your efforts and through the assistance of some other friends the Bengali translation of the "New Era" is ready for publication. He hopes you will be soon able to send it to the press, as he feels that the circulation of this valuable book can highly stimulate the spread of the Cause.

Shoghi Effendi was also much pleased to learn that you have successfully completed your history of the rise and progress of the Cause in India and Burma. He trusts that the Indian National Spiritual Assembly will be pleased over it and will approve of its being sent to Tihran. This is undoubtedly a real and abiding contribution you have been able to make to the Faith. May it fully serve its purpose and become a means whereby our Indian friends can be strengthened and inspired in their labours for the promotion of the Cause . . .

Dear and precious co-worker:

The work you have recently accomplished is highly meritorious in the sight of God, and will no doubt attract fresh and still greater blessings from the throne of the Almighty. You have, in the evening of your life, added fresh laurels to the crown of immortal glory which your many services to the Faith have won for you and which future generations will gratefully and Joyfully remember. I will continue to pray for you, for your dear wife and your devoted collaborators in that land. Rest assured, be happy, and persevere in your high endeavours. Your true brother,

Shoghi[8]

December 17, 1934

The Guardian wishes me to thank you for your deeply appreciated letter of December 4th with its enclosures, all of which he has carefully read and considered.

With reference to the Bengali translation of "Bahá'u'lláh and the New Era," he wishes me to convey to you, and to dear Mr. A. Islam as well, his hearty congratulations and grateful thanks for your splendid, sustained and successful efforts in this connection. He feels certain that nothing short of divine assistance, and of your painstaking and continued labours, could have brought this task to a successful consummation. He fully approves and deeply appreciates Mr. A. Islam's wish to defray the expenses for the printing of the book, and sincerely hopes that in this he will receive the whole-hearted collaboration and encouragement of the National Spiritual Assembly. He wishes you to urge the National Assembly to return the manuscript as quickly as they can to Amiru'l Islam so as to expedite its publication.

The Guardian was also gratified to learn of the important Bahá'í publications which you have translated into Burmese. He advises you to keep these manuscripts, or, in case you wish, to send them to the National Spiritual Assembly for publication in the future.

As regards your account of the history of the Cause in India and Burma, he hopes that the National Spiritual Assembly will soon find a way for forwarding your manuscript to the Tihran Assembly. He feels that, in view of the fact that the entry of Bahá'í literature is banned in Persia, it would be safer to send the manuscript through the care of a reliable person, preferably a believer.

In connection with your chairmanship in the National Spiritual Assembly, Shoghi Effendi has no objection if you, for reason of health or for any other important consideration, feel it essential to present your resignation as chairman of the Assembly. He would request you, however, to retain your membership in that body at any cost, even though you may feel unable to attend the sessions of the Assembly. Your membership in the National Spiritual Assembly he considers as a unifying force which is of essential importance to its effective working and progress.

With his renewed greetings and thanks and with his prayers for you, and for dear Mr. Amiru'l Islam.

Dearly beloved co-worker:

Your letter profoundly touched me. I grieve to learn of your increasing infirmities, and my heart is filled with inexpressible gratitude as I recall the long and distinguished record of service which will forever remain associated with your dear self and name. I am asking the National Assembly to relieve you of the Chairmanship of their Assembly and am sending a message of love and gratitude to dear Amiru'l Islam for his remarkable work and his generous offer. Rest assured that my thoughts and prayers are often with you and your dear wife and at the Holy Shrines I constantly remember you and pray for you. You belong to the heroic age of our Beloved Faith—an age to which you have so richly contributed. Rest assured and be happy.

Shoghi[9]

1935

First All-Burma Convention, 1935

I was planning to attend the All-Burma Bahá'í Convention in Kungyangon and did not send a personal congratulatory telegram on the occasion of the auspicious marriage of the beloved Guardian. I want to send one on behalf of all the friends.

The first All-Burma Convention under the auspices of the National Spiritual Assembly of India and Burma was scheduled from 6–11 April 1935. Everyone was invited to gather in the village of 'Abdu'l-Bahá, Daidanow. It was decided that I should go there before the start of the Convention to assist for its arrangement.

I left Mandalay on 3 April by second class rail, and, without resting in Rangoon, boarded the boat and arrived in Daidanow on 4 April. The Mayor of the village and the Bahá'í friends had decorated the Bahá'í Hall so beautifully that it shined with flowers and lamps.

This aroused the jealousy of the fanatic Muslim neighbors. They decided to dispatch the headmaster of the Muslim school to Rangoon to see the chief mullá. He reported the Bahá'í activities to the mullá and asked him for a fatwa. The chief mullá declared that the gathering of the Bahá'ís should not proceed under any circumstances. On his return to the village, the headmaster approached the wealthiest merchant of the village, who sponsored the Muslim school, and asked his assistance for 500 rupees to organize the people against the Bahá'ís. They told the merchant: "Their leader Siyyid Muṣṭafá has come here. He is a sorcerer and will deceive all the Muslims of the village to accept his heretic religion." The merchant replied, "I have known this man for many years. He is a respected person in Rangoon and in this village and will not do anything to harm Islam. This is a gathering of the Bahá'ís and has nothing to do with the Muslims. Go home and don't embarrass yourself."

With great anger the headmaster left him and approached another merchant. This man did not know me and gave them fifty rupees. From others they gathered some more money that altogether came to about 200 rupees. The group then approached the chief solicitor, a man named Mr. Khán. He was greatly agitated with their report and immediately arrived in Kungyangon by car.

The chief of police in Kungyangon is the grandson of the late chairman of the Local Assembly and is a Bahá'í and one of the organizers of the Convention. He met Mr. Khán, who had brought two of the solicitors of Kungyangon with him. I also immediately went to Kungyangon and met him. One of the solicitors knew me well and had seen me in Rangoon thirty years ago. He introduced me to the others. They asked whether we were Muslims. I told them that we were Bahá'ís and gave them the book *Bahá'u'lláh and the New Era*. I then explained the tenets of the Faith and told them that we respected all religions. I explained that the reports to Rangoon were given by the Indian Muslims of Kungyangon, and that no one from the village has opposed the Bahá'ís.

The next day the three of them visited the village and went to the Muslim Quarters. No one came to see them. They asked me if we needed the protection of the police. I answered, "if anyone attacks me personally, of course I will not retaliate as it is our directive. However, if they attack the Bahá'ís as a group, then according to law they will defend themselves." The officials went to the headmaster and warned him not to start anything, otherwise he would be arrested.

On 8 April many friends from Rangoon and the villages of Kungyangon arrived. A large white banner was hung at the gate announcing the All-Burma Bahá'í Convention in Burmese and English. We had sent invitations to all people of different religions and decided that from 12:00 noon to 3:00 p.m. there should be talks under the supervision of this humble servant. In the morning three policemen came to observe the proceedings. After the chanting of prayers and singing Bahá'í songs, talks started.

Meanwhile, a group of Muslims, mostly trouble makers who were known to the police, entered the meeting and said they had come to listen to Bahá'í songs. However, the police, knowing that they did not understand the Burmese language and only wanted to make trouble, ejected them.

The next two days were also spent in prayer and consultation about teaching and how to deepen the Bahá'ís in their understanding of the writings and to prepare them for future persecutions. The Convention also decided to open a new school in the name of the beloved Guardian.[10]

In answer to a report, the following letter was addressed to Siyyid Muṣṭafá on behalf of the beloved Guardian:

June 27, 1935
On behalf of the Guardian I wish to thank you most heartily for your welcome letter of the first instant with enclosures, all of which he has read with genuine interest and deepest appreciation.

The news of the success of the first all-Burma Bahá'í Convention held on April last in "'Abdu'l-Bahá's Village" at Daidanaw has particularly rejoiced his heart, and imparted added strength and stimulus to his hopes concerning the future of the Cause in Burma. It is, indeed, quite splendid and fully indicative of the mysterious and all compelling power of the Faith that in the face of all the malignant opposition of the Muslim divines the friends in Burma should have succeeded in holding such an important and truly historic gathering. He hopes that now that the first step in that direction has been definitely taken it will be easier for the believers to organize such conferences in the future, especially with the help and cooperation of the Indian National Spiritual Assembly, which has contributed so much towards the success of this year's Convention.

From the enclosed report prepared by your Secretary the Guardian has learned with deep appreciation of the emphasis laid by the friends at the Convention of the importance of organizing the Bahá'í school at Daidanaw. He trusts that the friends both in India and Burma will whole-heartedly respond to the Educational Committee's appeal for raising the necessary funds for that purpose. He particularly values the financial assistance extended in this connection by the National Spiritual

Assembly, and is confident that its example will be followed by the rest of the believers.

As to the name of the school, the Guardian would advise that this institution should be dedicated entirely to 'Abdu'l-Bahá's name, as it was during his days that the village was first established. The new section that you are planning to open very soon for the teaching of English, Arabic and Urdu will, no doubt, be of an invaluable addition to the school's already rich record of service. The Guardian is specially praying on behalf of the new teacher of English that has been appointed to take charge of the new school by the name of Mohammad Iqbal Khan. He wishes him full success in this highly responsible task he has been appointed to perform.

With the assurance of his prayers on your behalf, and with his greetings to you and to all the friends in Mandalay and throughout Burma.

Dear and prized co-worker:

I am delighted with your recent achievements. At your advanced age you have truly performed a work which the Concourse on High will extol and magnify. I am enclosing the sum of £30 as my contribution for the school recently established. The friends in Burma have proved themselves worthy of the great love and blessings our departed Master has lavished upon them. I will continue to pray for them from the depths of my grateful heart. To you, in particular, I feel greatly indebted. Kindly extend to all the friends in that far-away country my love, my congratulations and abiding gratitude for their magnificent efforts.

Shoghi[11]

November 15, 1935

On behalf of the Guardian I wish to thank you for your letter of October 19th with enclosure, and to renew his appreciation of your self-sacrificing and sustained efforts for the consolidation of the Faith throughout Burma. He specially values the continued care and attention with which you are assisting in the development of the Bahá'í school at Daidanaw. He has read with much interest the report of the school's progress which you had submitted to him under separate cover, and feels rejoiced at the realization of the active support which some of the Indian believers, and particularly the Poona Assembly, are extending to that institution. It is his hope that through the generous contributions and help of all individuals and assemblies in India and Burma the school's fund will steadily increase, and will thus enable you to carry out in their entirety, your plans for the wider penetration of the message in Kunjangoon and its surroundings.

The Guardian wishes me also to convey to you his thanks and appreciation for your painstaking efforts in connection with the preparation of two manuscripts on the Cause in Urdu. He trusts that the National Spiritual Assembly will soon find the means for their publication. . . .

May the Almighty, whose Cause you promote and safeguard with such tender solicitude, such firm constancy and magnificent devotion, reward you and your dear collaborators in Burma, and fulfil all your wishes in the service of His invincible Faith. Your true and grateful brother,

Shoghi[12]

1936

My wife and I are both getting feeble and old. I am now eighty-four years old and she is seventy-six. We are alone in this world and are without anyone to care for us, so we have decided to arrange a place for our mortal permanent abode. With consultation with the friends we have prepared and bought a place for our burial.[13]

July 16, 1936

Many thanks for your very kind letter of June 8th, which I have just received, and also for the enclosed cash account of 'Abdu'l-Bahá's school at Daidanaw-Kalazoo, both of which I have, at your request, presented to our beloved Guardian for his information.

He is indeed sorry to learn of the financial difficulties facing that school, and he is fervently praying that you, as well as your devoted co-workers in that institution, may be given the wisdom, energy and means you need to head for the furtherance of that institution.

He is enclosing a draft for thirty English Pounds as his contribution towards the expenses of the school. He is also impressing the National Spiritual Assembly of the Bahá'ís of India and Burma with the necessity of maintaining their contributions to the School's fund. He hopes that through their co-operation and through your energetic endeavours as well, the financial problem facing the Daidanaw school will be speedily and satisfactorily solved.[14]

September 16, 1936

Our beloved Guardian wishes me to thank you for your very kind letter of August 27th, the contents of which he has deeply enjoyed reading. He is truly gratified to learn that 'Abdu'l-Bahá's School at Daidanaw is progressing satisfactorily, and that his small contribution to the school's fund has been of some help to the friends in meeting the expenses incurred in connection with the maintenance of the English Section. His hope is that through the united cooperation of the Indian National Spiritual Assembly that institution will steadily grow and expand, and will attract the attention of all the non-Bahá'í neighbours in Daidanaw and its surroundings. The school should be maintained at any cost, and especially the new English Section which, if run properly, can be of immense teaching value to the Cause. No sacrifice is too great for this vital and highly-meritorious task.

The question of the School registration is obviously a very important one, and every effort should be exerted to have this step taken without the least possible delay. . . .

My well-beloved co-worker:

I rejoice to learn of your determination to prosecute, in collaboration with your devoted co-workers, the historic work which you have so gloriously initi-

ated, extended and consolidated in the course of your magnificent career in the service of the Cause of Bahá'u'lláh. Future generations will glorify and extol your services rendered with such devotion, zeal and love. I feel extremely grateful to you, and am proud of your record of service. Affectionately,

Shoghi[15]

November 9, 1936

Our beloved Guardian wishes me to thank you for your letter of the 31st October just received. Its contents, particularly the news of the completion of the publication of the Bengali version of "Bahá'u'lláh and the New Era," have greatly rejoiced his heart. On his behalf I wish to thank you, and also your able and dearly beloved collaborator Mr. Amiru'l-Islam of Chittagong, for your long and successful efforts for the publication of this volume, the circulation of which, he hopes, will further intensify the extension of the Cause throughout India and Burma. He is filled with gratitude to you both for the sacrifices you have so patiently endured for the sake of expediting the printing of the book. You should feel confident that your labours will be fully repaid as through them thousands of eager and ready souls who have been hitherto deprived of the blessing which the knowledge of the Cause confers, will be enabled to know and perhaps recognize and accept the Faith. You have left behind a historic work of immense value to the teaching work throughout India and Burma, and should therefore feel abidingly grateful to Bahá'u'lláh for having assisted you in its accomplishment.

The Guardian is fervently praying on your behalf and also on behalf of Mr. Amiru'l-Islam, that the Beloved may give you ever widening opportunities of service to the Faith.

My well-beloved co-worker,

I have just received the copy of the Bengali version of the "New Era" beautifully bound and splendidly printed. My heart is filled with joy and gratitude. I eagerly await the fifty copies I have asked to be sent to be placed in the Mansion of Bahá'u'lláh at Bahjí and in the various libraries established in the Holy Land. Kindly assure my dearly-beloved brother, Amiru'l-Islam, of my deep and abiding appreciation of this outstanding and unforgettable service to the Abhá Revelation. I will continue to pray for you both from the depths of my heart. Your true and grateful brother,

Shoghi[16]

December 7, 1936

Your letter of November 29th, has just arrived, and the news of your illness and that of Mrs. Roumie brought indescribable grief to the heart of our beloved Guardian. On his behalf I hasten to offer you both his sincere good wishes for your speedy and complete recovery, and wish also to assure you not to feel grieved over your inability to travel to Rangoon, in order to meet and welcome Mr. Schopflocher. Had he known of your severe indisposition he would have never asked you to undertake such a long and tiring journey, no matter how important and fruitful it may be in its results. For there is no consideration more vital at present than your own good health, and that of your dear wife. You should feel quite justified in curtailing some of your Bahá'í activities, in case you feel that they interfere with your health, and tax unduly your physical energies and resources. Your paramount duty now is to keep yourself and your wife in as good physical condition as possible, even at the expense of some temporary suspension or retardation in your labours for the Cause.

The Guardian is, meanwhile earnestly supplicating at the Holy Shrines on your behalf and on behalf of Mrs. Roumie, that Bahá'u'lláh may continue to protect and sustain you in your services, and may completely and speedily restore your health which, as you know only too well, is a real asset to the Faith in India and Burma. He is specially entreating Him to disband and completely crush the forces which the enemies of the Faith in Mandalay and its surroundings are so bitterly arraying against you and your beloved and humble co-workers. Do persevere, therefore, with the utmost cheer and tenacity in your task, for victory is surely yours, since Bahá'u'lláh has promised it to everyone of His steadfast and loyal servants throughout the world.

Dearest co-worker:

Do not feel disturbed, for I well realize your difficulties and the obstacles that stand in your way. For your own dear and precious self, as well as for your dear wife I will specially pray at the Holy Shrines. My heart overflows with gratitude for all that you have achieved in His path. Your true brother,

Shoghi[17]

1937

AUGUST 31, 1937

MARTHA ROOT ARRIVING BOMBAY SEPTEMBER SIXTEENTH URGE INDIVIDUALS LOCAL NATIONAL ASSEMBLIES VIGOROUSLY PARTICIPATE ENSURE TRIUMPHANT SUCCESS HER EXTENDED STAY ACCORD MAGNIFICENT WELCOME BEST BELOVED STAR SERVANT BAHA'U'LLAH.

SHOGHI[18]

[To Daidanaw Local Spiritual Assembly]

December 7, 1937

Dear Bahá'í Friends,

The Guardian was deeply rejoiced to receive your Assembly's message of November 21st, and to know of the very cordial reception you have arranged in honour of Miss Martha Root. The warm welcome you have so lovingly extended to that well-beloved servant of Bahá'u'lláh is certainly in keeping with the tradition of hospitality which the Daidanaw believers have set on previous occasions and which has won them the sympathy and admiration of the entire Bahá'í world.

The Guardian has also learned with profoundest satisfaction of the public meeting you had organized in honour of Miss Root, and in which several notables of the Kunjangoon village had accepted to participate. He sincerely hopes and ardently prays that the publicity which the Cause has received as a result will be further stimulated through the organized and energetic efforts of your Assembly.

Assuring you also of his supplications on behalf of each and all the friends at the Holy Shrines, and with cordial greetings.

Dearly-beloved friends:

My heart is filled with joy and gratitude whenever I recall your exemplary devotion to the Cause of God and your steadfastness in His path. I will continue to pray for you from the depths of my heart, that you may each and all be graciously assisted to mirror the glory and splendour of this Divine and most holy Revelation. Your true and grateful brother,

Shoghi[19]

APRIL 28, 1938

RIDVAN FESTIVAL CLOUDED BY PASSING HOLY MOTHER MUNIRIH KHANUM. WITH SADDENED HEARTS BAHÁ'ÍS EAST AND WEST CALL TO MIND INVALUABLE SERVICES WHICH HER HIGH STATION EMPOWERED HER RENDER DURING STORMIEST DAYS 'ABDU'L-BAHÁ'S LIFE. ADVISE ALL CENTRES BEFITTINGLY COMMEMORATE HER PASSING. SHOGHI[20]

We sent the following message of condolence to the beloved Guardian:

> We the mourning servants in Burma held the memorial service for our most beloved Holy Mother after receiving the Haifa Persian News Letter in June.[21]

July 7, 1938

The expression of loving sympathy conveyed in your letter of June 20th addressed to the Guardian on the occasion of the ascension of the Holy Mother has been very deeply appreciated by him, and he indeed wishes me to assure you, and through you the believers throughout Burma, of his profoundest thanks for the condolences you have been moved to express to him in his very sad bereavement.

Grief-stricken as the believers throughout the world must certainly feel at this heavy and indeed cruel loss, yet they should derive comfort at the thought that she is now re-united with her Lord, and is enjoying the blissfulness and peace which the great World Beyond alone can confer.

Her mortal remains, the friends will surely be pleased to know, have been laid to rest in a spot over-shadowed by the resting-place of the Greatest Holy Leaf on Mt. Carmel.

In closing I wish to renew to you the Guardian's loving and abiding gratitude for your painstaking and devoted labours for the Faith in Burma. He will continue to pray, that despite your advancing age and the attending difficulties and obstacles of your life, you may be given many more years of active service in the Cause.

Dear and prized co-worker:

It is always such a joy and comfort to hear from you. You are, I assure you, often in my thoughts and prayers. I long to hear of the fruits which your incessant labours are yielding. You have set an inspiring and unforgettable example to the rising generation. The Concourse on high is proud of and extols your splendid achievements. Be happy and comforted. Your true and grateful brother,

Shoghi[22]

In these turbulent times in which Burma is going through unprecedented problems, I do not have a moment to answer letters sent to me or write a supplication to the beloved Guardian of the Faith. In the last days of July, a great uprising started in Rangoon and has spread to all other cities and villages in Burma. The largest of the troubles is in Rangoon and Mandalay. Buddhists attacked foreigners and burnt some mosques. . . . It is not safe until now. The government has announced Martial Law. The situation continued until the end of July and the uprising reached Kunjan which is where we live. They attacked everything and looted stores. There is a police station behind our house. But although several times we sent someone to inform them that our house had been attacked, no one helped. At about 11:00 p.m. several police cars arrived at the stores behind our house, which we have gifted in the name of the beloved Guardian. They started arresting people. I went to the door and to the chief of police to beg him for help. He ordered me to immediately go back inside, lock the door, and stay there; otherwise I would be killed.

On 31 September 1938, the rabble attacked houses in our area again and broke doors and looted everything. When they came to our house, they could not break the door and left. That night at the insistence of my ailing wife, we moved to the house of a Muslim neighbor who was a policeman. We stayed awake the whole night but because this house was next to the police station we were not harmed. We went home in the morning and locked all the doors and stayed inside. Although friends and neighbors insisted that we move to the policeman's house, I did not agree because he did not want me to take the box of my books and papers with us. We remained in our own house with our Burmese servant. He had been with us for a long time. Some Muslims at night wanted to attack our house and the shops, but some others prevented them and said these belong to a Siyyid and should not be looted.

It was our beloved Guardian who saved us. Our meetings and gatherings are curtailed and we are alone in the house and have no one, but I rely on the bounty of my beloved Guardian. The people of the village of 'Abdu'l-Bahá, Kungyangon, are safe and continue their life and work. Route 34, where the Bahá'í Center is located, is safe. All uprisings were around here. But praise be God, we are safe. No one is paying rent anymore and people are hungry and miserable. We need prayers . . .[23]

March 2 1939 [To Mr. Vakil]

. . . I trust that by now a better understanding and more substantial cooperation has been attained by the friends of India and Burma. It is for the delegates who are to be chosen by them this year, to elect those whom they think are best qualified for membership of the National Spiritual Assembly, and once elected, the unity and efficiency of this body must at any cost be maintained. I cannot but pray that they may be guided in their choice and discharge honourably their functions. For yourself, I shall offer with a grateful heart my fervent prayers. Your true brother,

Shoghi[24]

2 October 1939

MARTHA'S UNNUMBERED ADMIRERS THROUGHOUT BAHÁ'Í WORLD LAMENT WITH ME EARTHLY EXTINCTION HER HEROIC LIFE. CONCOURSE ON HIGH ACCLAIM HER ELEVATION RIGHTFUL POSITION GALAXY BAHÁ'Í IMMORTALS. POSTERITY WILL ESTABLISH HER AS FOREMOST HAND WHICH 'ABDU'L-BAHÁ'S WILL HAS RAISED UP FIRST BAHÁ'Í CENTURY. PRESENT GENERATION HER FELLOW-BELIEVERS RECOGNIZE HER FIRST FINEST FRUIT FORMATIVE AGE FAITH BAHÁ'U'LLÁH HAS AS YET PRODUCED. ADVISE HOLD BEFITTING MEMORIAL GATHERING TEMPLE HONOR ONE WHOSE ACTS SHED IMPERISHABLE LUSTER AMERICAN BAHÁ'Í COMMUNITY. IMPELLED SHARE WITH NATIONAL ASSEMBLY EXPENSES ERECTION MONUMENT SYMBOLIC SPOT MEETING-PLACE EAST WEST TO BOTH WHICH SHE UNSPARINGLY DEDICATED FULL FORCE MIGHTY ENERGIES.[25]

According to the instruction of the beloved Guardian, the friends of Rangoon and Daydanaw convened special memorial meetings in remembrance of our dear sister Martha Root.

December 8, 1939

Your very kind message . . . expressing your profound sorrow and sympathy at the passing away of our beloved sister Miss Martha Root has just reached our dear Guardian, and he feels indeed most deeply touched by the very thoughtful words which you had been moved to convey to him. The loss which the entire Bahá'í world has come to sustain through her untimely departure from this world is indeed enormous, and can be compensated only partially by the self-sacrificing efforts which our dear Bahá'í teachers in East and West are now exerting in their respective fields of teaching.

The Guardian's hope, however, is that, spurred by the noble example of Martha's life and character, the friends in every land will make a supreme and united effort to carry onward the great teaching task which she had so untiringly been endeavouring to accomplish during all these years, and thus bring eternal joy and impart infinite hope and solace to her heart in the other world.

I deeply appreciate, and am greatly touched by, the noble sentiments you have expressed. The passing of dearest Martha, that distinguished hero of the Cause of Bahá'u'lláh, is indeed a great loss to those who labour for His Cause, both in the East and West. May her glorious example continue to inspire the friends in India and Burma to tread in her footsteps, and to extend the work she so nobly initiated.[26]

After months of illness, my dear wife, Ḥalímih Khánum, the faithful servant of the beloved Guardian passed away peacefully. She was eighty-one years old. . . .[27]

1940–41

I am now eighty-eight years old. My eyes are weak, and writing has become difficult. However, I have translated some Bahá'í books into the Burmese language. . . . Burma is completely different now and most of the people are in difficulty. I have been to my eye doctor, and, with the blessings of Bahá'u'lláh, with his medication I can see well. He had to operate on my left eye and I am using drops regularly in both eyes. . . .[28]

- 19 -

PASSING TO THE ABHÁ KINGDOM OF SIYYID MUṢṬAFÁ RÚMÍ

HONORED BY THE GUARDIAN AS HAND OF THE CAUSE OF BAHÁ'U'LLÁH, APOSTLE OF BAHÁ'U'LLÁH, PIONEER, AND MARTYR

Siyyid Muṣṭafá was now alone and, as he wrote, "feeble." However, in spite of physical difficulties and turmoil in the country, he valiantly continued to translate the Bahá'í writings into Burmese, hoping that one day they would be published and distributed.

The Guardian continued writing to the National Spiritual Assembly of India and Burma about Burma and Siyyid Muṣṭafá, although his letters and telegrams reached the friends after a long delay:

November 28, 1940

To NSA of India and Burma

Dear valued co-workers:

I regret that owing to present circumstances arising from the war and its grave repercussions, the activities, particularly in the teaching field, connected with the Six Year Plan, so spontaneously initiated by your

Assembly, have had to be curtailed. I wish to appeal, however, to all its members, and through them to the general body of the devoted friends in India and Burma, to make a united and supreme endeavour to overcome, while there is yet time, the obstacles that stand in their way, and to refuse to allow the perils, the uncertainties and anxieties that face and afflict their country to deter them from carrying out the original plan they have so nobly conceived. Let them remember that a firm resolution on their part, an absolute re-dedication of their resources, and an actual attempt to translate into action their meritorious intentions, coupled with perseverance in the discharge of their duties, would suffice to ensure the success of the mission to which they are now committed. The time is indeed ripe, and the minds and hearts of the suffering multitudes are being mysteriously prepared for the Great Message that can alone redeem, exalt and regenerate a sore tried and bewildered humanity. I will specially and fervently pray for the success of any and every effort the dearly beloved friends in India and Burma may arise to exert. Your true and grateful brother,

Shoghi[1]

DECEMBER 12, 1941

WIRE NEWS SAFETY FRIENDS RANGOON MANDALAY PARTICULARLY DISTINGUISHED BELOVED SIYYID MUSTAFA ASSURE THEM FERVENT PRAYERS.

SHOGHI[2]

FEBRUARY 22, 1942

WIRE SAFETY FRIENDS MANDALAY ASSURE THEM CONTINUED PRAYERS.

SHOGHI[3]

MARCH 26, 1942

ANXIOUS NEWS MANDALAY FRIENDS. ASSURE THEM CONSTANT REMEMBRANCE FERVENT PRAYERS.

SHOGHI[4]

MAY 4, 1945

ANXIOUS NEWS DEARLY BELOVED BAHA'I FRIENDS MANDALAY RANGOON PARTICULARLY SEYYED MUSTAFA.

SHOGHI[5]

These telegrams reached the friends after the martyrdom of Siyyid Muṣṭafá, which occurred on 13 March 1945. The Bahá'ís on several occasions had begged Siyyid Muṣṭafá to leave Kungyangon for a safer place as his life was at risk. He refused to do so and preferred to remain with his spiritual children in 'Abdu'l-Bahá's village.

On 13 March 1945, the village was attacked by a mob of 3,000 people who surrounded it in order to "purge it from all foreign influence." The Bahá'í school, the Ḥaẓíratu'l-Quds, and many Bahá'í homes were burned to the ground and property was looted. Eleven Bahá'ís were killed in the attack. The mob offered to let Siyyid Muṣṭafá leave the village due to his advanced age, but he refused to do so.

They then burned his home with all his precious papers and books, and took his life. Later the Bahá'ís gathered his remains and buried him in front of the burned Bahá'í Center.[6] The news of this tragic event was sent to the Guardian but reached him after significant delay. In response the Guardian, in a telegram to the National Spiritual Assembly, expressed the following:

JULY 14, 1945

HEARTS GRIEF STRICKEN PASSING SUPREME CONCOURSE DISTINGUISHED PIONEER FAITH BAHA'U'LLAH DEARLY BELOVED STAUNCH HIGH MINDED NOBLE SOUL SIYYID MUSTAFA. LONG RECORD HIS SUPERB SERVICES BOTH TEACHING ADMINISTRATIVE FIELDS SHED LUSTRE ON BOTH HEROIC AND FORMATIVE AGES BAHA'I DISPENSATION. HIS MAGNIFICENT ACHIEVEMENTS FULLY ENTITLE HIM JOIN RANKS HANDS CAUSE BAHA'U'LLAH. HIS RESTING PLACE SHOULD BE REGARDED FOREMOST SHRINE COMMUNITY BURMESE BELIEVERS. ADVISE HOLDING MEMORIAL GATHERINGS

THROUGHOUT INDIA HONOUR HIS IMPERISHABLE MEMORY. URGE INDIAN BURMESE BAHA'IS PARTICIPATE CONSTRUCTION TOMB. CABLING THREE HUNDRED POUNDS MY PERSONAL CONTRIBUTION SO PRAISEWORTHY PURPOSE.

SHOGHI[7]

August 9, 1945

. . . He was deeply grieved to hear of the death of our very dear and esteemed Bahá'í brother, Siyyid Mustafa. He was truly an example of steadfast devotion and one of the outstanding pioneers the Faith produced during the first century of its existence. He was also very sad to hear of the ruin of the Bahá'í Hazíratu'l-Quds and the plight of the Bahá'ís in general. He wishes your Assembly to exert its utmost in alleviating the suffering of the Burmese friends, and assisting them in every way possible. Convey to them all the assurance of his ardent and loving prayers on their behalf, and for the speedy re-establishment of the Faith and its institutions in Burma . . .[8]

November 7, 1945

GREATLY DEPLORE TRIBULATIONS AFFECTING DEARLY BELOVED BURMESE FRIENDS. PROFOUNDLY MOVED CIRCUMSTANCES ATTENDING ASSASSINATION HEROIC APOSTLE BAHA'U'LLAH SEYYED MUSTAFA AND ASSOCIATES. ADMIRE UNQUENCHABLE SPIRIT ANIMATING LONG SUFFERING BRETHREN RANGOON MANDALAY DAIDANAW ASSURE THEM ADMIRATION GRATITUDE STRONG ATTACHMENT. FERVENT PRAYERS REVIVAL ACTIVITIES. SOON TRANSMITTING ONE THOUSAND POUNDS MY CONTRIBUTION RELIEF, REBUILDING INSTITUTIONS PROMOTION TEACHING ACTIVITIES. URGE NATIONAL ASSEMBLY DEVOTE IMMEDIATE CONCENTRATED CONTINUAL ATTENTION PROMOTION VITAL INTERESTS BURMESE COMMUNITY.

SHOGHI[9]

December 18, 1945

. . . He was very sad to read of the sufferings of the beloved Burmese friends, of the death of that bright star of the Faith, Siyyid Mustafa, and of the murder of many other of the friends! At the same time his heart swelled with pride when he saw that already the believers have re-assembled, elected an Assembly, and started their school again. This shows how deep their faith is, and presages a glorious future for the Cause there. . . .[10]

August 2, 1946

[In the Guardian's handwriting.]

. . . *A special effort must simultaneously be exerted to provide whatever is required to reestablish the long-suffering and dearly loved Burmese Community on a secure foundation. The dispatch of competent teachers and visitors, to that sorely-tried land; the extension of the necessary relief to those who are still in need; the reconstruction of the administrative headquarters and the re-establishment of the Bahá'í school; the construction of the memorial to the beloved and unforgettable pioneer and martyr Siyyid Mustafa; the formation of Assemblies and Groups in as many localities as possible—these constitute the immediate tasks confronting your Assembly in addition to the responsibilities you are called upon to discharge under the new Plan.*

No sacrifice can be deemed too great for the achievement of this dual purpose, no effort should be spared in order to carry out in its entirety this twofold objective. May the Beloved grant you the strength you require for the accomplishment of your historic task. Your true brother,

Shoghi[11]

Exterior of the Shrine of Hand of the Cause of God Siyyid Muṣṭafá Rúmí.

Interior of the Shrine.

The headstone of the grave of Siyyid Muṣṭafá Rúmí. The date of the martyrdom of Siyyid Muṣṭafá appears to be incorrect on his headstone as it is reported to have taken place on 13 March 1945. Based on the birthdate he gives in his memoirs, 5 January 1852, he would have been ninety-three years old at the time of his passing. However, his gravestone indicates his age to have been ninety-nine. There are also instances in his correspondence where he gives his age but it doesn't align with his date of birth. It is possible, as was common at the time, that his date of birth was uncertain.

APPENDIX I
VISITORS TO BURMA

The following accounts of prominent Bahá'í visitors to Burma are from the memoirs of Siyyid Muṣṭafá Rúmí.

1904

In 1904 A.D., Áqá Mírzá Maḥmúd Zarqání came to Burma from India; and, thereafter between 1904 and 1905 a group of Oriental and Occidental friends visited Burma. Mr. Harris, Mr. Ober, Mr. Remey and Mr. Struven, all Americans; Mr. Dreyfus Barney from Paris; Jináb-i-Adíb and Jináb-i-Ibn-i-Abhar from Tehran, Persia; and Mírzá Maḥram from Bombay with Mr. Sydney Sprague. They gave many lectures in Rangoon, which were duly printed and published by the Bahá'í Assembly of Rangoon. They also went to see the Mandalay friends, and after sowing the seeds of the great Cause, returned to their respective countries, entrusting the service of watering the plants to the Bahá'ís of Rangoon. No. 20 Sparks Street was publicly declared to be the Bahá'í Hall.

1913–14

On 28 March 1913, I was invited by Rev. Armstrong of the American Baptist Mission in Rangoon to give a speech in Urdu and English in their union hall about the universal Bahá'í Movement to an audience of all denominations: Muslims, Hindus, Buddhists, and Christians. In November of the same year I visited Daidanow Kalazoo, Kungyangon village and joined with friends in the sacred meeting of the day of 'Abdu'l-Bahá, and returned to Mandalay. After my arrival I received a telegram, dated 6 December 1913 from Lua Getsinger, stating that she and Dr. Getsinger were in Bombay at the instruction of the Master to teach the Cause in India. I was asked to join them as soon as I could.

This was just after the passing of our revered teacher, Mírzá Maḥram, in Bombay on 9 December 1913. I left immediately and arrived in Bombay on the fifteenth via Calcutta and Jabalpur. I met Dr. and Mrs. Getsinger and also the revered Mrs. Stannard. Mr. Shírází of Karachi invited Mrs. J. Stannard to go to Karachi to attend the various ongoing conferences. She kindly asked me to accompany her and we left for Karachi via Ahmedabad, Marwar, Hyderabad (Sindh), and Kotry junctions. On the afternoon of 20 December we arrived in Karachi where Prof. Shírází was awaiting us at the railway station.

In Karachi we were the guests of Prof. Shírází. On the evenings of December 21, 22, and 23 Mrs. Stannard gave eloquent speeches in the Theosophical Hall before an audience of hundreds. On 26 December 1913, through the introduction of Prof. Shírází, we had the opportunity to meet the leaders of the Brahma Semaj Society in the house of Mr. Sen, the photographer and president of the Karachi Semaj, who is the elder brother of Mr. Promo Tolall Sen, chief of the society in Calcutta, the follower of the late Keshub Chandra Sen. The other guests consisted of: Mr. Cowar, the editor of The New Dispensation, of Calcutta; Mr. Hassaram, the secretary of this society in Karachi, which is celebrated at the Theistic conference; Mr. Shinde, the secretary of the Pararthana Semaj Bombay, "Rao Bahadur"; Mr. Chanravarkar, the minister of the state of Indore India; and, the Rev. Dr. Sunderlal, a representative of the Unitarians of America. In Prof. Shírází's house we also met with Dewan Tara Chand Mukhim and Mr. Phool Chand, president of the municipality of Hyderabad (Sindh). Prof. Shírází kindly provided a dinner on 2 January 1914.

Mrs. Stannard was asked to speak in the Theistic conference about the Bahá'í Cause. Dr. Sunderlal highly commended her speech. We had the privilege of seeing Mr. Bernard Temple of London, then editor of the Sind Gazette, Karachi. I asked Mrs. Stannard's permission to return to Bombay as I had nothing to do in Karachi. On 3 January I left for Bombay. I met many dignified souls on the train who were returning from the Congress and delivered the Bahá'í Message to all of them. On the morning of 5 January I arrived at Bombay. Here Mrs. Lua Getsinger and I met many honorable personages from different communities. She gave several speeches in the Bombay Theosophical Society hall and the Parathna Semaj hall. She gave the Message to many souls who became interested in the Cause. Mr. Vakil invited her to go to Surat and she visited many people and was invited to their homes for dinner and tea parties.

The Collector of Surat, a high government official, who was a European, in his remarks mentioned the names of two American Bahá'í ladies who had visited Bombay and Poona some time ago. . . . The British government had not been happy with their activities. Consequently, he suspected our revered sister Lua also. She tried her best to pacify him, but he insisted on his skeptical ideas and opposed her giving speeches anymore in Surat. She told him plainly that erelong he will suffer the consequences of such selfish motives. Within a month, he was suspended and had to come to Bombay to answer some serious charges brought against him. Lua met the ruling prince of Baroda state in the Bombay Taj Mahal hotel, and delivered the holy message to him. He was a very tolerant personage, with a liberal mind and devoid of prejudice. He promised to follow the sacred Teachings, but as a principal standard bearer of the state he could not change his hereditary faith of Hinduism. He went to Europe within a week and promised to see Bahá'í friends there and assist the Cause.

Dr. Getsinger also was busily engaged in the divine service; he had awakened the Bombay Parsees from their long slumber by publishing his effective articles in the renowned and widely circulated Gujrati Vernacular and in English papers and magazines of the Bombay Parsee Community. His booklet entitled "Universal Religion" and his three articles that were published in one of the daily papers called *Jám-i-Jamshíd* were witness to his extended services in Bombay.

1923

On 2 January 1923, our revered Bahá'í sister Mrs. J. Stannard arrived in Mandalay from Rangoon. She was cordially received and according to her direction we engaged a house for her in the Bahá'í neighborhood. She was taken to her house, which was on the highway near the Bahá'í Hall and was decently furnished by the Bahá'í friends of Mandalay. She stayed for a few months and was busy in delivering the great message to the interested souls who visited her. She gave many lectures in the Theosophy Hall and then went to live in Maymyo,[1] a summer hill resort in Burma. She lived there for a couple of months and after doing some splendid work for the holy Cause returned to Rangoon. She went to Europe via India and the Holy Land. In India she also rendered great services to the Cause.

1924

About the end of April 1924, Mrs. Schopflocher of Montreal, Canada, visited Rangoon. During her short stay in India and Burma she wrote beautiful articles about the Cause in leading newspapers in Rangoon and Calcutta and spoke at the Theosophical Society. Her addresses were received with great enthusiasm. She met the Bahá'ís in Daidanow Kalazoo village, Kungyangon, and Mandalay. Everyone who met her had a new spirit to serve the Cause. She also interviewed Sir Harcourt Butler, the Governor of Burma, in the Government House, where she was honorably received.

1925

Revered sisters Mrs. Greeven of New York and Mrs. Haggarty with her young daughter and sister-in-law, arrived in Rangoon on 22 January 1925. The friends in Rangoon were extremely happy to meet them. I had the privilege of first meeting Mrs. Cook at the Holy Land in 1921 in the holy presence of our beloved Master 'Abdu'l-Bahá. On 27 January they gave a short visit to the Bahá'ís of Kungyangon, returning the same day to Rangoon.

I informed the village friends about our visit and requested that they provide a Persian dish for our guests. It was ready on our arrival and all of us enjoyed the gathering with utmost pleasure. The missionaries helped

Mrs. Cook to take some group photographs with a little camera she had brought with her. The missionaries proceeded with their further journey and Mrs. Cook delivered her eloquent loving discourse for an hour. They left for home on 29 January 1925.

On 24 March 1925, we were blessed by the arrival in Rangoon of our dearly revered Bahá'í friend Mr. S. Schopflocher of Montreal Canada. On the following evening he attended the meeting of the Bahá'í Assembly of Rangoon and delivered a most impressive speech on the teaching of the Cause. His zeal, his earnestness, and his firmness infused a new spirit in all of us and afforded a fresh incentive to serve the august Cause under whose influence such union of the East and West has become possible. Early on the morning of the 26th, accompanied by Mírzá Maḥmúd Zarqání, S. M. Roumie, and other friends from Rangoon he proceeded to Daidanow Kalazoo, Kungyangon and spent the whole day there in the pleasant company of those modest but extremely dear friends who live a quiet but happy and peaceful life in the little village. He attended the meeting of the Spiritual Assembly of Rangoon and before bidding farewell to the friends delivered a beautiful address on the life and teachings of his holiness the Prophet Muḥammad, which deeply moved the few Muhammadan enquirers who happened to be present. On the afternoon of the 28th, he left Rangoon for Calcutta en route to Bombay and other cities of India.

1926

Áqá Mírzá Munír Nabílzadeh, a distinguished Bahá'í teacher of Persia, was sent by the beloved Guardian of the Cause to India. In November 1926 he arrived in India. It was arranged that he should stay in India for a year. Burma was also included in his tour. He stayed for about three or four months, mostly in Bombay, and paid occasional visits to other places. On 12 November he visited Surat, and on the 13th he addressed the students of a Persian class of the M.B.T. art college on the past and present of Persia. He met the principal and professors of the college and discussed the Bahá'í Cause and its teachings. He attended the Arya Semaj

Conference at Lahore and delivered a most impressive address on salvation that was translated by Maḥfúẓ'ul Ḥaq Ilmí, editor of the Bahá'í journal in Urdu, *Kaukabi Hind.* During his stay in the Elphiustone Hotel, Lahore, many interested enquirers came to see him to discuss the history and the Bahá'í principles. Jináb-i-Nabílzadeh, accompanied by Jináb-i-Ilmí, also paid visits to the leading citizens of the Lahore town and interested many of them in the Bahá'í Cause.

1927

Jináb-i-Nabílzadeh and his nephew 'Alí-Muḥammad, known as Professor Nabílí of Calcutta, arrived in Rangoon on 17 May 1927 and were the guests of Áqá Siyyid 'Abdu'l-Ḥusayn Shírází throughout their stay in Rangoon. On 22 May they went to Daidanow Kalazoo village, Kungyangon, and returned to Rangoon on 24 May 1927. They left Rangoon again on 28 May, reaching Mandalay on 29 May 1927.

The young men of Mandalay had their own meeting called "Ánjuman-i-Khádimin-i-Mítháq," or the "Assembly of the Servants of the Covenant," established and confirmed by a holy Tablet of our beloved Master 'Abdu'l-Bahá. Jináb-i-Nabílzadeh, in proposing many reforms, newly established a committee called "Khádimat" or "Service" under the auspices of the Local Assembly.

Jináb-i-Nabílzadeh returned to Rangoon on 7 June, and on 11 June he delivered a public lecture in the Y.M.C.A. Rangoon town branch and on 12 June at the Rangoon Theosophical Society. His subject was "Bahá'ism and its need in the world." The addresses in both places were as inspiring and instructive as they were eloquent and impressive and were translated into English by his nephew, Professor Nabílí. At the request of the Bahá'í Assembly of Rangoon, his excellency the governor graciously granted an interview to Jináb-i-Nabílzadeh on 13 June 1927. A group photograph of the Rangoon Bahá'ís was also taken on 12 June, and on the morning of 14 June all the friends met at the Rangoon wharf to bid farewell to both distinguished guests on the day of their sailing for Calcutta. During his stay in Rangoon, Jináb-i-Nabílzadeh proposed various suggestions for the advancements of the Cause in Burma, which were appreciated by the Rangoon friends.

The following proposals were carried out by the Rangoon Bahá'ís:

1. The opening of a children's class for religious teaching.
2. The establishment of a women's committee.
3. The construction of a Mashriqu'l-Adhkár in Rangoon. The last proposal is now carried out in 1932 with our dear generous Bahá'í brother Áqá Siyyid Maḥmúd Shírází—son of the late Áqá Siyyid Isma'il Shírází and the grandson of Jináb-i-Áqá Ḥájí Siyyid Mihdí Shírází, the first Bahá'í in Rangoon—having built a Ḥaẓíratu'l-Quds Bahá'í prayer hall independently with his own money at the cost of 15,000/- or thereabouts.

Our Bahá'í sister Mrs. Schopflocher of Canada visited Rangoon again on 25 February 1927. She is said to have come from the Holy Land via Baghdád and thenceforth by airplane to India. In accordance with the directions received from the Guardian of the Cause she proceeded to the new Bahá'í village, Kyigon in the Shwebo District of upper Burma, visiting the friends at Mandalay on her way. Thus she left for Mandalay on the 26th, arriving there on 27 February 1927. She was cordially welcomed by the Mandalay Bahá'ís, who were lovingly waiting to receive her at the railway station on her arrival.

In the company of several friends from Mandalay, with Miss Mya Mya to translate her talks into Burmese, she left for Kungyangon on the same day. Jináb-i-Khalífa Muḥammad Yúnis, alias Ko Po Thwai of Mandalay, sent his son Yúsuf before her arrival to arrange everything for her reception. Bahá'ís and non-Bahá'ís all were present at the railway station to welcome her with motorcars and several bullock carts. Khalífa Ṣáḥib of Mandalay came and delivered the message to the villagers and introduced her to them. Three young men declared themselves Bahá'ís during her visit.

Mrs. Schopflocher, in writing about her experience of the village states, "It was a beautiful village of about three hundred inhabitants, the houses were made of bamboo and nestled among papaya, tamarind and palm trees. The whole village came to visit me and the headman, a Buddhist, was very kind and invited me to return sometime. He said he believed in justice and would do what he could for the Bahá'í believers. I told him I was a Bahá'í, and as Bahá'u'lláh said, 'Justice is loved above all.' He was delighted; we had great success in every way. The government has a nice rest-house one mile away where we all slept for the night and took bullock carts in the morning to the village. The whole village had been cleaned up overnight and was expecting us."

After staying a day in the village she went to Rangoon. She generously paid for two copies of *The Dawn* to be sent to two friends in Kungyangon, whose names and addresses she had given, simply for establishing a spiritual link between the village Bahá'ís and the Rangoon friends. Mrs. Schopflocher arrived in Rangoon from Mandalay on the afternoon of 4 March and left by a mail boat for Calcutta on the morning of 5 March 1927.

1928

TEACHING TOUR OF JINÁB-I-MAWLAWÍ FAḌIL SIYYID MAḤFÚ'UL ḤAQ ILMÍ

Jináb-i-Maḥfúẓ'ul Ḥaq Ilmí, editor of the Bahá'í Urdu journal, *Kaukabi Hind,* left his headquarters in Delhi on 5 August 1928. He visited Aligarh, Cawnpore, Etawah, and Allahabad and delivered the divine message in these cities. He then attended the centenary of the Brahmo Semaj, held in Calcutta on 19 August 1928. At this conference, delegates representing the Zoroastrians, Arya Semajis Theosophists, Hindus, Brahmo Semajis, Buddhists, Christians, Rama Krishna mission, Salvation Army, Muslims, and Bahá'ís were present. The delegates who represented the Bahá'ís were:

1. Mr. N.R. Vakil, BA LLB, President and Treasurer of the Bahá'í National Spiritual Assembly of India and Burma.
2. Mr. Isfandíyár K. B. Bakhtíyárí, President B.S.A. Karachi.
3. Mr. Isfandíyár Bahram, President B.S.A. Bombay
4. Mr. Bahmard Behram, a member B.S.A. Bombay
5. Mr. Mihribán Khodadad

6. Mr. Firaydún Húrmuzdíyár
7. Mr. Khusraw Húrmuzdíyár, Secretary B.S.A. Karachi
8. Jináb-i-Maḥfúẓ'ul Ḥaq Ilmí, editor of the Bahá'í Urdu journal, Delhi
9. Mr. S. Ḥishmatu'lláh Qurashí, Secretary N.S.A. India and Burma

Jináb-i-Ilmí, after leaving Calcutta, proceeded to his native home, Chittagong, where he addressed several meetings of the enlightened citizens on the Bahá'í Cause and created great interest. He is a learned scholar and is well versed in Arabic, Persian, and Urdu.

He arrived at Rangoon on 11 September 1928. He was the guest of Siyyid Jináb-i-'Alí, the chairman of the Rangoon Bahá'í Spiritual Assembly. He left for Daidanow Kalazoo, Kungyangon on the 16th with a party of friends, and returned to Rangoon the next day. His arrival was announced in two leading English papers, "Rangoon Gazette" and "Rangoon Times," inviting enquirers about the Bahá'í religion.

On 27 September 1928, he delivered a most impressive address on "The Message of Love and Peace" at the hall of "Khalsa Anglo-Vernacular School," under the auspices of Ajut Mirind Kumar Sabha. Dr. Anup Singh was president of the said Sabha who arranged everything to make the meeting successful. The meeting was presided over by Dr. Randheer Singh. Mr. Ilmí dwelt at length on the history of the Bahá'í martyrs who manifested the highest form of love, namely love of God. He quoted some passages from the religious books of the Sikhs by way of illustration, which was very much appreciated by the audience.

At the conclusion of the address the president in a few well-chosen words expressed his great appreciation of the speech of Mr. Ilmí and the principles advocated by the Bahá'ís. Then the chairman of the Spiritual Assembly of Rangoon conveyed the appreciation of the Bahá'ís of Rangoon to the management of Ajit Mirgind Kumar Sabha.[2]

He left Rangoon on 28 September 1928, accompanied by two very promising Bahá'í youths, Siyyid Maḥmúd Shírází and Siyyid Ḥishmat 'Alí, a medical student in the Burma University and the son of Dr. Siyyid

Maẓhar 'Alí S̲h̲áh, who accepted the Cause during the time of Jináb-i-Mírzá Maḥram while he was in Burma.

On the following day, 29 October, they arrived in Maymyo, which is the summer residence of the Government of Burma. On the way they were met at the Mandalay railway station by some of the members of the Bahá'í Spiritual Assembly of Mandalay. At Maymyo they were the guests of Siyyid Maẓhar 'Alí S̲h̲áh, who was a medical officer in charge of the staff in the government house. Soon after their arrival at Maymyo, several Muslims—both Sunní and S̲h̲í'ih, as well as members of the Aḥmadíyyih sect—interviewed Jináb-i-Ilmí, and a lively discussion on the various phases of the Bahá'í movement followed. He answered all their questions completely and satisfactorily. On 2 October he was invited to talk in the Muslim Library, where he met a selected number of enlightened Muslims. Here he delivered a very stirring speech. His theme was that every religion at its source is perfectly pure; it infuses in people a new spirit and ushers in a new civilization. As time passes its potentiality gradually is lost and fails to exercise the same influence on the life of the people. The decline of its pristine power becomes more and more noticeable. At such a period the Almighty, in the interest of the preservation of the human race, reveals a new order and instills new life. Blessed are those who avail themselves of the quickening influence of the new Revelation. It is no good to speak proudly of your achievements and admire them. Take stock of your present position, then only you will realize that what you possess does not satisfy your present requirements.

In the course of his address he cited numerous verses from the Holy Qur'án in support of his statements. The speech was highly impressive.

On 4 October Jináb-i-Ilmí delivered a lecture in the United Club. He spoke in Urdu on the "Present Needs of the World" and Siyyid Ḥis̲h̲mat 'Alí translated his talk into English. At the conclusion of his talk the president of the club, a member of the Brahmo Semaj, spoke very highly of the principles and teachings advocated by the Bahá'í movement and said that he considered Bahá'ism to be at the forefront of all religions in the present age.

Jináb-i-Ilmí left Maymyo on 6 October for Mandalay. He and his companions were given a most cordial reception by the Mandalay Bahá'ís.

On 10 October Jináb-i-Ilmí delivered a lecture at the Theosophical Society Hall. His subject was "The Light of the New Day." The speech created great interest and some of the audience asked questions, which were answered very satisfactorily.

Owing to breaks in the railway line, they could not proceed to Kyigon, Shwebo district,[3] where a new Bahá'í center had been recently formed. They decided to go to Monywa,[4] in response to the invitation received from our Bahá'í brother, Dr. M. A. Latiff, who was employed in the government hospital of that city.

On 10 October 1928, they left for Monywa, reaching there on the 11th. They stayed there as Dr. Latiff's guests until the 14th. On Friday the 12th, Jináb-i-Ilmí delivered a sermon after their usual Friday prayer, in the mosque at Monywa, in response to the request of the mullá, who was a very broadminded and enlightened gentleman. Our friend, as a true Bahá'í, availed himself fully of this opportunity and spoke in a most impressive language on the Bahá'í teachings of universal peace, universal love, the oneness of the world of humanity, and the abandonment of all prejudices. On the same day at about 8:00 p.m., Dr. Latiff arranged a lecture at the Arya Semaj. This was Jináb-i-Ilmí's only public lecture at Monywa. The audience was a mixed one consisting of Hindus, Muslims, Sikhs, Arya Semajists, and a few Christians. They all rejoiced to hear the glad-tidings and the twelve basic Bahá'í principles. The president of the meeting, who was a Sikh gentleman and a leader of the Sikh community, was very much impressed and in his closing remarks stated that what really struck him was the broad ideas and high ideals of the Bahá'í religion.

The party reached Mandalay on 15 October 1928, with the intention of proceeding to Taunggyi, Southern Shan State, where they were invited by two Bahá'í residents. However, at the repeated request of friends in

Mandalay, Jináb-i-Ilmí consented to speak again. Accordingly a lecture was arranged at the Theosophical Society Hall on the 18th. It was further arranged that Miss Hla Hla, the first Bahá'í lady graduate of Burma, would speak on the "History of the Bahá'í Movement." The subject of Mr. Ilmí's address was "We Are One." His address was translated from Urdu into English.

On 19 October 1928, Jináb-i-Ilmí, with Siyyid Maḥmúd Shírází, left Mandalay for Taunggyi.[5] This was a long and arduous journey of about 170 miles from Mandalay. On the morning of their departure it became known that, as was the case at Kyigon, there was a breach on this line also. But Mr. Ilmí this time was determined to go to Taunggyi at any cost and declined to cancel this journey. On arrival at the railway station, they heard about the unsafety of the road to Taunggyi, which was again ninety-six miles from their halting station. In spite of all this disheartening news, with great difficulty they boarded a bus that was already overcrowded and departed for Taunggyi. They were welcomed warmly by Mr. 'Abdu'l-Rashíd, who had accepted the Bahá'í Cause in Rangoon and settled there as a P.W.D. contractor. They stayed in Taunggyi until the 27th, during which period there were two public lectures and daily discussions with individual enquirers. They left Taunggyi and returned to Rangoon on 28 October 1928 after a successful tour of one month.

On the morning of 6 November 1928 Jináb-i-Ilmí left by mail boat for Calcutta and returned to Delhi to resume the duties of his editorship of the Urdu Journal, *Kaukabi Hind.*

The majority of the audiences at these lectures was comprised of Indians who temporarily domiciled on business or government service in Burma. Except the educated Burmese who know English, the language of the people of Burma is Burmese—both Buddhist and Muslim communities speak, read, and write in Burmese, so it is very difficult to deliver the message to them in other languages. We found, therefore, that though so many great learned and experienced teachers occasionally visited Burma, we were not able to draw a single soul to the Bahá'í fold during their blessed tours in Burma, but the Holy Cause was widely promulgated.

1932

February 11 1932 [from a letter on behalf of Shoghi Effendi]

> . . . Mrs. Ransom-Kehler has informed us of her trip to India. Shoghi Effendi hopes that the friends will give her all the necessary facilities to make of her tour a real success. The report of her work in Australia and New Zealand has been brilliant. There is no reason why she should not do the same in India and Burma if she is given the chance, and be put in touch with really open-minded and interested people. In America she is considered among the first class national teachers and is well informed as to the progress of modern thought and the teachings of the Cause. Maybe she will be able to give a new impetus to the teaching work. . . .
>
> He trusts that through the efforts of you and the other members of the National Assembly the Cause will take a real lead in uniting the different elements existing in India and turn the face of its people to the light of God shining through Bahá'u'lláh.

Your most welcome letter interrupting a prolonged silence on your part, has brought joy and strength to my heart. I will most assuredly pray for your complete recovery, for in you the Cause in India has an invaluable asset which I, for my part, greatly value and prize. I trust and pray that Mrs. Kehler's visit will lend a fresh impetus to the work which you are so ably conducting. I would certainly advise her to prolong her stay in your midst if it is practicable for her to do so. It is a splendid opportunity which the friends in India should utilize to the utmost possible extent. May the Beloved bless and reinforce your high endeavours, remove every obstacle from your path, and enable you at once to broaden and reinforce the foundations of the Faith in that troubled land.

Mrs. Keith Ransom-Kehler arrived at Rangoon on 24 February. We welcomed and cordially received her. She arrived in Mandalay at 6:20 a.m. on 17 February, and was escorted by all the Mandalay Bahá'í friends to the house where Miss Martha Root had stayed. She delivered a lecture in the theosophical lodge at 6:30 p.m.. Her subject was "Is universal brotherhood possible?" the meeting was presided over by Mr. Pertab Singh, Cantonment Executive Officer of Mandalay. There was a large number of people and all of them were highly interested in her eloquent speech. Although she is advanced in age, about sixty-six years, she sacrificed herself in the service of the Beloved and the well-being of mankind.

She delivered a lecture in the town public library in China street, and her subject was "The Great Message of Bahá'u'lláh." The chairman was the secretary of the Mandalay municipality. A large multitude was present, and, except for an American Christian missionary lady who was the head-mistress of the Christian girls high school, all were highly interested. The said lady was exceedingly annoyed, especially when she heard that Keith was to deliver a lecture the next day at Maymyo. She was astonished by Keith's magnetic speech, particularly when she heard her answering very ably all questions put to her by several inquirers of different denominations and creeds.

The Maymyo people invited her once more for delivering a lecture and many cultured people, even from Mandalay, went to attend this meeting. The government Anglo Vernacular high school was selected as the venue and her subject was "The Universal Brotherhood."

Mrs. F. E. Schopflocher and Mr. L. H. Loveday also safely arrived from Bhamo and accompanied Mrs. Keith Ransom-Kehler to Maymyo. As she had no time, according to her program, to stay any longer, she left Mandalay for Rangoon and Daidanow Kalazoo, Kungyangon with Mrs. Schopflocher and Mr. Loveday. Mr. Faqír Muḥammad, of the Mandalay Bahá'í Spiritual Assembly also accompanied them.

The Rangoon friends arranged three more lectures for Mrs. Kehler, the announcement of which was duly published in two leading daily papers—"Rangoon Times" and "Rangoon Gazette"—and a large number of hand bills advertising her lectures were also printed and promptly circulated. The following was the program of her lectures:

1. February 27th, under the auspices of the Bahá'í Spiritual Assembly of Rangoon at the Brahmo Samaj Hall in Rangoon. Subject; "Man's Great Expectation."

2. February 28th, under the auspices of the Theosophical Society of Rangoon. Subject: "The Divine Adventure."

3. February 29th, under the auspices of "Hindu Young Men and Women Association" at the Theosophical Society. Subject: "Women and World Affairs"

All addresses delivered by the learned teacher Mrs. Kehler were extremely impressive; the audience composed of men and women of different beliefs and backgrounds were highly interested. She answered all questions asked her after every lecture so wisely that everyone was satisfied. Both Mrs. N. Sen and Mr. B. R. Rao, who took the chair, expressed their profound appreciation of the glorious principles and teachings advocated by the Bahá'í movement.

The reporter of the *Rangoon Times* who had an interview with Mrs. Kehler, wrote an article to be published with her photograph in the paper.

A meeting of the Bahá'í ladies of Rangoon was held on the evening of 28 February at Áqá Siyyid 'Abdu'l-Ḥusayn Shírází's residence, where Mrs. Kehler addressed the ladies on the teachings of the holy Cause and proposed to them various measures for their spiritual advancement. Before they left, Mr. Loveday took moving pictures of some of the Bahá'í friends of Mandalay including this humble servant.

All of us went to the railway station to see them off and bid farewell with feelings of Bahá'í loving sentiments and grief of separation from these divinely noble souls who are real servants of the world of humanity and the beloved Guardian. On the morning of 1 March 1932, Mrs. Keith Ransom-Kehler left Rangoon for Calcutta in accordance with her program. All the friends of Rangoon went to the wharf to bid her farewell.

CALCUTTA

On 3 March 1932, Mrs. Kehler arrived in Calcutta where she was received by Prof. Pritam Singh, the secretary of the National Spiritual Assembly of the Bahá'ís of India and Burma, who had especially been deputized from Lahore to arrive for her tour program in India. On the evening of that day, the Bahá'ís of Calcutta had arranged a reception at their assembly room, 33 Elliot Road, where prayers were chanted in Urdu, Persian, and English by the friends, and a warm reception and cordial welcome was extended on behalf of the Bahá'ís of Calcutta.

On 4 March she addressed a meeting in the Albert Hall on the "Great Message of Bahá'u'lláh" and spoke like one who is inspired; and in a most learned style she replied to all question which were asked by the audience.

On 5 March 1932, she was invited to a tea party by Dr. B. C. Sinha at his own residence and before a large gathering of Dr. Bengalee's Hindu friends and the Calcutta Bahá'í group, who were invited also. She, in her impressive talk, emphatically established the truth of the Bahá'í Cause to the audience. Dr. Sinha, who for some years past had been taking a keen interest in the divine teachings of Bahá'u'lláh, expressed his great joy for her visit to his home as he was eager to meet the Bahá'í teacher in Calcutta.

Contacts were made in Calcutta with three Hindu organizations on the evenings of 6, 7, and 8 March respectively. At the Theosophical Hall in College Square she spoke on the subject of "Divine Adventure" before a very learned Theosophist audience. They listened to her speech with great interest and attention. She impressed on them the doctrine of "Prophetic Cycles" as enunciated by Bahá'u'lláh. The next contact was made with the Arya Semaj, a reform movement recently introduced by a great learned sage known as Dayanand Saraswati, more than half a century ago. Her subject was "Bahá'í Solutions to World Problems." On the evening of 8 March 1932, Mrs. Kehler spoke on the subject of "Universal Brotherhood" from the platform of the Brahma Semaj, where the Bahá'í twelve basic principles were explained vividly.

[From a letter written on behalf of Shoghi Effendi:]

Shoghi Effendi wishes me to acknowledge the receipt of your letter dated March 14th 1932 informing him about the arrival of Mrs. Ransom-Kehler to Calcutta. He was very glad to know that her visit was successful and that it has very much stimulated the teaching work in that city. He sincerely hopes that as a consequence a number of souls will enter the Cause and be inspired by its divine teachings and ennobling spirit.

Such teachers of the Cause who, with all sincerity and determination, undertake such long trips, should be very much helped by the resident believers if real progress is to be achieved. They ought to be assisted to reach important people, speak to intelligent and receptive audiences, and obtain interviews with persons whose heart is open to the light of God. Otherwise, during their short stay they would, like a helpless man in a strange country, be impotent to achieve their purpose.

Shoghi Effendi is very glad the friends have taken the necessary step to assist Mrs. Ransom-Kehler by appointing Professor Pritam Singh to accompany her in her trip through India. May God help her and help you in proclaiming the Word of God through the length and breadth of that vast land.

BENARES

Mrs. Kehler and Prof. Pritam Singh left Calcutta for Benares on 9 March 1932. Prof. Gurmukh Nihal Singh of the University of Benares had arranged a talk in the club room. The message of Bahá'u'lláh was given to the learned gathering in an impressive style. The next morning, a visit was made to the engineering college and various other colleges within this big Hindu University of Benares—the Theosophical Society Hall, which is the headquarters of the Indian sector, and an old Hindu college, both established by Dr. Annie Besant and raised subsequently in

1915 to the status of a University. Our distinguished teacher Keith delivered a lecture on the "Divine Adventure" to the Theosophists. Prof. K. T. Telang, the general secretary of the Theosophical Society, was present.

LUCKNOW

The next stop was at Lucknow, the seat of another young University in northern India. The first meeting there was arranged by Prof. Radha Kawal Mukerjee. The university arranged an extensive lecture for Mrs. Kehler on the subject of "The youth and the Changing World Order." Prof. Radha Kawal Mukherjee chaired the session.

Another lecture was delivered at the Brahma Semaj Mandir of Lucknow on 13 March 1932, where the message of the Bahá'í movement and its divine teachings was given in a spirit of . . . devotion, inculcating a high spiritual dynamic principle, enunciated by Bahá'u'lláh more than sixty years ago. She left Lucknow for Aligarh the same morning, arriving there in the afternoon. The party met Dr. M. S. Burney at the station and were taken to the officer's rest-house, as there was no hotel in that city.

ALIGARH

Aligarh is a big university center for the Muslim community of India, having been founded in 1885 by Sir Siyyid Aḥmad Khán, a great reformer among the Indian Muslims, under the name of "Muhammadan Anglo-Oriental College, Aligarh." About ten years ago this college was raised to the status of "Muslim University" and it is now the biggest seat of learning for the Muslim community in Asia. It is larger than the Al-Azhar University of Cairo.

Keith and Pritam Singh were pleased to meet the students of this university, who did not let Mrs. Kehler leave Aligarh until she had told them all about the Bahá'í movement. The following three lectures were delivered at the University:

1. March 14th at the university students union. Subject: "The Youth and the Changing World Order."

2. March 15th morning at the university training college. Subject: "Trends in Modern Education."

3. March 15th afternoon at the university intermediate college. Subject: "Character Building."

In the evening, she met a group of the faculty of Aligarh University and gave them an informal talk on the teachings of Bahá'u'lláh. Dr. Burney succeeded in bringing her in touch with the members of the Bar Association of Aligarh, where the message of Bahá'u'lláh was given to some sixty erudite lawyers and barristers practicing law. This contact proved very useful as they asked many questions regarding the Bahá'í movement and received satisfactory answers.

AGRA

On the afternoon of 16 March, they arrived in Agra and were met at the railway station by Mr. Osman Ghani, the telegraph manager of Agra, who had accepted the Cause about ten months earlier. Since no lecture could be arranged in the Agra College owing to the absence of Mr. S. Ḥishmatu'lláh Qurashí from that city, Mrs. Kehler visited the Taj Mahal toward the evening and a second time in the moonlit night when this beautiful monument looks simply superb.

DELHI

On 17 March, Mrs. Kehler and Prof. Pritam Singh arrived at Delhi, the metropolis of India. But as Delhi was in a state of political agitation at the time, in consultation with Bahá'í friends, the idea of lecturing in the city was given up. This city has a Local Spiritual Assembly with a learned and sincere Bahá'í group that was established during Riḍván of 1932 under the auspices of our revered Bahá'í brother Jináb-i-Maḥfúẓ'ul Ḥaq Ilmí. They met this group and also met Mr. Qurashí, who was in Delhi at the time. A prayer was offered and after the story of Mrs. Kehler's coming into the Cause had been told by her, they left Delhi on the night of the 17th and arrived the next morning in the famous city of Amritsar, the seat of Sikh culture.

AMRITSAR

On the morning of 18 March, Mrs. Kehler visited the Golden Temple of the Sikh community of the Punjab, who are said to be about four million in number and established in 1526–30 A.D. Its founder was Guru Nanak, a glorified divine personage. Mrs. Kehler joined their service, involving chanting the Sikh prayer accompanied with music and the offering of flowers to the holy book of the Sikhs. It created a deep impression upon the devout spirit of Keith and Prof. Pritam Singh and his friend Prof. Rajinder Singh. Mrs. Kehler prayed in this temple with the same earnestness and devotion as she had displayed in the Muhammadan Mosque at Aligarh University a few days earlier when she prayed for the unification of religions and faiths in the worship of the one true God, the Glorious and the Forgiving.

By the kindness of the Sikh friends of Prof. Pritam Singh, a meeting had been arranged at the Khalsa college of Amritsar, the seat of learning for the Punjab Sikhs. The subject offered there was "The Trend in Modern Education." About 400 undergraduates and the whole faculty were present and listened to the lecture with rapt attention. From Amritsar they motored down to Lahore in the car of Mrs. Pritam Singh's uncle.

LAHORE

On the afternoon of 18 March, they arrived in Lahore, and, as Mrs. Kehler always liked to stay in Bahá'í homes, she was the guest of Prof. Pritam Singh. She spent two delightful days with the family of Prof. Pritam Singh, during which she fulfilled three important engagements, although she had not been well since leaving Aligarh.

The first lecture was delivered at the Lahore Y.M.C.A. hall and the subject was "The Message of Bahá'u'lláh." The speech was very eloquent and instructive. Prof. Sirájud'd-Dín of F. C. College was in the chair. The second lecture was on "The Solution to World Problems" and had been arranged by an old friend and fellow classmate of Prof. Pritam Singh, Principal Brij Narain, M.A. of Sanatan Dharma College of the Hindu community, who also presided. About 200 students were present at this lecture and Bahá'í solutions to the agrarian, the industrial, the racial, and the religious problems were offered in a very clear and simple manner. The chairmen offered a few appreciative remarks and expressed a desire to hear in detail about solutions to economic problems. In response to that wish, Mrs. Ransom-Kehler sent him an article on the "Bahá'í Economic Plan," which was published in the "Bahá'í Weekly," dated 9 April 1932.

On 19 March 1932, a tea party was arranged by Prof. Pritam Singh in his own residence on behalf of the National Spiritual Assembly of the Bahá'ís of India and Burma in honor of Mrs. Keith Ransom-Kehler's visit to Lahore. About forty guests were present and an interesting talk was given about the abolition of all kinds of prejudices with an explanation of the Bahá'í basic principles.

The next morning Mrs. Kehler left Lahore for Karachi to fulfill an important engagement on 21 March 1932, the first day of the new Bahá'í year.

KARACHI

The important engagement in Karachi was for Mrs. Kehler to dedicate and open the new Ḥaẓíratu'l-Quds, or Bahá'í Hall, recently erected through the sacrifice and sincere efforts of the Bahá'í friends of Karachi. This she did on the day of her arrival, 21 March, the Naw-Rúz feast day. She dedicated the Bahá'í Hall in a very glorious manner in the congregation of guests and Bahá'í friends. Mr. Jamshíd Mehta, the four-time elected mayor of Karachi, was invited to take the chair. He first called upon Mr. Isfandíyár Ba<u>kh</u>tíyárí, who was the moving spirit in the construction of the building, to open the meeting with a prayer, which was chanted in Persian. Then Mr. Jamshíd read passages from 'Abdu'l-Bahá's writings concerning the purpose and influence of the Bahá'í places of worship. Mr. 'Abbásí gave a brief account of the manner in which the Ḥaẓíratu'l-Quds was built. Then Mrs. Kehler was called upon to make the dedication address. After a brief summary of the basic teachings, mostly based on quotations from the sacred utterances, she led the way to the front door of the building and said: "To the Glory of God and the brotherhood of man I declare this Hall open for public worship and may Bahá'u'lláh richly bless all who enter here."

BOMBAY

Mrs. Kehler arrived in Bombay on the *SS Ellara* from Karachi on 31 March 1932, and was warmly received by the Bahá'í friends at the dock. On the same evening she met a large number of believers in the Bahá'í Hall and addressed them in English; which was translated into Gujerati by Mrs. Shirin Fozdar.

On 1 April she spoke on "The Interesting Personalities I have Met in the Orient" at the Marwadi Vidyalia Hall. The hall was full of men and women of different beliefs and backgrounds and her speech was greatly acclaimed by all.

On the evening of 2 April, the Theosophical Hall was full to capacity to hear this most distinguished and brilliant lady speak on "The Spiritual Basis of Citizenship" under the chairmanship of Mr. F. J. Ginwalla. She spoke with such energy that the audience was spellbound.

On the evening of 3 April, she spoke again exclusively to a confirmed group of the believers at the Bahá'í Hall. Her speech was translated into Gujerati by Mr. H. K. Modi, and into Persian by Mr. Rustam Khusraw. This evening she gave them the message of our beloved Guardian and in the same day a group photo of the believers with Mrs. Keith Ransom-Kehler was taken in the University garden.

On the evening of 4 April, she spoke to the multitude at the Prarthna Semaj and talked about "The Great Message of Bahá'u'lláh."

On 5 April, she delivered a lecture on the Bahá'í teachings that make a person a better follower of his own religion. This was at Sir Cawasji Jehangir Hall, which was full of men and women of all nationalities, under the chairmanship of Shamsul Ulama Dr. Sir Jiwanji J. Mody. He introduced her to the audience in very glowing terms.

On this day she appealed to her audience to practice love toward God and toward men. She emphasized the fact that Bahá'u'lláh has renewed the spiritual vitality of His followers, not by taking from them their most cherished beliefs but by emphasizing a new version of the fundamental teachings of the great faiths of the world.

On the evening of 6 April she spoke at the Theosophical Hall, which was crowded with an interested and appreciative audience, under the chairmanship of Mr. F. J. Ginwala. The subject was "Is Universal Brotherhood Possible?" The learned men who were present listened to her speech attentively with utmost interest. At the end of her speech, some questions were asked and they were satisfactorily answered.

The Sir Cawasji Jehangir Hall was again a scene of great enthusiasm and animation on the evening of 7 April when she spoke on "The Bahá'í Solution to World Problems." Dr. (Mrs.) Hirabai Gildar chaired the meeting. She said that unless we can speedily find some basis for adjustment among men, the social structure cannot much longer withstand the storm of our hatred, animosity, and strife.

The leading papers of Bombay—such as *The Times of India, The Bombay Chronicle, The Radical of Bombay,* and others—were full of her inspired talks and glorious visit to Bombay.

On 7 April 1932, she left Bombay by the Madras Mail for Deccan, Hyderabad, where she was the guest of the state.

During her stay in Bombay, she rendered a dynamic service by holding a free study class every morning in the Bahá'í Hall that was attended regularly by those who were interested in the practical solution to the world's grave problems, as enunciated by Bahá'u'lláh.

POONA

Mrs. Kehler visited Poona three days prior to the Riḍván Feast. She spent three days with the Bahá'í friends in Poona in service to the holy Cause. Her first lecture at the Theosophical Lodge was titled "Is Universal Brotherhood Possible?" Although there was extreme heat, her address was soul stirring.

Her second lecture was at the Petil Hall, on "The Spiritual Basis of Citizenship." The Hall was packed by cultured people of all denominations, particularly the Zoroastrian Parsee Community. It was highly impressive.

The third and last lecture was given at a hall in the heart of Poona city with a seating capacity of 500 people. Over 600 had gathered in the Hall, and despite extreme discomfort, not one would leave. The subject was "The Bahá'í Solution to World Problems" and throughout the lengthy address the audience sat with rapt attention. All questions were satisfactorily answered.

The citizens of Poona who heard her lectures, particularly the Bahá'í friends, highly commended and appreciated her speeches. They said that she spoke as one inspired with the Holy Spirit, for the whole atmosphere was filled with the spirit of love and devotion. After these lectures she left Poona for Bombay to celebrate and join with the congregation of the friends in the Riḍván Feast. At the invitation of Mr. N. R. Vakil, the Chairman of the National Spiritual Assembly of Bahá'ís of India and Burma, Mrs. Kehler left Bombay for Surat.

SURAT

Mrs. Kehler visited Surat and there delivered two lectures on 27 and 28 April 1932 on the following subjects:

1. At Naginchand Hall on 27 April, subject: "Is Universal Brotherhood Possible?" Under the chairmanship of Dewan Bahadur Thakar, Ram Kapil, Ram government attorney, Surat.

2. On 28 April, subject: "The Bahá'í Solution to World Problems." Under the chairmanship of 'Alí Muḥammad Khán Dehlevi.

The lectures were very well attended and were highly appreciated by the audience.

Mrs. Keith Ransom-Kehler spent ten weeks in Burma and India, and during this period visited Mandalay; Rangoon; Daidanow Kalazoo, Kungyangon; Calcutta; Benares; Lucknow; Aligarh; Agra; Delhi; Amritsar; Lahore; Karachi; Bombay; Hyderabad (Deccan); Poona; and Surat.

She set sail from Bombay on 30 April 1932 for the Holy Land. Thus ended her first trip to India and Burma. According to her letter from Persia dated 18 July 1932, she longed to once more visit India and Burma for a second time, as she was already commanded by the beloved Guardian.

> [From a letter written on behalf of Shoghi Effendi to N. R. Vakil:]
> March 28, 1932
> He was very glad to learn of the plans you made for Mrs. Ransom-Kehler. He sincerely hopes that in these meetings and public lectures delivered in so many cities, she has been able to attract some new souls to the Cause and confirm people who until now have been merely interested. We should admit, however, that the time at her disposal was too short to give her the chance of doing her best. A teacher ought to remain at least a few months in the same city if he wants to really confirm souls. Mere passing and giving a lecture or two is not sufficient unless there are resident Bahá'ís to continue the work that was merely started. Anyhow Mrs. Ransom-Kehler is expected to reach Haifa in about 3 weeks and Shoghi Effendi will hear the report of her journey from herself.[6]

APPENDIX II
N. R. VAKIL AND PRITAM SINGH

NARAYNRAO VAKIL,
THE FIRST BAHÁ'Í OF HINDU ORIGIN IN INDIA

Naraynrao Vakil was born in the year 1866, in a well-known and prominent Hindu family of Navsari, an important principality of Baroda, which later became known as the state of Gujarat. He received his Bachelor of Arts degree from the renowned Elphinston College of Bombay in 1908 and later graduated from the School of Law of Bombay University.

It was at Elphinston College in 1909, that Vakil came in contact with a fellow student, M. R. Shírází, who introduced him to the great Bahá'í teacher Mírzá Maḥram. Although Vakil had been raised as an Orthodox Hindu, he was so attracted to the Teachings of Bahá'u'lláh as presented by Mírzá Maḥram, that after a short while he declared his faith. He was the first Indian of the Hindu background to accept the Bahá'í Faith.

Almost immediately he started to teach the Faith to his friends and when confronted with difficult questions he brought them to Mírzá Maḥram. In 1910, a large conference was held in Allahabad which included an all-India Religious Conference. Siyyid Muṣṭafá Rúmí was to represent the Bahá'í Faith at the Conference, which had attracted thousands of people from across the country, but at the last moment he developed a sore-throat and could not read his talk. Vakil replaced him and his address strongly affected the crowd. This was the first of many conferences that Vakil would attend to represent the Faith of Bahá'u'lláh.

In 1914, Vakil had the privilege to be invited by 'Abdu'l-Bahá to travel to the Holy Land. During this trip he kept a detailed diary of his meetings with the Master, Who spoke to him through a translator: "From

India I have received many letters praising and commending you. Now I see with My own eyes that, praise be to God, those praises and commendations are not only fully manifest in you but . . . you are greater than the picture portrayed in the letters. . . . From our first meeting you have become very dear to Me. Are the members of your caste investigating, searching, or are they satisfied with their old customs? . . . I hope that when you leave this Holy Spot you will become the cause of their guidance and, God willing, your very breath shall have a great effect on their hearts. . . .

"Do not look at your own weakness, but look to the confirmations of God. . . . You are a tree planted by the hand of Providence and watered by the vernal rains of Divine bounty. . . . You will bear luscious fruits from which all the people of India will benefit. . . . Bahá'u'lláh has crowned you with a crown of jewels. You will awaken multitudes."

During this pilgrimage Vakil supplicated 'Abdu'l-Bahá to visit India. 'Abdu'l-Bahá replied that He would send Vakil instead, with special spiritual powers. He should show people that he was a Bahá'í, through his conduct. "People must see that you are different from others. Do not become too engaged in your work; devote some of your time to business and some to the Cause. . . ."

After the ascension of 'Abdu'l-Bahá, Vakil was drowned in sorrow and despondency. The loving and consistent communications of the Guardian were his sole source of strength. Although he suffered from poor health, the never-ending prayers and concern of the Guardian helped to restore his well-being and uplift his soul, to be able to render great services to the advancement of the Faith of Bahá'u'lláh. He had the bounty to be called "Family" by the beloved Guardian. In him the Guardian had a loyal and able friend whom he could trust with many difficult missions.

The Executive Committee of the Bahá'ís of India was elected in 1922 and Vakil was appointed as its auditor. This Committee was renamed the National Spiritual Assembly of the Bahá'ís of India at the instruction of the Guardian and Vakil was elected its Chairman. He occupied this post, except for one year, until his passing.

Many of the letters of Shoghi Effendi to India are addressed to Vakil and they illustrate the Guardian's constant concern for his health. In 1929, the Guardian welcomed Vakil and his family, which now included his two daughters, to the Holy Land. . . . He returned with a revived sense of mission, continued to serve his beloved Guardian and attracted a great number of prominent Hindu personalities to the Cause of God. In 1943, the Bahá'í community of India suffered the loss of its most prominent and dedicated native son, who had been compared by Shoghi Effendi to the martyrs.[1]

PROFESSOR PRITAM SINGH THE FIRST BAHÁ'Í OF SIKH BACKGROUND IN INDIA

Pritam Singh, whose name meant "Lion of the Beloved," was born on 16 November 1881, in a highly cultured and wealthy Sikh family of Sialkot, Punjab, now a part of Pakistan. His father, Sardar Sahib Chatter Singh, was a judge of the High Court of Lahore and a prominent businessman.

Pritam Singh finished his primary studies in his hometown and obtained his Bachelor of Arts degree in History, Economics and Political Science from the University of Lahore in 1904, and his post graduate degree with honors from the University of Calcutta in 1909. It was in this year that he met Mírzá Maḥmúd Zarqání, who, at the behest of 'Abdu'1-Bahá had established his residence in Lahore to teach the Faith. Pritam Singh, was so entranced with the Teachings of Bahá'u'lláh, that he decided to devote most of his time to the promotion of his new-found Cause.

Pritam Singh was fluent in several Indian languages and wrote many articles and books explaining the tenets of the Faith. At the instruction of the Guardian he translated "Bahá'u'lláh and the New Era" into Indian languages.

The letters of the Guardian to him show how Pritam Singh's services were valued: "I deeply appreciate your outstanding and constant services to our beloved Faith, admire the spirit that animates you, and sympathize with you in your cares and difficulties. I will pray for their removal from the depth of my heart. Rest assured and persevere in your historic and unforgettable services."

Pritam Singh's incessant activities in promoting the Faith, particularly among the Sikh community, incited the ire of the priests and caused the opposition of the fanatics, who, at one time, severely beat him and forbade him to talk about the Faith in the Sikh Temples.

He was not dissuaded and in 1927 resigned his post as a lecturer in the University to devote all his time to the service of the Cause. He accompanied international Bahá'í teachers such as Martha Root and Keith Ransom-Kehler throughout India, acting as their guide and translator and assisting them in teaching the Faith.

He started a Bahá'í weekly magazine at his own expense, the first Bahá'í periodical in India which was well received by the intellectual society. His articles appeared in publications such as the "World Order," "Kawkab-i-Hind" and "Payámbar." In 1932 he was appointed by the Guardian as an editor of the "Bahá'í World," representing India and Burma.

Pritam Singh traveled throughout India, visiting universities and colleges and attending conferences where he could bring the Faith to the attention of the educated circles. He was known to many of the Vice-Chancellors and university professors and so could reach the intellectual strata of the Indian society quite easily and naturally. Shoghi Effendi encouraged Pritam Singh to continue to bring the message of Bahá'u'lláh to the educated people of India.

Pritam Singh's way of life greatly displeased his wealthy and religious family and his father disowned him. In an article in "The Bahá'í World" Vol. XIII, it is recorded that: "His family was embarrassed that he, with all his brilliant career and bright future, should leave not only his comfortable way of life, but also his hereditary religion. Therefore, they started to place [him] under economic and other pressures. However, when their persuasions flavored with the promise of a large fortune to be bequeathed to him by his father, failed, they even begged Professor Pritam Singh to remain a Bahá'í if he wanted to, but at least for the sake of the reputation of the family, to give up his public lectures and teaching tours." Pritam Singh did not succumb to the pressures.

Isfandíyár Bakhtiyárí, a close friend and associate of Pritam Singh recalled: "After the partition of the country into India and Pakistan, some well-known individuals who had occupied important positions in Pakistan came over to India. Among them were admirers of Pritam Singh who held him in high regard and came to meet him. One of these was Lala Ishwardas, an ex-judge of the Lahore High Court who had left a lot of property behind in Pakistan and had been given suitable compensation from the Government of India. He lived in a palatial residence in Delhi with his two sons, one of whom was an Ambassador and the other a highly-placed government official.

"One day this gentleman came to the Bahá'í Center where Pritam Singh and I shared a room, and invited Pritam Singh to his house. . . . He returned and told me 'Do you Know what Lalaji told me? He said "What is this life that you are leading there along with an Írání in the corner of an office? Anyone can enter your room at any time and there is no privacy." Then he said as he had a large and commodious house and many servants, he would be glad to give me comfortable accommodation in his house and free board for the rest of my life, if I would only give up the Bahá'í Faith. . . ." I told him do you expect me to undo what I have achieved in a whole lifetime? I am very happy where I am. This corner of an office is very dear to me and I shall not exchange it for a big palace. . . ."

For the last few years of his life, Pritam Singh pioneered to Amritsar where there were no other Bahá'ís. He worked as a proofreader in a printing press and gave all his spare time to the promotion of the Faith. He lived alone in a humble garage, without any means of comfort, and refused to leave his pioneering post despite his old age and declining health.

A representative of the National Spiritual Assembly who had gone to visit him reported:

"He wore a white turban, white shirt, white pants and white canvas shoes. He looked worn out; his cheeks were hollow, his eyes had sunk in their sockets. He smiled and embraced me and expressed his joy and gratitude that I had gone to see him. Then he said: 'The call may come any moment now. I am eager to attain the presence of Bahá'u'lláh to submit my reports to Him. God alone knows how I have tried to serve His Glorious Cause! I am but a humble servant and rely on the mercy of the Manifestation of God.'"

This was just a fortnight before Pritam Singh passed peacefully to the Abhá Kingdom, in his sleep, on August 25, 1959. He was buried according to Bahá'í rites.

The Hands of the Cause of God residing in the Holy Land, sent the following cable to the National Spiritual Assembly of the Bahá'ís of India:

> GRIEVE LOSS OUTSTANDING INDIAN BELIEVER PRITAM SINGH DISTINGUISHED TEACHER ADMINISTRATOR FAITH MUCH LOVED PRAISED BY BELOVED GUARDIAN. HIS DEVOTED UNTIRING SERVICES SO LONG PERIOD SO MANY FIELDS UNFORGETTABLE. PRAYING SHRINES RICH REWARD.[2]

NOTES

Siyyid Muṣṭafá wrote his memoirs in English and Persian and sent copies of the completed manuscript to the National Spiritual Assembly of the Bahá'ís of India and Burma to be preserved in its National Archives. All other papers of Siyyid Muṣṭafá—including his unpublished translations of the Bahá'í writings into Urdu, Bengali, and Burmese languages—were destroyed and burned during the attack by a mob on his home, which resulted in his martyrdom.

I translated sections of his Persian memoirs not found in the English version and merged them together. Siyyid Muṣṭafá had sent some of his memoirs for publication in the Bahá'í magazine *Star of the West* and had asked the editors to correct his English as it was not his first language. In accordance with this request, in the editing of his memoirs I made minor changes to the English sentences for clarity; however great care was taken not to alter the substance of his words.

Many articles have been written about Siyyid Muṣṭafá and his efforts for the Faith. Some have mentioned discrepancies between details in his memoirs and the accounts of historians. While I was compiling these memoirs it became apparent to me that Siyyid Muṣṭafá kept detailed records of his activities and movements, and because his memoirs offer a firsthand account of events, they can be treated as a reliable historical document. Of course, it should be noted that any accounts concerning interaction with 'Abdu'l-Bahá are to be considered the recollections of the author, and treated as "pilgrim notes," and not as authenticated renderings of 'Abdu'l-Bahá's words and actions.

All of the provisional translations of the Tablets of 'Abdu'l-Bahá included in this book have been reviewed and approved by a committee at the Bahá'í World Center.

Iran Furútan Muhájir

Foreword

1. Nabíl-i-A'ẓam, *The Dawn-Breakers: Nabíl's Narrative of the Early Days of the Bahá'í Revelation,* p. 589.

2. Ibid., p. 590.

3. Ibid., pp. 302–5.

4. Adib Taherzadeh, *The Revelation of Bahá'u'lláh, vol. 4,* pp. 180–81.

5. 'Abdu'l-Baha, *Memorials of the Faithful,* pp. 134–35.

Introduction

1. In a letter to a friend, Siyyid Muṣṭafá Rúmí explains that he has written a complete account in Persian at the request of the National Spiritual Assembly of Iran and will forward it to them when the situation of the Bahá'ís in Iran allows it. The present book is compiled from both the Persian and English versions.

Chapter 1: Childhood and Youth

1. The Janissary corps was originally staffed by Christian youths from the Balkan provinces who were converted to Islam on being drafted into the Ottoman service. Subject to strict rules, including celibacy, they were organized into three unequal divisions (*cemaat, bölükhalkı, segban*) . . . In the late sixteenth century the celibacy rule and other restrictions were relaxed, and by the early eighteenth century the original method of recruitment was abandoned. The Janissaries frequently engineered palace coups in the seventeenth and eighteenth centuries, and in the early nineteenth century they resisted the adoption of European reforms by the army. Their end came in June 1826 in the so-called "Auspicious Incident." On learning of the formation of new, westernized troops, the Janissaries revolted. Sultan Mahmud II declared war on the rebels and, on their refusal to surrender, had cannon fire directed on their barracks. Most of the Janissaries were killed, and those who were taken prisoner were executed. [Encyclopedia Britannica Online]

2. Siyyid Javád-i-Karbalá'í had met Shaykh Aḥmad-i-Aḥsá'í in Karbilá and studied fiqh and jurisprudence in the classes of Siyyid Káẓim-i-Rashtí. After returning to Iran he had the bounty of being in the presence of the Báb when he was about ten years old. In his travels Siyyid Javád visited Bombay and stayed there for a while. During the years that the Báb was in Búshihr, Siyyid Javád was also there and met Him several times. He also attained the presence of Bahá'u'lláh and was the recipient of Tablets revealed by Him.

3. The sixth Imám of <u>Sh</u>í'ih Islam.

Chapter 2: The Arrival of Jamál Effendi in India

1. Rohilkhand is a region of the northwestern Uttar Pradesh state of India, named after the Rohilla Afghan tribes. [Encyclopædia Britannica Online].

2. Siyyid Muṣṭafá Rumi copied about forty Tablets of Bahá'u'lláh that were revealed at that time for the new believers.

3. In 1877, when Queen Victoria assumed the title "Empress of India," Durbar was a ten-year-old prince. Mahboob Ali Khan was the nizam of Hyderabad and came to Delhi with his regent, the formidable Sir Salar Jung. —*The Cyclopedia of India and of Eastern and Southern Asia,* pp. 897.

4. Karnataka, north of Bangalore.

5. Kashipur, Uttarakhand is a city and a municipal corporation in the Udham Singh Nagar District in the state of Uttarakhand, India. Moradabad is a city in the northern Uttar Pradesh state in northern India. Lucknow is the capital city of the Indian state of Uttar Pradesh.

6. "Consider, that even the year in which that Quintessence of Light is to be made manifest hath been specifically recorded in the traditions, yet they still remain unmindful, nor do they for one moment cease to pursue their selfish desires. According to the tradition, Mufaḍal asked Ṣádiq saying: "What of the sign of His manifestation, O my master?" He made reply: "In the year sixty, His Cause shall be made manifest, and His Name shall be proclaimed."

"Of these, Ṣádiq, son of Muḥammad, hath said: 'The religious doctors of that age shall be the most wicked of the divines beneath the shadow of heaven. Out of them hath mischief proceeded, and unto them it shall return.'"

". . . Ṣádiq, son of Muḥammad, that he spoke these words: "Knowledge is twenty and seven letters. All that the Prophets have revealed are two letters thereof. No man thus far hath known more than these two letters. But when the Qá'im shall arise, He will cause the remaining twenty and five letters to be made manifest."—Bahá'u'lláh, the Kitáb-i-Íqán, ¶281, 271, 272.

7. "Jabulqa and Jabulsa are two mythological cities mentioned in Shí'ih Ḥádith. In the early *Basa'ir al-darajat,* these cities were inhabited by archetypal believers who were waiting for the appearance of the Qá'im. In the *Kitab al-haft wa-l-azilla* (8th–11th century C.E.), transmitted by Nasayri Shí'a, the sixth Imám al-Ṣádiq states that the Qá'im will live in these cities. Each city has 12,000 gates, each of which is guarded by 12,000 men until the Day of Resurrection, when the Qá'im will appear."—Orkhan Mir-Kasimov, *Unity in Diversity,* pp. 140–41.

8. "In the days of Bahá'u'lláh, during the worst times in the Most Great Prison, they would not permit any of the friends either to leave the Fortress or to come in from the outside. . . .

It was at such a period that the Afnán, Ḥájí Mírzá Muḥammad-'Alí—that great bough of the Holy Tree—journeyed to 'Akká, coming from India to Egypt, and from Egypt to Marseilles. One day I was up on the roof of the caravanserai. Some of the friends were with me and I was walking up and down. It was sunset. At that moment, glancing at the distant seashore, I observed that a carriage was approaching. 'Gentlemen,' I said, 'I feel that a holy being is in that carriage.' It was still far away, hardly within sight.

'Let us go to the gate,' I told them. 'Although they will not allow us to pass through, we can stand there till he comes.' I took one or two people with me and we left.

At the city gate I called to the guard, privately gave him something and said: 'A carriage is coming in and I think it is bringing one of our friends. When it reaches here, do not hold it up, and do not refer the matter to the Governor.' He put out a chair for me and I sat down.

By this time the sun had set. They had shut the main gate, too, but the little door was open. The gatekeeper stayed outside, the carriage drew up, the gentleman had arrived. What a radiant face he had! He was nothing but light from head to foot. Just to look at that face made one happy; he was so confident, so assured, so rooted in his faith, and his expression so joyous. He was truly a blessed being. He was a man who made progress day by day, who added, every day, to his certitude and faith, his luminous quality, his ardent love. He made extraordinary progress during the few days that he spent in the Most Great Prison. The point is that when his carriage had come only part of the way from Haifa to 'Akká, one could already perceive his spirit, his light.

After he had received the endless bounties showered on him by Bahá'u'lláh, he was given leave to go, and he traveled to China. There, over a considerable period, he spent his days mindful of God and in a manner conformable to Divine good pleasure. Later he went on to India, where he died." —'Abdu'l-Bahá, *Memorials of the Faithful,* pp. 16–18.

9. Bahá'u'lláh, in Shoghi Effendi, *Messages to the Indian Subcontinent,* p. 431.

10. Provisional translation by Siyyid Muṣṭafá Rúmí.

Chapter 3: First Visit to Burma

1. Village head.

2. Dhaka, present capital of Bangladesh.

Chapter 4: Travels in Celebes and Macassar

1. All parts of Cassia Fistula trees are used in traditional medicines.

2. The first successful smallpox vaccine to be developed was introduced by Edward Jenner in 1796.

Chapter 5: Return to Rangoon from South Asia

1. Bahá'u'lláh, in Shoghi Effendi, *Messages to the Indian Subcontinent,* p. 434.

2. Ibid., p. 433.

Chapter 6: Return of Jamál Effendi to Burma

1. Lahej was a Sheikdom based in Lahej in Southern Arabia. The Sultanate became self-ruled in 1728 and gained independence in 1740. In 1839, the Sultanate became Aden Protectorate of the British Empire, though nominally the 'Abdali sultan retained his status. The Aden Protectorate was briefly ruled again by the Ottomans during World War I, but was regained by the British and absorbed into the Federation of South Arabia in 1963. The 'Abdali dynasty was officially abolished in 1967, with the proclamation of South Yemen.

2. Refers to Qur'án 2:261: "The similarities of those who lay out their substance for advancing the religion of God, is as a grain of corn which produceth seven ears, and in every ear an hundred grains, for God giveth twofold unto whom he pleaseth: God is bounteous and wise."

Chapter 7: Áqá Mírzá Maḥram

1. Rice before threshing or in the husk.

Chapter 8: First Pilgrimage, 1903

1. Translated by Siyyid Muṣṭafá Rúmí.

Chapter 9: Events of 1904–1906

1. Qur'án 2:214.

2. He remained a devoted Bahá'í, and corresponded until the end of his life with Siyyid Muṣṭafá and assisted him in translating Bahá'í literature into the Bengali language.

3. According to Buddhist tradition, Maitrya is a bodhisattva who will appear on Earth in the future, achieve complete enlightenment, and teach the pure dharma. According to scriptures, Maitrya will be a successor to the present Buddha, Gautama Buddha (also known as Sakyamuni Buddha). Horner, *The Minor Anthologies of the Pali Canon,* p. 97.

Chapter 10: Arrival of the Faith at Daidanow Kalazoo Village

1. From *Star of the West,* Vol. 1. Dec. 12, 1910, Masa'il No. 15:

". . . The number of believers is swelling day by day and the new school for the Bahai boys, which was recently opened by our revered brother Seyad Mustafa Roumie, though in a very primary scale, is well attended and has caused great zeal among the servants of God all over India. Also, our brother Aga Seyad Mehdi Behahani, who, since his return from the holy land of Acca in October, has been residing in Bombay, has just arrived in Rangoon and will go to inspect the school, and in all probability will be placed in charge there to train the boys.—*A. S. Ismaeel.*

Chapter 12: Second Pilgrimage to the Holy Land

1. 'Abdu'l-Bahá, in Shoghi Effendi, *Promised Day Is Come,* ¶30.

2. *Barasat* is the Indian monsoon.

3. Famous Bahá'í poet.

Chapter 13: Events of 1914–1920

1. World War I is recorded as starting on 28 July 1914 in Europe.

2. Refers to the Qur'án 2:261: "The similarities of those who lay out their substance for advancing the religion of God, is as a grain of corn which produceth seven ears, and in every ear an hundred grains, for God giveth twofold unto whom he pleaseth: God is bounteous and wise."

3. The Qur'án 54:20.

4. The Karen tribe was the first to convert to Christianity. Its people are often sent to other tribes as Christian missionaries. Seventy percent of Karen are Buddhist, Buddhist-animist, or animist. About twenty to thirty percent are Christian.

Chapter 14: Third Pilgrimage to Holy Land, 1921

1. The two quotes are taken from a letter of Siyyid Muṣṭafá Rúmí to Isfandíyár Bakhtíyárí in 1935.

2. This marriage seems to have taken place after Siyyid Muṣṭafá Rúmí's pilgrimage. It is possible he mentions it here because of the young groom's Burmese roots. "On the last Friday morning of his stay on earth (November 25th) he said to his daughters: 'The wedding of Khusraw must take place today. If you are too much occupied, I myself will make the necessary preparations, for it must take place this day." . . . Later in the evening of Friday he blessed the bride and bridegroom who had just been married. He spoke impressively to them. "Khusraw," he said, "you have spent your childhood and youth in the service of this house; it is my hope that you will grow old under the same roof, ever and always serving God." —*The Passing of 'Abdu'l-Bahá* by Shoghi Effendi and Lady Blomfield.

Chapter 15: The Ascension of 'Abdu'l-Bahá

1. It seems plausible that Siyyid Muṣṭafá Rúmí's arrival in the Holy Land may have been delayed due to the unreliability of communication and travel at the time.

2. The Bibby Line was founded in 1807 by John Bibby (1775–1840). It has operated in most areas of shipping throughout its 200-year history, and claims to be the oldest independently owned deep sea shipping line in the world.

3. Mírzá Munír Zayn was the son of the well-known Bahá'í scribe Zaynu'l-Muqarrabín.

4. Shoghi Effendi, letter to the editors and publishers of "The Dawn," dated 7 Febraury 1925, in *Messages of Shoghi Effendi to the Indian Subcontinent, 1923–1957,* p. 14.

Chapter 16: My Second Marriage, 1929

1. Bahá'u'lláh, The Hidden Words, Persian, no. 43.

2. Letter written on behalf of Shoghi Effendi, dated 6 January 1930, *Dawn of a New Day,* p. 27.

3. Ibid., dated 7 May 1930, in *Messages of Shoghi Effendi to the Indian Subcontinent, 1923–1957,* p. 64.

4. Ibid., dated 3 January 1931, in *Messages of Shoghi Effendi to the Indian Subcontinent, 1923–1957,* pp. 68–69.

5. For detailed accounts of Martha Root's visit to the region, as well as the visits of several other prominent Bahá'ís, see Appendix 1: Visitors to Burma.

Chaapter 17: The Ascension of Bahíyyih Khánum, the Greatest Holy Leaf

1. Shoghi Effendi, cable dated 14 July 1932, in *Messages of Shoghi Effendi to the Indian Subcontinent,* 1923–1957, p. 85.

2. Shoghi Effendi, in *Bahíyyih Khánum,* p. 22.

3. Letter written on behalf of Shoghi Effendi to Siyyid Muṣṭafá Rúmí, dated 25 August 1932, in *Messages of Shoghi Effendi to the Indian Subcontinent, 1923–1957,* p. 85.

Chapter 18: Extracts from Correspondence, 1931–41

1. Siyyid Muṣṭafá Rúmí, letter to Isfandíyár Bakhtíyárí, dated 1931. Translated from the Persian by Iran Furútan Muhájir.

2. Ibid, dated 1933.

3. Letter written on behalf of Shoghi Effendi to Siyyid Muṣṭafá Rúmí, dated 10 September 1933, in *Messages of Shoghi Effendi to the Indian Subcontinent, 1923–1957,* pp. 102–3.

4. Siyyid Muṣṭafá Rúmí, letter to Isfandíyár Bakhtíyárí, dated 1933. Translated from the Persian by Iran Furútan Muhájir.

5. Letter written on behalf of Shoghi Effendi to Siyyid Muṣṭafá Rúmí, dated 5 October 1933, in *Messages of Shoghi Effendi to the Indian Subcontinent, 1923–1957,* pp. 103–4.

6. Siyyid Muṣṭafá Rúmí, letter to Isfandíyár Bakhtíyárí, dated 1934. Siyyid Muṣṭafá Rúmí's age has been corrected here based on his date of birth, 5 January 1852. In this letter he refers to himself as being eighty-six years old. Translated from the Persian by Iran Furútan Muhájir.

7. Siyyid Muṣṭafá Rúmí, letter to Isfandíyár Bakhtíyárí, dated 1934. Translated from the Persian by Iran Furútan Muhájir. The translation of the extract from the Tablet of 'Abdu'l-Bahá included here has been approved by the Universal House of Justice.

8. Letter written on behalf of Shoghi Effendi to Siyyid Muṣṭafá Rúmí, dated 19 February 1934, in *Messages of Shoghi Effendi to the Indian Subcontinent, 1923–1957,* pp. 110–11.

9. Ibid., dated 17 December 1934, in *Messages of Shoghi Effendi to the Indian Subcontinent, 1923–1957,* pp. 121–22.

10. Letter of Siyyid Muṣṭafá Rúmí, translated from the Persian by Iran Furútan Muhájir.

11. Letter written on behalf of Shoghi Effendi to Siyyid Muṣṭafá Rúmí, dated 27 June 1935, in *Messages of Shoghi Effendi to the Indian Subcontinent, 1923–1957,* pp. 126–27.

12. Ibid., dated 15 November 1935, in *Messages of Shoghi Effendi to the Indian Subcontinent,* 1923–1957, p. 134.

13. Siyyid Muṣṭafá Rúmí, letter to Isfandíyár Bakhtíyárí, dated 1936. Translated from the Persian by Iran Furútan Muhájir.

14. Letter written on behalf of Shoghi Effendi to Siyyid Muṣṭafá Rúmí, dated 16 July 1936, in *Messages of Shoghi Effendi to the Indian Subcontinent, 1923–1957,* p. 144.

15. Ibid., dated 16 September 1936, in *Messages of Shoghi Effendi to the Indian Subcontinent, 1923–1957,* p. 146.

16. Ibid., 9 November 1936, in *Messages of Shoghi Effendi to the Indian Subcontinent, 1923–1957,* p. 150.

17. Ibid., 7 December 1936, in *Messages of Shoghi Effendi to the Indian Subcontinent, 1923–1957,* pp. 151–52.

18. Shoghi Effendi, cable, dated 31 August 1937, in *Messages of Shoghi Effendi to the Indian Subcontinent, 1923–1957,* p. 160.

19. Letter written on behalf of Shoghi Effendi to the Daidanow Local Spiritual Assembly, dated 7 December 1937, in *Messages of Shoghi Effendi to the Indian Subcontinent, 1923–1957,* p. 163.

20. Shoghi Effendi, cable, dated 28 April, 1938, in *Messages of Shoghi Effendi to the Indian Subcontinent, 1923–1957,* p. 168.

21. Siyyid Muṣṭafá Rúmí, letter to Isfandíyár Bakhtíyárí, dated 1938. Translated from the Persian by Iran Furútan Muhájir.

22. Letter written on behalf of Shoghi Effendi to Siyyid Muṣṭafá Rúmí, dated 7 July 1938, in *Messages of Shoghi Effendi to the Indian Subcontinent, 1923–1957,* p. 171.

23. Siyyid Muṣṭafá Rúmí, letter dated 1938.

24. Letter written on behalf of Shoghi Effendi to N. R. Vakil, dated 2 March 1939, in *Messages of Shoghi Effendi to the Indian Subcontinent, 1923–1957,* p. 180.

25. Shoghi Effendi, cable, dated 2 October 1939, *Messages to America,* p. 30.

26. Letter written on behalf of Shoghi Effendi to Siyyid Muṣṭafá Rúmí, dated 8 December 1939, in *Messages of Shoghi Effendi to the Indian Subcontinent, 1923–1957,* p. 185.

27. Siyyid Muṣṭafá Rúmí, letter to Isfandíyár Bakhtíyárí, dated 1939. Translated from the Persian by Iran Furútan Muhájir.

28. Ibid., dated 1940–41. "During the British rule, Burma was a part of India from 1824 to 1937. In 1937 the British government separated Burma from India and granted it its own constitution, independent of that of India; the masses interpreted this as proof that the British planned to exclude Burma from the next phase of Indian reform. The Japanese advanced into Burma and by the end of 1942 had occupied the country." —*Britannica*

Correspondence between Burma and the Holy Land had become curtailed after the turmoil and the occupation by the Japanese. Bahá'ís from Rangoon and Mandalay, including Siyyid Muṣṭafá, had moved to the Kungyangon area to be with the large Bahá'í community of nearly 800 for safety.

Chapter 19: Passing to the Abhá Kingdom of Siyyid Muṣṭafá Rúmí

1. Shoghi Effendi, *Messages of Shoghi Effendi to the Indian Subcontinent, 1923–1957,* p. 191.

2. Ibid, p. 216.

3. Ibid., p. 214.
4. Ibid., p. 217.
5. Ibid., p. 259.
6. See Barron Harper, *Lights of the Spirit,* p. 127.
7. Shoghi Effendi, *Messages of Shoghi Effendi to the Indian Subcontinent, 1923–1957,* p. 260.
8. Ibid., p. 261.
9. Ibid., p. 263.
10. Ibid., p. 264.
11. Ibid., p. 274.

Appendix I: Visitors to Burma

1. Maymyo, also called Pyin Oo Lwin town, central Myanmar (Burma). The town, named for Colonel (later Major General) James May of the 5th Bengal Infantry stationed there in 1886, served as the summer capital during the British administration. . . . Maymyo is reached by road from Mandalay. —*Brittannica*
2. Sikh society established in the 1860s in Punjab.
3. Kyigon is a village in Kale Township, Kale District, in the Sagaing region of western Burma.
4. Monywa is a capital city and the largest city in the Sagaing region, Myanmar, located 136 km northwest of Mandalay on the eastern bank of the River Chindwin.
5. Taunggyi is the capital and largest city of Shan State, Myanmar.
6. Letter written on behalf of Shoghi Effendi to N. R. Vakil, dated 28 March 1932, in *Messages of Shoghi Effendi to the Indian Subcontinent, 1923–1957,* p. 81.

Appendix II: N. R. Vakil and Pritam Singh

1. *Messages of Shoghi Effendi to the Indian Subcontinent, 1923–1957,* pp. 438–41.
2. Ibid., pp. 441–45.

ABOUT THE COMPILER AND EDITOR OF THIS VOLUME

Knight of Bahá'u'lláh Mrs. Iran Furútan Muhájir has pursued an active life of service to the Bahá'í Faith. At the inception of the Ten Year Crusade she accompanied her husband, Dr. Muhájir, to the pioneering post of Mentawai Islands in Indonesia, and both were honored by the beloved Guardian with the accolade of Knight of Bahá'u'lláh.

She has traveled to more than fifty countries in service to the Bahá'í Faith and has served on a variety of Bahá'í institutions and Spiritual Assemblies, including the National Spiritual Assembly of the Bahá'ís of the Philippines. She resided at the Bahá'í World Center in the company of her father Hand of the Cause of God Mr. Furútan for more than ten years and undertook special projects for the Universal House of Justice. She continues to work on a number of international Bahá'í assignments.

Mrs. Muhájir is the author of the biographies of Hands of the God of God Mr. Furútan and Dr. Muhájir, and has compiled several important Bahá'í books, including *The Mystery of God* (a portrait of 'Abdu'l-Bahá), and *Dawn of a New Day,* which she expanded into *Messages of Shoghi Effendi to the Indian Subcontinent.*

She holds a Master's degree in Middle Eastern Studies from Harvard University.

She lives in Maryland with her daughter Gisu; her son in law, Robert W. Cook; and her grandchildren, John and Amelia.

INDEX